UNDERSTANDING
OPTIONS

UNDERSTANDING
OPTIONS

Second Edition

Michael Sincere

New York   Chicago   San Francisco   Athens   London
Madrid   Mexico City   Milan   New Delhi
Singapore   Sydney   Toronto

1 2 3 4 5 6 7 8 9 0   QFR/QFR   1 0 9 8 7 6 5 4 3

ISBN	978-0-07-181784-4
MHID	0-07-181784-0
e-ISBN	978-0-07-181787-5
e-MHID	0-07-181787-5

This publication is designed to provide accurate and authoritative information in regard to the subject matter covered. It is sold with the understanding that neither the author nor the publisher is engaged in rendering legal, accounting, securities trading, or other professional services. If legal advice or other expert assistance is required, the services of a competent professional person should be sought.

—From a Declaration of Principles Jointly Adopted by a Committee of the American Bar Association and a Committee of Publishers and Associations

Library of Congress Cataloging-in-Publication Data

Sincere, Michael.
    Understanding options / by Michael Sincere. — 2e [edition].
      pages cm
    Includes indexes.
    ISBN-13: 978-0-07-181784-4 (alk. paper)
    ISBN-10: 0-07-181784-0 (alk. paper)
    1. Options (Finance)   I. Title.
    HG6024.A3S562 2014
    332.64'53—dc23   2013032442

To my mother, Lois, whom I will always remember for her compassion and generosity, who asked for so little while accomplishing so much; and to my father, Charles, for his kindness and positive attitude.

To Anna Ridolfo, a close friend and loyal New Yorker, who devoted her life to helping others.

Contents

Preface

A Much Improved Options Book

Because of the success of the first edition of *Understanding Options*, my editor at McGraw-Hill asked me to write a second edition. I want to thank the thousands of readers who bought my book and wrote to me with suggestions. Because of their ideas, this second edition is even better.

I listened to the readers who wrote and said they wanted to learn more about intermediate and advanced strategies. In this edition, I added chapters on exercise and assignment, collars, writing cash-secured puts, buying straddles and strangles, the Greeks, implied volatility, protective puts, and spreads. I also included advanced strategies such as iron condors, calendar spreads, the butterfly spread, and trading options on exchange-traded funds (ETFs).

Finally, I discuss popular products such as weekly options and mini-option contracts. Obviously, the second edition is a lot longer. Still, I did my best to introduce all the strategies using understandable language.

If you are learning about options but are not familiar with the stock market, I suggest you read my book *Understanding Stocks* (McGraw-Hill, 2nd Edition). That should help answer most of your questions, and it's written in the same reader-friendly voice as this book.

Finally, while you are reading this book, if you have any questions about options, I include a toll-free phone number that you can call Monday through Friday. It may be hard to believe but all your options questions will be answered by calling this number. You can also chat online with an options professional. The cost? Free.

Who Should Read This Book

If you are thinking of trading stock options or you are already trading them but losing money, this could be the most useful book you ever read. I have taken the classes, read the books, talked to the pros, and made the trades, so I can teach you what I learned. Like my other books, I try to explain options as if you were sitting across from me at the kitchen table. My goal is to save you time and money while educating and entertaining you.

An options book that is entertaining? I know it sounds ridiculous, especially if you have slogged through the dozens of other options books that are supposedly for beginners. Most of the option books I have read sound as though they were written for lawyers or mathematicians. They make options seem a lot more confusing than they actually are. Perhaps it's because option contracts are legal contracts that include specialized terms. As much as possible, I leave most of the lawyerly talk out of the book.

I have one friend who is afraid to take risks and another one who is a speculator. When I told my timid friend that he should consider trading options, he immediately snapped, "Are you crazy? That's way too complicated for me! I don't want to lose all my money." He was an experienced stock market investor who liked to buy and hold stocks and index funds. He believes that options are a get-rich-quick scheme that operates like a casino. He was convinced that options were not friendly to risk-averse investors.

My speculator friend, a successful dentist, is addicted to the Vegas-style action of the stock market. When the stock market wasn't exciting enough, he and his wife enrolled in an options seminar, plunking down $4,000 for the two-day course (not including the $2,000 software that supposedly chose winning options). The instructor pressed all the right buttons, and by the end of the class my friend was ready to plunge into options using sexy strategies like naked puts, calendar spreads, and straddles. He was convinced that he could quickly make a fortune in options by using the most sophisticated strategies. He believed that the more complicated the strategy, the more money he'd make. Fortunately, he talked to me first.

I wrote this book for my two friends and thousands more like them. If you think that options are too complicated or dangerous, give me a chance to change your mind. The good news: there is an options strategy that will meet the needs of both of my friends, from the risk-averse defensive investor to the risk-loving speculator. In addition, if you are reading this book not to make money, but for education or entertainment, I believe the book will meet your needs.

If you are thinking of taking an expensive options course, then read this book first. It could save you thousands of dollars. Even if you still decide to take the class, you'll be much better prepared. Also, if you are one of the 10 million employees who receive stock options from your employer, this book could help you to understand the benefits and risks of stock options.

And finally, if you are concerned that this book is too basic, there are plenty of intermediate and advanced strategies in the last two sections to whet your appetite, including a dynamic interview with an options guru. I describe all these strategies with my usual "reader-friendly" style.

What's So Great About Options?

What if I told you that you could use options to make money every month or every quarter? And what if I told you that you can use options as insurance, for example, to protect your stock portfolio? In fact, minimizing risk is one of the best ways to use options. And if, on occasion, you wanted to speculate, you could leverage your money to double or triple your profits. It will cost you a lot less than if you bought stocks. And, finally, if you like to short stocks, it is safer to use options strategies than to use the stock market.

Speaking of safety, did you know the single best reason for choosing options is that you know in advance how much you can lose? You are in control of how much risk you are willing to take. If this is done properly, you can use options to generate income, to protect your stock portfolio, to hedge against risk, and to speculate. By the time you finish this book, you should have a good idea of what options can do for you and whether you want to trade them.

For example, one of my friends who just started trading called to tell me he experimented with a sophisticated options strategy called a *straddle* (explained later in this book). After investing $2,000, he sold the option for a $25,000 profit the next day. Perhaps it was beginner's luck but it goes to show that you can hit a home run on occasion. Another friend has been using a conservative options strategy called *selling covered calls* to receive monthly income.

One reason you'll like options is that you can make money no matter what the market conditions. This doesn't include all the intermediate and advanced strategies that are discussed in detail throughout the book. Options are powerful tools that, if used properly, can be used in conjunction with the stock market to enhance or protect your portfolio.

At the very least, it's smart to learn everything you can about this fascinating and flexible financial instrument. When you hear that options are flexible, it simply means that you can trade them under any market condition and that the strategies can be as simple or as complicated as you want to make them.

Do you think a particular stock is going to explode higher? There is an option strategy for that, and it will cost you little up-front money. How about a crash? There's an option strategy for that, too. And if you think the market is going sideways, there are option strategies that can bring in income. Can you think of any other financial instrument besides stocks that meets the needs of investors no matter what their income level or financial goals?

There is another reason why you should learn about options: They can help reduce your financial fears. For example, in the midst of a bear market, many people predict the worst. You can use options to protect your stock portfolio if you're uncomfortable with the market. Options aren't perfect, but in the hands of knowledgeable investors, options are a powerful tool.

How the Book Is Organized

The book is divided into six parts. The first part, "What You Need to Know First," includes a thorough overview of options. In Parts 2 to Part 4, the book is organized the same way as you would trade, from beginner

Level 1 strategies to advanced Level 4 strategies. I start slowly, patiently teaching you how to sell covered calls, buy calls, and buy puts.

In Part 5, you will learn intermediate strategies such as spreads, straddles, strangles, cash-secured and naked puts, the Greeks, Weeklys, and mini-options. I worked hard to make these strategies understandable to a novice trader. Then the pace quickens as I introduce advanced options strategies such as the iron condor, calendar spreads, and the butterfly spread.

In Part 6, you'll enjoy the must-read interview with Sheldon Natenberg, bestselling author and a recognized options expert. Finally, I include an updated list of books, classes, software, and other resources for those who want to continue studying options. (If you have questions while reading this book, I include a toll-free phone number in Chapter 26 you can call that will give immediate answers.)

Some of you might wonder how it's possible to write a relatively short book when many options books are well over 500 pages long. First, most of those books are aimed at experienced traders, not beginners. Second, other authors devote hundreds of pages to explaining how options are constructed using complicated formulas. Although I do introduce pricing formulas, my theory is you don't have to learn how an engine works to drive a car.

Although analyzing options formulas might be interesting to mathematicians, I'd prefer to keep my eye on the bottom line: to teach you how to successfully trade options. Trading options is not as hard as many people think, but it's also not as easy as some want you to believe.

How to Contact Me

I congratulate you for taking the time to learn about options. Trading stocks is like playing checkers, while trading options is similar to playing chess. If this is your first book on options, I'm honored to be the first to teach you about this fascinating product. After you've read my book, other books about options will make a lot more sense.

It is estimated that only 5 percent of the population actually understands how options work. It's easy to understand why. After all,

it takes skill, knowledge, experience, and perseverance to be a successful options trader. By the time you finish the book, you'll have joined
this small group of knowledgeable traders.

Thanks again for reading my book. I tried hard to make it the
most useful options book you ever read. You still may have to read it
a few times before you truly understand options.

Finally, if you have questions about my book or notice any errors,
feel free to e-mail me at msincere@gmail.com or visit my website,
www.michaelsincere.com. I always enjoy hearing from you.

UNDERSTANDING
OPTIONS

PART ONE

WHAT YOU NEED TO KNOW FIRST

1

Welcome to the Options Market

I'm delighted that you decided to join me as we learn more about options and options trading. Options can be deceiving—something like walking through quicksand. At the beginning, it may seem straightforward and uncomplicated. But as you get in deeper, it can get murkier, and before long you find yourself sinking under the weight of options terminology.

As you become more familiar with the strategies, it gets easier. But don't get me wrong. Learning about options is like learning a new language. The good news is that you don't need an advanced degree in mathematics to be a successful options trader. Most of the math is basic. If sophisticated calculations are needed, you can find the answers on your computer or mobile device.

The best way to learn about options is in small steps, strategy by strategy, which is exactly how I present the information. If you are like my speculator friends, you will want to jump right into trading options. But I urge you to take the time to understand the purpose and uses of options first before putting real money into the market.

Suggestion: In addition, before you trade options, it's essential that you have a working knowledge of the stock market. Because stocks and options are linked, you should know how to buy and sell stocks before you trade options. If you are new to the stock market, I recommend my previous book, *Understanding Stocks* (McGraw-Hill, 2nd ed.), which quickly and easily covers what you need to know about the stock market. There are many other books on this subject at your local or online bookstore.

The Advantages of Trading Options

Before we discuss options in detail, let's take a closer look at the reasons you may want to participate in them. Did you know that options were created thousands of years ago? And they were popular well before the first stock market was created? You also might be surprised to learn that options can be included in anyone's portfolio, from defensive, risk-averse investors to speculators. Many traders love trading options because of their flexibility and low cost. No matter what your reason, you can find a way to use options—for income, insurance, hedging, or speculation.

Income

In Part 2 I discuss income strategies thoroughly, but for now remember that options can be used quite effectively to generate income or cash flow. Basically, instead of buying options, you sell options on stocks that you already own. In a way, you are renting your stocks to other people (options buyers), and they pay you for the privilege. This can be a profitable way to use options, similar to an annuity, where you can receive cash each month just for holding the stocks.

Protection

Another effective use of options is to protect or insure your investments. Let's say that you have a rather large position in one stock. If you prefer to reduce your risk, you can use options to protect your stock position in case of disaster. And just like an insurance policy, you hope you don't have to use it. Originally, options were created for just this purpose.

Using options to protect your stocks is one of the more conservative ways to use the options market.

Hedging

Similar to buying stock insurance, you can hedge against risk. Let's say you are worried that the market is going to plunge during the next year and take a bite out of your stock and mutual fund profits. You can hedge your entire portfolio by buying options on *exchange-traded funds* (ETFs) that follow major indexes such as the S&P 500, Dow Jones Industrial Average, Nasdaq-100, or Russell 2000. As the market goes down, your options gain value. The pros routinely use options to hedge their stock portfolios, and you can, too.

Speculation

Options have a reputation as a "get-rich-quick" casino because speculators get so much media attention. For very little up-front money, you can leverage your investments with the chance to make many times more than you invest. With this strategy, you are controlling a lot of shares of stock for a little bit of money. The best part of these options strategies is that you always know in advance how much you could lose.

Another advantage of trading options is that you can make money in any market environment. You can create options strategies that attempt to profit from a bull, bear, or sideways market.

Let's Keep It Simple

Perhaps you believe that the only people making money in options are those who use the more advanced strategies. This isn't true! For the retail options trader, sometimes the simpler the strategy, the more money you'll make. And the more complicated strategies come with more risk. Just stick with strategies that you are comfortable with— the ones that don't keep you up at night. This pertains to the stock market as well as to options.

More than likely, it's too early to know the best way to use options. Many options traders use a combination of strategies: they employ options for income or cash flow and also for hedging against potential disasters. Obviously, many people are attracted to options because they can make many times their initial investment.

Buying an Option on a House

This short story should give you a better understanding of how options work.

Let's say that you are thinking of buying a particular two-bedroom house that is listed for $100,000. You really like this house and think the price is fair. You are eager to lock in the price at $100,000 in case it goes higher. If you can lock in the price, you'll have time to look at other houses and also time to act if you decide to buy.

So you approach the owner of the house to see if she will sign an options agreement. When she agrees, you sit down to discuss the terms. After a short conversation, the owner of the house agrees to hold the house for you for three months. During this time, no one else will be allowed to buy it. It also means that no matter how high other offers may be for the house, you are allowed to buy it for $100,000. Even if a Realtor puts the house on the market for $120,000 within the next three months, you, and only you, are allowed to buy it for $100,000. The owner still pays the bills, but you control when, if, and for how much the house will be sold. What a great deal.

But what if the house goes down in value to $90,000, for example? According to the rules of the options contract you signed, you can just walk away. In lawyer talk, you have the "right" to buy the house for $100,000, but you are not "obligated" to buy it. That means that no matter how much the house is worth, higher or lower, you can buy the house for $100,000 or choose to walk away from the deal. (By the way, you will hear the word *right*, a lot, because options give you the right to buy or sell.)

Perhaps you're thinking, "What does the owner get out of this transaction?" That's a good question. Because the owner is holding the house for you and can't let anyone else buy it, she will want compensation; that is, she wants money. Typically, the owner will want a small percentage of the purchase price, perhaps 2 percent, or $2,000. So for $2,000, she will hold the house for you for three months. (Note: the $2,000 you pay the owner is called the *premium*.)

The owner is pleased because she gets $2,000, which she can use as she pleases. You're happy because for three months you know you won't have to pay more than $100,000 for the house. In your opinion, $2,000 is a small price to pay for the right to hold this house. And if you change your mind during the next three months, although you will lose the premium you paid to the owner, you are free to look for another house.

Let's see what could happen in real life. If the value of the house zooms up to $120,000, you decide to buy the house for $100,000 as previously agreed. You just made a $20,000 paper profit.

If you change your mind or the price of the house drops below $100,000, you aren't obligated or forced to buy it. You walk away from the deal with a $2,000 loss, but it's better than owning a house that has dropped in value. But what about the owner? She doesn't care if you buy the house; she's happy to receive the $2,000. And when the three months are up, if you don't buy the house, she could write another options agreement with someone else. This way she can continue getting these tidy little premium checks from potential buyers.

Note: If the price of the house goes up, there is another action you can take: You can sell the profitable options contract to someone else. With this outcome, you take the $20,000 profit and walk away without owning the house. Why $20,000? The difference between the buy and sell prices represents your profit.

Buying Options on Snow Shovels in Chicago

To give you another example of how people use options in the real world, I have another story. Let's say that you own a hardware store in Chicago. You know that you'll probably need snow shovels in December. After all, last year there was a huge December snowstorm. Within weeks, you ran out of snow shovels, costing you profits and annoying your customers. This year, in August, you arrange an options agreement with the snow shovel manufacturer, Shovels, Inc.

The options agreement specifies that Shovels, Inc., will provide you with 100 snow shovels for $15 each, although it normally charges much more. The options agreement specifies that you have the right to buy the snow shovels for $15 each until the third Friday in December. You don't have to buy the shovels, but you can if you want to.

If it doesn't snow by the third Friday in December, you probably won't buy the snow shovels. Remember the premium in the first story? The manufacturer will charge you a $300 premium for holding the 100 snow shovels at $15 each. No matter what happens, whether you take delivery of the snow shovels or not, you pay that $300.

Why would Shovels, Inc., sell you an option on snow shovels? First, the company receives the $300 premium from you. Second, the company knows there is a chance you may decline to buy the snow shovels, so an option to buy is better than nothing.

Let's see what happens in the real world. If there is a brutal snowstorm in November and everyone needs snow shovels, the price of shovels will go up. You are delighted because you have the right to buy the snow shovels for $15 each. You accept delivery of the snow shovels and sell them to your customers for an even higher price. That will be very profitable for you.

Let's say the Chicago winter turns out to be very mild. In this case, you don't want the snow shovels at all. You don't accept delivery of the shovels, and the option contract expires. In this worst-case scenario you lost the $300, but at least you aren't stuck with delivery of 100 unneeded snow shovels. In a way, the options contract was an insurance policy.

If it's a mild winter, Shovels, Inc., keeps your $300 and the 100 shovels. In fact, the company will try to sell a similar option to someone else as soon as you refuse delivery on the 100 shovels. The money the manufacturer receives for each options contract will help it get through the mild winter.

You might not realize it, but options contracts are written on thousands of products, from corn, soybeans, and oil to houses, snow shovels, and stocks.

A Very Important Question

Think about the following question: Would you rather be the options buyer or the options seller? The buyer is in control of when (or if) the property or product is bought or sold. But the seller receives the premium and must follow the terms of the contract. As we examine stock options further, you will learn strategies for both buyers and sellers. Meanwhile, think about which you'd rather be—the options buyer or the options seller.

The Early Years

The Bible has the first recorded option transaction (in the book of Genesis), involving a marriage agreement between Jacob and one of Laban's daughters, Rachel. The date of this transaction is estimated to be about 1700 BC. Under the terms of this options agreement, Jacob had the "right" to marry Rachel but only if he agreed to seven years of labor. Apparently, Laban changed the terms of the agreement and insisted that Jacob marry his older daughter instead. Jacob was so determined to marry Rachel that he took out another option agreement for another seven years of labor. Finally, after fulfilling the terms of the contract, Jacob was allowed to marry Rachel.

Many years later, Aristotle (384–322 BC) wrote a story about Thales of Miletus, a poor Greek astronomer, mathematician, and philosopher, which is the first written record of option speculation.

According to Aristotle, Thales studied the stars to make unusually accurate predictions about future weather conditions, coming to the conclusion that the olive crop would be "bountiful," in other words, there would be an excellent season in the fall. Thales was clever enough to take advantage of his prediction. Although he didn't have a lot of money, he quietly approached the owners of the olive presses (the presses were used to convert olives into olive oil) to make an offer.

He paid each owner a deposit (or premium) to reserve the olive presses during the harvest. For a small deposit, the owners would hold or reserve the olive presses exclusively for Thales during the autumn. Because no one believed that Thales could predict the weather nine months into the future, no one bid against him. Therefore, Thales paid very little for the right to reserve the olive presses.

As it turned out, Thales's prediction was correct. It was an excellent year for olives, and the demand for the olive presses was enormous. Thales sold his option contract (which was the right to use the olive presses) to the olive farmers for a huge profit.

The moral of the story: Thales proved to the world (and himself) that philosophers or speculators can become rich if they are clever enough to figure out how to use options in the real world. (It also helps to do your research before you invest.)

Eighteenth Century

The first options market in the United States began in 1791, when the New York Stock Exchange (NYSE) opened. Because options were still not considered part of the regular market, transactions were arranged in the less prestigious "over-the-counter" market. Obviously, it wasn't easy to match buyers and sellers, especially before computers and phones. There was no central place that buyers and sellers could meet to trade options. To help match buyers and sellers, broker-dealers would meet in an over-the-counter market. Sometimes broker-dealers placed ads in financial journals to help generate interest in a specific option contract.

Nineteenth Century

By the turn of the century, stock options were traded through a loose organization of over-the-counter dealers known as the Put and Call Broker Dealers Association. One of the problems was that no one knew what was considered a fair price for an option. Therefore, it was quite easy to make a bad deal and lose money. In addition, because no one guaranteed the option contract, traders were basically on their own. Finally, negotiating an option contract was difficult because the terms for each contract were unique. Unfortunately, traders had to wait another 100 years before the first organized options exchange was created.

Now that you have a general idea of how to use options, in the next chapter you'll learn how to open an options account.

2

How to Open an Options Account

The two most common questions that people ask when they are interested in options are, "How do you open an account?" and, "How much money do I need to get started?" Both questions are answered in this short but important chapter.

By now, you may be eager to place your first options trade. The wise traders, however, wait patiently for the best investment or trading opportunities. If you step into options without knowledge or experience, you could lose money. Take the time to study options thoroughly before you place your first order. With that in mind, let's get started on learning what you need to do to open an account.

The Five Steps to Opening an Options Account

Because your brokerage firm handles all your options trades, you must begin with a brokerage account. After you have opened your brokerage account, you are then ready to open an options account. You can fill out the forms online or have them mailed to you. Once again, you must have at least a basic knowledge of the stock market to successfully trade options.

After you've opened your brokerage account with the required minimum (the exact dollar amount varies with each brokerage firm, but typically you'll need a minimum of $2,500), the brokerage firm will determine exactly how much money you need to open an options account.

Step One: The Brokerage Firm

In the old days, you had to rely on a stockbroker to make an options trade for you, but you paid dearly for the privilege. Because of the Internet, it's almost required that you make your own trades. This is one of the reasons why option commissions have dropped so dramatically, to as little as $10 a trade (or lower) in recent years.

Nevertheless, when you first get started with options, there is nothing wrong with using the brokerage firm and a representative (they are no longer called stockbrokers) to place the trade for you. The broker also confirms the trades that you make. (It costs a little more if the representative makes the trade.)

Although you should consider the expense of commissions when choosing an online brokerage firm, you also want knowledgeable customer service representatives who will help guide you through the trades and discuss option strategies. You also want a brokerage firm that has sophisticated options software and tools that can route your trades quickly to the market with the best bid and ask price. In addition, you want access to online educational materials like webinars and articles. It is also helpful if the customer service reps are available at least 12 hours a day to answer questions for you.

Choose the brokerage firm that offers all the above. If you stick with well-known brokerage firms, they have options professionals willing and eager to help you set up and manage your options account.

Step Two: The Margin Agreement

If you borrow money from a brokerage firm to purchase stocks, you are "buying on margin" and need to open a margin account.

If you do decide to open a margin account at your brokerage, you will first have to fill out a margin agreement, which is similar to a credit application. The brokerage firm will run a credit check and require you to truthfully fill out a detailed questionnaire. The brokerage wants to make sure you have the financial resources and knowledge to handle margin. It also wants you to understand the possible risks. If your credit is good, you should have no problem getting the application approved.

If you are using Level 1 and Level 2 option strategies (explained below), you will *not* need to fill out a margin agreement. When buying options, margin is not used because you must pay for the purchase in full. On the other hand, if you want to use more advanced options strategies, it is required that you have a margin account. (This will be clear when you read about advanced strategies.) In fact, if you are new to options, it's not necessary to open a margin account.

Another interesting fact: Margin agreements are not usually allowed on an IRA, a tax-deferred 401(k), or a trust account (you are required to have what is called a *cash account*). However, some firms do allow it. Nevertheless, you are still allowed to have an options account in your IRA or tax-deferred account. The only catch is that you may be limited to using basic options strategies. Later on, you'll learn that this isn't necessarily a disadvantage. Best advice: check with your brokerage firm for the specific rules regarding margin.

Note: Just because you can trade options in a retirement account doesn't mean that you should. There are defensive option strategies you will read about that make sense, but do not speculate with money you can't afford to lose.

Step Three: The Options Agreement

The options agreement must be completed if you want to trade options. The purpose of the options agreement is to determine how much knowledge and experience you have. (After you've read this book, you will have no problem with the options agreement.)

The brokerage firm wants to know that you fully understand the risks of trading options and that you have the financial ability to take care of any losses. It will ask you questions about your net worth, your bank, your employer, your experience and knowledge with trading stocks and options, and how much risk you are willing to take.

If you have never traded options before, you will be approved for only Level 1 and Level 2 options trading. Before I tell you why, let's go over the options trading levels, which could vary depending on your brokerage firm:

- Level 1: Selling covered calls
- Level 2: Buying calls and puts, buying straddles and strangles, collars, selling cash-covered puts; buying options on ETFs and indexes
- Level 3: Credit and debit spreads
- Level 4: Selling naked puts, selling straddles, and selling strangles
- Level 5: Selling naked indexes and index spreads

As I mention above, the brokerage firm will be very cautious about approving a newcomer for anything higher than Level 2. It will want to make sure that you have enough experience and financial resources to use advanced strategies.

At the end of the agreement, you have to sign and date the form. I don't know why, but most people sign even though they don't read the agreements thoroughly. You should read this form before you sign it.

Step Four: The Brochure

Every brokerage firm is required to give you a copy of the tedious and technical brochure *Characteristics and Risks of Standardized Options* (also called the *options disclosure document,* which you can download). It's not an easy read, but it is filled with useful information and calculations. I have a feeling that although everyone agrees to read this brochure, few really do. Nevertheless, if you read the brochure carefully, you will learn all the risks involved in trading options. After you read about all the potential risks, you might change your mind about trading options!

Suggestion: I strongly suggest that you first read this entire book before you read the brochure *Characteristics and Risks of Standardized Options*. After reading this book, the brochure will make a lot more sense.

Step Five: The Standardized Option Contract

All option contracts are standardized, which means that the terms of the option are the same for all contracts. In the old days, option contracts were created on an individual basis, so it was every person for himself or herself. As soon as the terms of the agreement were standardized, then it became a relatively level playing field.

By the way, when you buy or sell an option, it is a legal contract. Basically, stock option contracts are an agreement that is insured by the OCC (Options Clearing Corporation). This organization guarantees that the contract will be honored. As long as you know the rules (your rights and obligations), you should have few problems. This is one of the reasons you are reading my book.

A Tarnished Reputation

In the United States, options were used in several schemes that were designed to take advantage of investors' lack of knowledge. At the time, there was little or no regulation. According to the book *Options*, by the Options Institute, brokers would recommend undesirable stocks to unsuspecting clients.

For participating in this scheme, options speculators would reward stockbrokers with large quantities of call options. As more and more clients bought the underlying stock, both the options and underlying stock would rise in price.

As is typical of these kinds of "pump-and-dump" schemes, the speculators and stockbrokers closed their positions while the clients were left holding the soon-to-be-worthless stock.

Another scheme involved creating an "option pool." Major stockholders would buy large amounts of options in an underlying stock. The options allowed them to manipulate and control the price of the stock. As a result, the price of the option would rise or fall based on rumors of what the option pools were buying or selling rather than on the financial expectations of the company.

After the stock market crashed in 1929, many of these schemes were exposed. At first, an angry Congress outlawed options completely because many investors had lost everything. During the investigation phase of the stock market crash, the options industry sent an experienced trader and representative, Herbert Filer, to testify in front of Congress.

Filer explained to a confused Congress that options were similar to insurance contracts to protect against market volatility. At the time, although most options were worthless when they expired, buying options was similar to paying an insurance premium on your house. "If you insured your house against fire and it didn't burn down, you would not say you had thrown away your insurance premium," Filer testified.

As a result of Filer's convincing arguments, Congress agreed that not all options trading was manipulated and, in fact, could be a valuable tool if used properly. The Investment Act of 1934 legalized option trading, and in 1935 the newly formed Securities and Exchange Commission (SEC) granted the Chicago Board of Trade (CBOT) a license to register the options market as a securities exchange. The Securities and Exchange Commission continues to regulate the options industry to this day. Ironically, the CBOT didn't actually take advantage of this license and register as an options exchange until 1968.

Now that you've learned how to open an options account, you're going to learn more about the fascinating characteristics of options.

3

The Fascinating Characteristics of Options

Remember when I said that learning about options is like learning a new language? You'll understand what I mean when you read this important chapter. Think of it this way. What if you had never seen or driven an automobile but had read everything you could about the steering wheel? No matter how much you read about this important and powerful device, you wouldn't know what it was like to use a steering wheel until you started driving. Learning about options is similar.

In this chapter, you'll discover that options really have their own special language that will seem unusual, at least at first. After you master the options language and start trading, it will all begin to make sense. So get ready for a unique experience as I introduce to you the fascinating characteristics of an extremely flexible and powerful financial instrument—the stock option.

The Official Definition of Stock Options

The official definition of a stock option from one of the options exchanges is rather technical. A *stock option* is "a contract that gives the owner the right, but not the obligation, to buy or sell a particular asset (the underlying stock) at a fixed price (the strike price) for a specific period of time (until expiration). The contract also obligates the writer to meet the terms of delivery if the contract right is exercised by the owner."

No wonder people think that options are complicated. A simpler definition would be that a stock option is "the right to buy or sell a specific stock at a certain price for a limited period of time." This is a much better definition, but if you are still confused, don't worry. By the time you finish this chapter, you will have a pretty good idea of what options are all about.

Stock Options Explained

You already know that stock options are contracts. Remember the stories about the house and the snow shovels? You had the right to buy the house, but you didn't have to buy it. In other words, you had the right but not the obligation to buy the house. It was the same with the snow shovels. According to the option contract, you had the right to buy the snow shovels, but you weren't obligated or forced to. You could let the contract expire and walk away.

Stock options are very similar. For example, an option contract gives you the right to buy stock, but you are not required to do so. In fact, many people don't buy the stock at all. They just buy and sell the option contracts. Also, unlike a share of stock, which is ownership of something real, an option contract is intangible.

This will make more sense if you allow me to tell one more story.

Let's say you are interested in a stock—YYY Manufacturing Company—that you think is going up. It is currently trading at $10 per share. You are sure it's going a lot higher within a few months. So you decide to buy an option contract.

According to the option contract, you have the right to buy 100 shares of YYY for $10 per share any time within the next three months. If YYY moves higher, to $11, $12, or even $15 a share, you can still buy shares of YYY for $10 each.

What if you are wrong and YYY goes down in price? In fact, if YYY is lower than $10, you definitely no longer want to buy it. You will buy it only if it's higher than $10 at the time the option contract expires. Just as with the house and the snow shovels, it seems to be a very good deal. The stockholder still owns YYY, but you control the shares.

So what does the seller of the option get? He receives money from you. Do you remember the name of the money that the owner receives? (In case you forgot, it's called the *premium*.) In the case of this stock option, the premium is rather cheap, perhaps no more than $50.

Basically, for only $50 you have the right to buy 100 shares of YYY for $10 per share within the next three months. You are not obligated to buy them, but you can if you want to. If you had bought stock instead of options, it would have cost you a lot more.

Let's see what happens in real life: YYY suddenly announces that it is developing a new product, a GPS tracking device, and the stock zooms higher. In one day YYY goes from $10 per share to $18 per share. Excellent! According to the option contract, you can buy YYY for $10 per share even though it's actually worth $18. That's a $750 unrealized profit (i.e., "paper profit"). The asset you own is worth more than you paid for it, but you have not yet sold it.

Here's something to think about. The premium on the stock option was $50 when the stock was selling for $10 per share. Now that the stock is selling for $18 per share, the premium increased by $750 and is now $800. The owner of YYY should be satisfied because he gets to keep the original $50 premium, although he is probably kicking himself a little for selling the option too soon and too cheaply.

You also have another choice, which is what makes options so fascinating. As the option buyer, you can also turn around and sell the option contract to someone else for $800. If you do this, you don't have to go through the trouble of buying the stock. In just a few weeks, you made a $750 profit without ever owning the stock.

Perhaps you think it's impossible to make money this quickly. Although it's not likely to happen, it's quite possible. I have a friend who made over $130,000 in three days by buying options in a biomedical company. He had read that the company might get approved for a new drug. Just on the rumor alone, the option premium rose by more than 400 percent. (Later in the book, I tell you what happened to his money.)

The Unique Characteristics of Options

Now that you have a general idea of how options work, let's look at some very unusual characteristics of options. Remember what I said. Sometimes the deeper you dig, the more confusing it gets. But to truly understand options, you have to learn their very specialized language. Although I can guarantee the next section will be educational, it will be a challenge to make it entertaining. I promise, however, to do my best.

Options have unique characteristics that are very important to understand. After we discuss these characteristics, I show you how the different pieces work together like a finely tuned financial instrument.

The Underlying Stock: "Without Me, You're Nothing!"

Without the *underlying stock*, there would be no option contract. Many people underestimate the importance of the underlying stock. In fact, one of the keys to success in the options market is choosing the correct stock.

By itself, an option isn't worth anything. If you think about it, stock options are only paper contracts that give you the right to buy or sell something. Think of it this way. Every option is linked or attached to a stock, which is the underlying stock. (Another term used to describe options is "derivatives," which means that option values are derived from, or based on, another financial instrument. In the case of stock options, the value is derived from a stock.)

You might wonder which stocks are allowed to have their options trade on an options exchange. Actually, there are options on more than 3,600 stocks trading on 12 option exchanges (and the list of stocks and exchanges keeps growing). The most well-known stocks have options, for example, General Electric, IBM, Apple, Google, Home Depot, McDonald's, to name only a few. The participant exchanges that allow options trading have very strict rules governing which stocks have their options listed for trading. Remember, not all stocks have options, but every option is linked to an underlying stock.

Penny stocks, that is, stocks that trade for under $3 per share, are not allowed to trade on an exchange. You know from the stock market that when you trade stocks that are under $3 per share, there isn't a lot of liquidity. It's the same with options. Generally, if you stick with well-known companies, you should get a lot of trading opportunities.

There is something else you should know about an underlying stock. Although I casually mentioned it earlier, you need to pay attention now because this is important. The following formula illustrates how options and stocks are linked.

1 option contract = 100 shares of stock

You can see from the formula that an option contract and the underlying stock are related. This is important when you're calculating what premium you are paying or receiving. To be technical, one option contract gives you (the owner of the option) the "right" to buy 100 shares of stock. You don't have to buy, but you can if you want to. (Hint: Later you will learn that most option traders do *not* buy the stock. We talk about this in more detail later in the book.)

Therefore, if you bought or sold two contracts, that would give you the right to buy 200 shares of stock. Five contracts equal 500 shares. If you bought or sold 10 contracts, that would be equal to buying 1,000 shares of a stock. Always remember to use 100 as a multiplier when calculating how many options to buy or sell.

One mistake that many beginners make is confusing contracts and shares. So when it comes time to enter the options order, instead of entering one contract, they become mixed up and enter 100 contracts. Do you realize what that means? They just attempted (if there is enough cash in the account) to buy the rights to buy or sell 10,000 shares of the underlying stock! I do my best to make sure you don't make that mistake when we discuss order entries.

When you are first starting out, you will practice by trading only one option contract (or 100 shares). This way, if something goes wrong, you won't lose very much. You won't earn much, either, but it's a small price to pay to gain experience.

Advanced note: In addition to trading options on individual stocks, you can trade options on exchange-traded funds (ETFs) such as SPY (S&P 500), QQQ (Nasdaq-100), DIA (Dow Jones Industrial Average), and IWM (Russell 2000). These are discussed in more detail in Chapter 23.

Note: You can also trade mini-options on certain high-priced stocks. With mini-options, 1 option contract = 10 shares of stock. Mini-options are discussed in Chapter 23.

The Secret of Options Is Revealed

There is something else you should know about an option's underlying stock. When the underlying stock goes up in price, the option goes up as well. Now you know the secret of options. In other words, if you pick an underlying stock whose price is rising, your option will usually go up in value. If the stock goes up high enough, eventually the stock and option will move together on a one-to-one basis. This is as sweet as it gets for an option owner.

Advanced note: The example above refers only to *call* options, which you'll learn about shortly. Also, there are times when the stock rises, but the call option does not.

No matter whether you are an options buyer or seller, the key to success in options is choosing the right underlying stock. Where the stock goes, the option almost always follows. And that is the secret of options that many people forget.

The Expiration Date

Near the stroke of midnight (ET) on Saturday following the third Friday of the month, I disappear forever.

Another unique characteristic of options is that they always expire. After a certain date and time, called the *expiration date,* options are nothing but a worthless piece of electronic paper. Options are wasting assets because they lose value over time and eventually no longer exist. As soon as you buy or sell an option contract, the clock begins ticking, like a scuba diver who has only a certain amount of air left in her tank.

The expiration date is listed on every option contract. What is the expiration date? It's officially 11:59 p.m. on the Saturday after the third Friday of each month. In other words, all contracts cease trading on the third Friday of each month at 4 p.m. ET (Eastern time), which is when the market closes. If you pay attention to the stock market, you'll notice that television commentators refer to it as "options expiration day."

Another interesting fact is that the third Friday of each *quarter* is referred to as "triple witching day" because thousands of stock options, index options, and future options expire simultaneously. On this day, the stock market is often volatile.

Unlike stocks, which exist indefinitely (unless a company goes out of business or merges), every option contract expires, sometimes in a month, sometimes longer. By the way, because all options eventually expire, they are a bit riskier to own than stocks. It's the time pressure that makes them riskier. Because you know in advance that the option will expire on a certain date, you have to make your profits quickly. In Part 2, I discuss how to use this time pressure to your advantage.

An expiration date secret: The more time that is left on an option contract, the more valuable the contract is.

Type: Call, Put, Buy, Sell (That's All You Have to Know)

Believe it or not, there are only two types of options: a *call* and a *put*. And with these two types of options, you can take only two actions: buy or sell. That's correct. Every option strategy is based on buying or selling calls or puts. Although there are dozens of fancy-sounding options strategies, all are based on buying or selling calls or puts. Call, put, buy, sell—don't forget these four words.

Although this entire book is devoted to buying or selling calls or puts, here is a brief description to get you started.

Call

A *call* option is similar to "going long" a stock (it means you believe the stock will rise). If you believe that the option's underlying stock will go up in price, you would buy a call. Remember the options secret? If the underlying stock goes up in price, the call option usually follows. The attractive part about call options is that you can participate in the upswing of a stock without actually owning the stock—and for a lot less money.

Put

Buying a *put* option usually refers to taking a short position in a stock (it means you believe that the stock will fall in value). In other words, if you believe that the underlying stock will go down in price or you want to protect your stock from a downward move, you will buy a put. Therefore, if the underlying stock goes down in price, the put option usually goes up. One huge advantage of buying a put option is that it's less risky than shorting stock—and less expensive.

The Strike Price: The Fixed Price

Hopefully, you already know that options give you the right to buy or sell something (such as houses, shovels, or stocks). When discussing stock options, the *strike price* is the fixed price at which you can buy or sell the underlying stock. Remember, when you buy a (call) option, you are actually buying the right to the underlying stock at a certain price— the strike price. When you sell a (call) option, you are actually selling the right to the underlying stock at a certain price—the strike price. Believe me, the strike price is a very important piece of information, which you'll discover when you first start trading, and as you keep reading.

To help you understand the strike price, let's review our examples. Remember when you bought an option on the house? The strike price was $100,000 (although you hoped the price of the house would go higher). And remember when you bought the snow shovels at a fixed price of $15, no matter how high the price of the shovels went up? The strike price was $15. And remember when you were willing to buy the stock in YYY for $10 per share? The strike price was $10.

By itself, the strike price is simply a number. You have a choice of many different strike prices. For example, although YYY is currently trading for $10 per share, you can choose strike prices from $5 all the way up to $25 (in the case of this stock, strike prices are available in 1 point or 2 ½ point increments).

> *First advanced hint*: If a stock is trading for $10 per share and
> you choose to buy a high strike price of $20, you must be
> brave or know something others don't know. This means that

by the time the option expires in a few months, you expect YYY to double in price and reach at least $20 per share. If you're right, you could make a small fortune. If you're wrong, well, you lose the cash you invested. Suggestion: Do not buy options that require stock prices to double.

Second advanced hint: The higher the strike price of a call option, the less the option will cost. If a stock is trading at $10 per share and you choose a $10 strike price, it will be relatively expensive. A $12 strike price will cost less. A $15 strike price will cost even less.

Final hint: Don't forget to pay attention to the strike price.

The Premium = The Price

As you know by now, the *premium* is extremely important to options traders. If you are a buyer, it is the price you pay for an option. If you are a seller, it is the price you receive. Just as in an auction, the premium constantly changes. It goes up and down based on the supply and demand of the market. If you are experienced with the stock market, you will understand that the options market also uses *bid* and *ask* prices. The final transaction price is the premium. Think of the premium as the price you paid or received for the contract.

The Basic Options Quote

Because options investors must know what options they are buying or selling, four options characteristics have been combined into a single description. For example:

SECOND
FRIDAY

MSFT December 13, 2019 25 Put

Underlying stock: Microsoft
Type of option: Put
Last day of trading: Third Friday in December 2019
Strike price: $25

YYY January 15, 2019 15 Call

> Underlying stock: YYY
> Type of option: Call
> Last day of trading: Third Friday in January 2019
> Strike price: $15

The Detailed Options Quote

Before the Internet existed, it wasn't easy to get access to options quotes. You had to wait for the next day's newspaper, visit your local brokerage firm, or call your stockbroker. Now you can retrieve options quotes instantaneously on your computer, mobile device, or phone.

In addition, before the arrival of computers, you had to be familiar with the letter and number option codes. Now the quotes are so user-friendly that it's easy to find what you need.

Option Chain

Let's begin by looking at the detailed options quote in Figure 3.1. By the way, the quote is called an *option chain* because it contains a series of options with different strike prices, in this case, for Boeing. The option chain also contains a variety of *expiration dates.*

The option chain contains extremely important information. Any website that has stock quotes also has the option chain, which you can read on your computer or mobile device. The option chain is your road map, and you will spend time studying it. It contains all the information you need to trade options.

It's essential that you learn how to read an option chain. After all, if you get confused, you could end up buying or selling the wrong option. For example, it is very common to make money-losing mistakes because you choose the wrong strike price or expiration date.

Note: Become familiar with the option chain because you will rely on it to find current option prices and correct expiration dates—something you must know when you're entering an order. It takes experience to find options with expiration dates that meet your needs. It also takes skill to find strike prices that pay you enough premium (if selling) or are a good value (if buying).

Although each brokerage firm might have slightly different ways of displaying an option chain, Figure 3.1 is an example of an option chain for the Boeing Company.

Your brokerage firm has the option chain on its website. If you don't have a broker, you can go to several sites that list the option chain. The most well known are the Chicago Board Options Exchange (CBOE) website (cboe.com), the Options Industry Council (OIC) website (optionseducation.org), Google (google.com/finance), or Yahoo! (finance.yahoo.com). There are dozens of other financial sites with free quotes.

To look up a free option quote, enter the stock symbol, such as BA, AAPL, GOOG, or IBM. On the left, select "options," and the option chain should be displayed. Options will be listed in order by the expiration date.

Note: The CBOE also has an excellent option chain app (application) you can read on your phone or mobile device while you're on the go. Your brokerage firm may have one, too.

Figure 3.1 is an example of an option chain for the Boeing Company.

The Option Symbol

Several years ago, the Options Clearing Corporation (OCC) modernized the option chain symbols. Each option symbol consists of the following information:

Underlying Stock	Expiration Y/M/D	Strike Price	Call or Put
YYY	20 07 20	55.00	C

Calls for BA Show Symbols | Show Analytics* ❷

Last	Change	Bid	Ask	Volume	Open Int	Action	Strike ▲
⊟ **Calls for May 18** 3ʳᵈ Week – Any Year							
4.30	+0.70	4.40	4.50	485	9,795	Select ▾	85
2.85	+0.71	2.79	2.82	1,157	14,723	Select ▾	87.5
1.60	+0.44	1.55	1.57	1,702	3,289	Select ▾	90
0.75	+0.20	0.77	0.79	27	517	Select ▾	92.5
0.36	+0.13	0.36	0.38	189	1,884	Select ▾	95
⊟ **Calls for Jun 22** → Always 4ᵗʰ Week – Any Year							
5.15	+0.80	5.05	5.15	31	510	Select ▾	85
3.50	+0.55	3.50	3.60	72	605	Select ▾	87.5
2.31	+0.45	2.30	2.32	329	3,808	Select ▾	90
1.38	+0.29	1.40	1.42	77	114	Select ▾	92.5

Puts for BA Show Symbols | Show Analytics* ❷

Strike ▲	Action	Last	Change	Bid	Ask	Volume	Open Int
⊟ **Puts for May 18**							
85	Select ▾	1.42	-0.29	1.42	1.44	430	2,412
87.5	Select ▾	2.30	-0.45	2.31	2.34	192	801
90	Select ▾	3.60	-1.21	3.60	3.70	114	219
⊟ **Puts for Jun 22**							
85	Select ▾	2.15	-0.40	2.19	2.21	13	454
87.5	Select ▾	3.20	-0.50	3.10	3.20	32	231
90	Select ▾	4.30	-0.75	4.40	4.50	23	238

Figure 3.1   Option chain for Boeing: a) call option, b) put option

Source: Fidelity Investments. © 2002 FMR LLC. All rights reserved. Used by Permission.

When you put it all together, this is what the quote looks like: YYY20072055C. This long, descriptive symbol simply means that the YYY call option has a strike price of $55 and expires on July 20, 2020. → 3ʳᵈ MONDAY

Fortunately, you no longer have to memorize option symbols because most brokerage firms hide the option symbols on their menu.

• •

Now that you have a general overview of the options market, you're going to learn how to trade. In Part 2 you will learn almost everything you need to know about a popular strategy called *selling covered calls*. For some of you, this might be the only options strategy you will ever use.

PART TWO

SELLING COVERED CALLS

4

The Joy of Selling (Writing) Covered Calls

You've waited a while to apply all the isolated bits of knowledge we've discussed so you can finally begin trading. Learning the strategies is not that difficult. The difficulty lies in the fact that for each strategy, you have many choices of what to do. In the stock market, you really have three decisions: buy, hold, or sell. But with options, you have more choices. (Why do you think they call them options?)

In Part 2 we discuss almost all you need to know about *selling* or *writing covered calls*. It's not necessarily easy to learn, although it's considered a conservative options strategy. Selling covered calls is mostly used to generate income or cash flow, which is why it's so popular with both professionals and individual investors.

This is the strategy that my risk-averse friends will appreciate (although there is risk when the market falls), which we discuss in Chapter 6. If you talk to certain speculators, they might claim that selling covered calls is boring. They prefer other options strategies in which they can do more leveraging. My answer to them is, "When is it boring to make money?" To use a baseball analogy, while you're waiting to hit a home run, why not hit a few singles?

I'll be straight with you: Part 2 is perhaps the most important section in the book. Why? Because much of what you wanted to know about options can be taught using covered calls. If you understand this strategy and learn to use it well, the other options strategies will seem relatively easy.

Nevertheless, this will be a challenging chapter. You may have to read it a couple of times before you truly understand it, even when we're using a so-called simple strategy like selling covered calls.

What It Means to Sell a Covered Call

Remember when I asked you earlier if you wanted to be a buyer or a seller? When you use the covered call strategy, you will be a seller. That's right—you are going to sell call options to people like my speculator friends. And even if you aren't interested in selling covered calls, it is important to understand how a seller thinks. This information can be useful no matter which side of the option contract you take—buyer or seller.

In options talk, *selling* a call is the same as *writing* a call. In the days before options traded on an exchange, call sellers had to write the orders on special forms, so the term *writing a call* stuck with many of the old-timers. In the options market, people use both terms interchangeably, saying that they are writing, or selling, a call. In this book, I use *selling calls* rather than *writing calls* because the term *selling calls* is used more often.

There is something else you should know about selling calls. When you sell a call on a stock that you own, it is known as a *covered call*. The word *covered* means that you own the stock whose options you are selling. Therefore, in this section I talk only about selling options on stocks that you have already bought and own.

The official definition of selling a covered call from the Options Industry Council (OIC) is, "An option strategy in which a call option is written against an equivalent amount of long stock." This is a good definition.

My explanation takes a little longer. When you sell a covered call, you are selling the buyer the right to buy your stock. To many people, it sounds weird to sell a right. Unlike investing in stocks, you are not holding a certificate or a piece of a company. Your only evidence that you bought or sold an option is what appears on your account statement or computer screen.

First of all, keep in mind that to sell one covered call, you must own a stock (100 shares). Basically, you have handed the rights to your stock to the call buyer until the expiration date. If you want to be technical, you have handed the rights to buy your stock to some random person who owns the same call that you sold. You are disconnected from the original buyer.

There is one main reason that you are willing to sell covered calls. You receive compensation, that is, money. Do you remember what the money is called that you receive from the buyer? If you do, you have a good memory. The compensation you receive from the buyer is called the *premium*. Collecting that cash is the main reason why you want to sell covered calls in the first place.

Many covered call sellers are preoccupied with receiving monthly or quarterly income. The premium is their compensation for selling the covered call to someone else. Later, when we go through the steps of selling a covered call, you will be able to calculate exactly how much premium you might receive.

What do you have to sacrifice in order to receive that money? When you sell covered calls, you accept the premium (cash) in return for agreeing to sell shares of your stock. This is your main obligation.

Do you remember the price you will sell the shares for? Answer: It is the *strike price*. There is an assortment of strike prices you can pick. And here's one key to being a successful covered call seller: Choose the right strike price, and you could make a decent profit. We talk more about choosing strike prices later in this chapter.

The Advantages of Selling Covered Calls

There are actually two main reasons to sell covered calls:

1. To bring in income or increase cash flow
2. As a method of selling stock that you own

When we talk about increasing income, it means that you sell covered calls to buyers to receive money. Instead of working for your money, your money is working for you. If you are fortunate, you can figure out ways to bring in relatively consistent income.

There are other advantages as well. Not only do you receive the premium, but you still own the stock. This means if the stock goes up in price, you may receive capital gains (depending on the strike price you choose). In addition, you also receive dividends from owning stock in the company (if the company pays dividends).

In addition, a very clever covered call strategy is to use the options market to sell stock you were thinking of selling anyway. You might as well receive a few extra bucks for doing so.

Selling covered calls is similar to buying a house and renting it to someone else. But instead of renting your house, you are renting your stocks. You need to think like a seller—much like the woman who sold an option on the house she owned and the manufacturing company that sold an option on snow shovels.

There are other good reasons for selling covered calls. It's one of the few option strategies that you can use in an IRA or in a tax-deferred account like a 401(k). Perhaps the best reason for selling covered calls in an IRA or 401(k) is that you won't be taxed on the revenue you receive (depending on the rules of the plan) until you take the money at retirement. Be sure to contact a tax advisor to make sure this information is applicable to you.

Perhaps you may be thinking that selling covered calls is too good to be true. Obviously, there are downsides to every strategy, and later, in Chapter 6, the risks of selling calls are thoroughly discussed. That's why I take so much time in the next three chapters to explain your various options (no pun intended).

Meanwhile, a lot of what you need to know about options can be learned with covered calls. And now, let's take a closer look at selling covered calls, an intriguing strategy I think you'll enjoy.

Background

The current date is April 10. Figure 4.1 illustrates the most active April call options for Boeing Company (NYSE: BA). The current price of Boeing is $88.10 per share (although it's guaranteed to change by the time you read this). You own 100 shares of the stock.

Understanding Covered Calls

You will sign onto your brokerage firm's account and enter the symbol of the underlying stock—in this case, BA. As soon as it is entered, the

Calls for BA   Show Symbols | Show Analytics* ❷

Last	Change	Bid	Ask	Volume	Open Int	Action	Strike ▲
⊟ **Calls for May 18**							
4.30	+0.70	4.40	4.50	485	9,795	Select ▼	85
2.85	+0.71	2.79	2.82	1,157	14,723	Select ▼	87.5
1.60	+0.44	1.55	1.57	1,702	3,289	Select ▼	90
0.75	+0.20	0.77	0.79	27	517	Select ▼	92.5
0.36	+0.13	0.36	0.38	189	1,884	Select ▼	95
⊟ **Calls for Jun 22**							
5.15	+0.80	5.05	5.15	31	510	Select ▼	85
3.50	+0.55	3.50	3.60	72	605	Select ▼	87.5
2.31	+0.45	2.30	2.32	329	3,808	Select ▼	90
1.38	+0.29	1.40	1.42	77	114	Select ▼	92.5
⊟ **Calls for Aug 17**							
6.04	+1.14	5.95	6.05	58	8,932	Select ▼	85
4.58	+0.48	4.50	4.60	38	1,128	Select ▼	87.5
3.20	+0.40	3.25	3.35	35	3,702	Select ▼	90
2.33	+0.33	2.30	2.34	29	1,084	Select ▼	92.5
1.54	+0.24	1.55	1.58	30	1,612	Select ▼	95

Figure 4.1   Option chain: Boeing calls

Source: Fidelity Investments. © 2002 FMR LLC. All rights reserved. Used by permission.

Boeing option chain appears on your screen (see Figure 4.1). You can find the option chain on your brokerage firm's site or on websites such as the OIC, CBOE, Google, or Yahoo!

The Premium

The option chain contains a great deal of information. First of all, we look at the *premium*, which is displayed as the *bid* and *ask* price. As sellers, we are focused on the premium that we collect (the bid price). The bid price simply displays the current highest bid price being published. Use it as a guideline, and do not expect it to be the amount of money you'll receive for your covered calls. Just as in the stock market, the bid and ask prices change constantly, especially on actively traded options.

The minimum premium you expect to receive (bid price) is displayed as "per share," from $0.77 to $5.95 in this example, but the

$0.36

premium ranges from pennies to hundreds of dollars depending on many factors. You may be wondering why there is such a wide range of premium prices. Welcome to the options market! Understanding how premiums are determined is one of the keys to being a profitable options seller (or buyer).

Remember that the current price for the underlying stock, Boeing, is $88.10. We'll choose the Boeing June 90 strike price because it's slightly above Boeing's current price. When you look at Figure 4.1, you see that the premium is currently displayed as $2.30 per share. This is what you can collect when you sell at the bid price.

Let's determine how much you'll receive if you sell the call. Remember that one option contract equals 100 shares of stock.

Calculating Premium (June 90 Call)

$2.30 per share premium (June 90 call)
× 100 shares of Boeing stock (or one option contract)

Total: $230 premium

Explanation: Because the premium is $2.30 per share and one contract equals 100 shares of stock, the premium is $230. If you sold two contracts, you would receive $460. If you sold five contracts, you would receive $1,150. If you sold ten contracts, you would receive $2,300. Remember that to sell 10 contracts, you must own 1,000 shares of Boeing.

Let's say that you wanted to sell the covered calls that expire in a later month. Take a look at the Boeing August 90 calls. When you look it up, the premium is higher that that of the June 90 calls—$3.25 per share. Do you know why the premium is higher?

Reminder: The later the expiration month, the higher the premium.

Calculating Premium (August 90 Call)

$3.25 per share premium (August 90 call)
× 100 shares of Boeing stock (or one option contract)

Total: $325 premium

Remember, calculating how much money you can potentially make is not the same as making money. Nevertheless, one day after you sell the covered call, the cash (premium) you receive goes into your brokerage firm's account marked as "Credit Received." (Note: Your brokerage firm may have a different wording.)

The first time you receive a juicy premium, it's exciting. As one reader said, "I feel like I'm getting paid to own a stock." But like any strategy, there are risks as well as benefits.

It's All About the Money

A few years ago, I discovered the beauty of selling covered calls. I sat down with my computer, looking up the premiums on dozens of options and calculating how much money I was going to make. It seemed like such an easy way to bring in extra cash (and from the comfort of my own home).

I figured I could bring in thousands of dollars in extra income every few months by selling covered calls on stocks I owned. But after jumping into it a bit too quickly, I realized that selling covered calls was a little more involved than I had originally thought. Although I made money every few months, it wasn't easy. Unfortunately, the books available at the time were either too technical or too unrealistic. I am determined to prevent you from making the same mistakes I did.

And now, I'd like to introduce a few important terms.

Introducing At-the-Money, Out-of-the-Money, and In-the-Money Options

It's important that you learn the terms, *at the money, out of the money*, and *in the money*. Fortunately, by the time you finish this book, you will be very familiar with these terms. When you begin trading, one of the factors that determines which option you buy or sell is whether an option is in, at, or out of the money.

To make it easier to understand these terms, let's bring up the Boeing option chain again. See Figure 4.2.

Calls for BA Show Symbols | Show Analytics* ❷

Last	Change	Bid	Ask	Volume	Open Int	Action	Strike ▲
⊟ Calls for May 18							
4.30	+0.70	4.40	4.50	485	9,795	Select ▼	85
2.85	+0.71	2.79	2.82	1,157	14,723	Select ▼	87.5
1.60	+0.44	1.55	1.57	1,702	3,289	Select ▼	90
0.75	+0.20	0.77	0.79	27	517	Select ▼	92.5
0.36	+0.13	0.36	0.38	189	1,884	Select ▼	95
⊟ Calls for Jun 22							
5.15	+0.80	5.05	5.15	31	510	Select ▼	85
3.50	+0.55	3.50	3.60	72	605	Select ▼	87.5
2.31	+0.45	2.30	2.32	329	3,808	Select ▼	90
1.38	+0.29	1.40	1.42	77	114	Select ▼	92.5
⊟ Calls for Aug 17							
6.04	+1.14	5.95	6.05	58	8,932	Select ▼	85
4.58	+0.48	4.50	4.60	38	1,128	Select ▼	87.5
3.20	+0.40	3.25	3.35	35	3,702	Select ▼	90
2.33	+0.33	2.30	2.34	29	1,084	Select ▼	92.5
1.54	+0.24	1.55	1.58	30	1,612	Select ▼	95

Figure 4.2   Option chain: Boeing calls

Source: Fidelity Investments. © 2002 FMR LLC. All rights reserved. Used by permission.

At-the-Money (ATM) Options

Rule: When the current price of the stock is the same as the strike price, the option is said to be at the money. People still refer to the option as at the money even if it's a few pennies away.

Look at the option chain in Figure 4.2. If Boeing were at $87.50, then the May 87.50, June 87.50, and August 87.50 options would be at the money. I'll give you another example. If the current price of General Electric (NYSE: GE) is $35 per share, what strike price is at the money? If you answered $35, then you are right. It could be the February 35, the March 35, or the April 35, but $35 is at the money.

Out-of-the-Money (OTM) Options

Rule: When the strike price of the call option is higher than the price of the underlying stock, the option is out of the money.

Using Boeing (which is $88.10 per share) as an example, the next closest strike price *above* $88.10 is out of the money for call options. (You can say that the option is one strike price away.) Therefore, the May 90 call is out of the money. So is the June 90. In fact, every call option with a strike price higher than 90 is out of the money. The May 92.5 is four points out of the money. The May 95 is seven points out of the money. What about the August 95? That is also seven points out of the money.

> *Hint:* Note that the more the call option is out of the money, that is, the *higher* the strike price, the *lower* the premium. For example, the May 90 premium is $1.55 while the May 95 premium is $0.36. The May 90 is more valuable.

In-the-Money (ITM) Options

Rule: When the strike price of the call option is lower than the price of the underlying stock, the call option is in the money.

In the example in Figure 4.2, the next closest strike price *below* $88.10 is in the money for call options. Therefore, the May 85 call is in the money. So is the June 85. The May 85 is three points in the money. The August 80 (not shown) is eight points in the money.

> *Hint:* Note that the more the option is in the money, that is, the *lower* the strike price, the *higher* the premium. For example, the June 85 call is more valuable than the June 90 call.

Which Option Should You Choose?

Assume that the underlying stock is at $40 per share. You choose whether you want an in-, out-of-, or at-the-money option. There are reasons for each choice.

The table below shows some of the options for a $40 stock one month before expiration. Remember that we are selling call options.

Stock Price	Strike Price	Call Option	Premium
$40	$50	Far out of the money	$0.10
$40	$45	Out of the money	$0.40
$40	$42	Slightly out of the money	$1.30
$40	$40	At the money	$2.70
$40	$35	In the money	$6.80
$40	$30	Deep in the money	$9.90

I know what some of you are thinking. Why not choose to sell the option with the juiciest premium? If you chose the $30 or $35 strike price, it would be nice to receive $6.80 or $9.90 per share premium for each contract you own.

In fact, choosing a deep in-the-money call is not recommended for beginners because the profit is minimal. Why sell your $40 stock for $30 or $35 per share just because the option price is high? (It's true, however, that some experienced traders sell in-the-money calls and believe in the strategy.)

Bottom line: In the above example, the $42 out-of-the-money strike price with $1.30 is an appropriate choice (note: as you gain experience, you may have other ideas of what is appropriate). If you choose the $42 strike price, you may become obligated to sell the stock at $42 per share, which is what you hope will happen. You also receive $130 in premium for selling one covered call.

Important note: Many believe that when you own an option that is in the money, it means that you (the option buyer) made a profit. A few of you may remember the old song, "We're in the Money." In the options world, just because an option is in the money doesn't necessarily mean that you make a profit.

The only factor that determines whether you earn a profit is whether the current price is higher than the price you paid to buy the option. The term *"in the money,"* simply refers to the relationship between the strike price and the stock price. It has nothing to do with profits and losses.

Before you go to the next chapter, I want to introduce a very important term: *assignment.* You'll be hearing this word a lot as you study the various option strategies.

Understanding Assignment

As a covered call seller, you have an important obligation. If the underlying stock is above the strike price at expiration (this means that the option is in the money), you are obligated to sell your underlying stock at the strike price. That is what happens when options owners *exercise* their rights. You (the option seller) will be *assigned* an exercise notice.

There is actually an official term for what happens to your stock when the buyer exercises the call option. Your account is assigned or the stock is *called away*. This means that you sell stock at the strike price. Because "called away" so clearly describes what happens to your stock, this is the term I use.

Once again, at what price does the call owner get to buy your shares? If you said at the strike price, then you are correct. If the buyer decides to exercise the option, the stock transaction always occurs at the strike price. This is according to the rules of the option contract.

As the covered call seller, it is theoretically possible to have your stock called away by the call buyer at any time, although it's almost always done at expiration. Don't expect to have your stock called away (sold at the strike price) before expiration, although there are times when it may happen. As the covered call seller, assignment is a good outcome. It means that your strategy has worked.

The main point is this: If you are going to sell covered calls, you should be prepared to sell your stock at the strike price. This is one reason why choosing the correct strike price is so important.

On the other hand, if you can't bear to have your stock sold at the strike price on the expiration date, then find another strategy. Many people sell covered calls on stocks they planned to sell. Your stock is sold, and you receive income. This is one reason why this strategy is so popular.

Important: Technically, your stock can be called away at any time, although it almost always happens at expiration. If your stock has been called away, you will be notified by your broker (no later than the opening of the market on the next business day) that your account has been assigned and that you no longer own the stock.

Note: You can always repurchase the stock and once again sell covered calls for the next month.

Note: For assignment to occur, the call buyer (also called the *call holder* or *holder*) must first *exercise* the option. First the buyer submits an exercise notice to his or her broker. Then the broker notifies the OCC (Options Clearing Corporation), which assigns that notice to a random person. If your account is randomly assigned an exercise notice, then the stock is called away. Remember that when you sell a call, you give up your right to decide when the stock is sold; that is, the option owner can decide to take your stock at any time.

When the call holder buys the stock from you, he or she is *exercising* the option. When the call holder *exercises* the option and if your account is assigned an exercise notice, you are obligated to deliver the shares of stock on which you sold calls. Don't worry—it's all done automatically by the OCC and your broker so you don't actually have to do anything. If you're still not sure how assignment works, I explain it in more detail in Chapter 8.

The Options Market Finally Gets Respect

It took almost 100 years, but an organized options market was finally created, based on the successful trading platform of the futures market. This is a short account of how the options market finally got the respect it deserved, after a very rough start.

1960s

During most of the twentieth century, trading in the over-the-counter options market was rather slow and tedious. Because there was no organized options exchange, trades were done by telephone. An options dealer arranged the deal between the buyer and seller. Unfortunately, there wasn't an organization to guarantee contracts. Also, traders didn't really know an option's fair price. Because of these limitations, the public had little interest in trading options.

The most annoying rule during this time was one mandating that if an option contract needed to be exercised, it had to be done in person. This means that if you missed the option exercise deadline, your option would be voided even if your option was profitable.

In 1968, the Chicago Board of Trade (CBOT) looked at the over-the-counter options market and concluded that changes needed to be made. It realized that at a minimum, all options contracts needed to be standardized; that is, the terms of a contract had to be the same for all contracts. In addition, the rule about exercising in person was eliminated.

1970s and Beyond

In 1973, after four years of study and planning, the CBOT applied to the SEC to create the world's first stock options exchange, called the Chicago Board Options Exchange (CBOE). The CBOE and the American Stock Exchange (which had allowed options trading on its floor) created an organization that would issue the contracts and guarantee the "settlement and performance" of the contracts. And thus the Options Clearing Corporation (OCC) was created to issue, settle, and guarantee option contracts. Officially, the OCC is a corporation owned by a number of U.S. exchanges that trade listed stock options.

With all the paperwork and politics out of the way, the CBOE opened for business on April 26, 1973. The first options trading room was actually the smoking lounge for CBOT members. According to the authors of *Options* (by The Options Institute), critics wondered how a bunch of "grain traders from Chicago thought they could successfully market a new trading instrument that the New York Stock Exchange had judged too complex for the investment public."

Call options were listed for 16 of the stocks in the most widely known U.S. companies. It would be another four years before put options were introduced. The first day, there was a total volume of 911 option contracts. By the next year, the average daily volume was 6,000 contracts with an annual volume of 1 million contracts.

By the end of 1974, after banks and insurance companies included options in their portfolios, the average daily volume in the options exchanges zoomed to over 200,000 contracts. Soon, other stock exchanges began trading listed options. Once the daily newspapers began listing options prices, volume multiplied even more.

With the introduction of computers, mobile devices, and additional options products such as index options, LEAPS, weekly options, mini-options, and options on ETFs, the average daily volume at the options exchanges exceeds 16 million and continues to grow. The annual volume now exceeds 4 billion contracts. Ironically, the volume of trading in the first half-hour often exceeds the volume of option contracts for all of 1974.

Now that you have been introduced to the covered call strategy, you will learn how to choose the correct covered calls.

5

How to Choose the Right Covered Call

By now, you might be feeling rather comfortable with the idea of selling covered calls. Maybe you think that the art of picking the right call is simply looking up the option with the most expensive premium and selling that option. Unfortunately, this is what some people do, but it's not the best method. Some people think the hardest part is deciding how much money they want to make!

What you may not realize is that there is an art to picking the correct covered call, and premium is only one part of the equation. In this chapter, we look closely at all the factors that lead us to make the right covered call.

Until now, most of our time has been spent looking at definitions. In this chapter, however, we do a lot more thinking and analyzing. This is what makes options so challenging. Selling covered calls, like other options strategies, is similar to playing a game of chess. You'll see why as we look at the main factors that affect the covered call, which are:

Market environment
Underlying stock
Strike price
Premium

Expiration date
Interest rates*
Dividends*

Advanced note: Interest rates and dividends are less important and are discussed in Chapter 11.

When you understand how each of these factors affects the covered call, then you will be on your way to becoming a knowledgeable covered call trader.

The Ideal Market Environment for a Covered Call Writer

If you trade stocks or invest in the stock market, you want the market to go up—and not just a little, but a lot. On the other hand, the one market environment that most people hate is a flat, slightly bullish market that appears to go in circles. In this type of market, stocks seem listless and out of breath, and no one seems to be making any money. The stock market could put you to sleep.

But there is one group of people that welcomes a sideways, somewhat slow market. Do you know who? If you guessed the sellers of covered calls, you are right. The ideal market environment for selling calls is when the market appears to be rising slowly. In this type of market, there is less danger that the market, or your underlying stock, will fall. Obviously, there are no guarantees, but your trade could be more successful when the market is a bit slow. While people are complaining they can't make any money in the stock market, you could be cleaning up.

Question: If the covered call seller prefers a slowly rising market, then you are right to assume that he or she likes stocks that act the same way. Do you know why? If you're not sure of the answer, you will be by the end of this chapter.

Searching for the Right Underlying Stock

At this point, you either already own stocks or are thinking of buying a stock, thus allowing you to sell calls. You already know that the underlying stock is important, but many people underestimate *how* important. In fact, the key to finding the correct covered call is finding a suitable underlying stock.

Actually, the underlying stock is essential no matter what option strategy you use. Most people mistakenly have this reversed. They first look at the option and then at the stock. They are led to believe that a profitable option is out there waiting to be discovered, like a winning lottery ticket. Unfortunately, they are looking in the wrong place. The right place, of course, is the underlying stock.

So which underlying stocks have the right characteristics for selling covered calls? For many years, investors and institutions sold covered calls on stocks of companies like General Electric, Microsoft, Coca-Cola, IBM, and Home Depot. These stocks fit the covered call profile. Many of the stocks in the Dow Jones Industrial Average (DJIA) were also perfect for this strategy. Although these stocks worked out well in the past, unfortunately there is no guarantee they will work in the future.

To find the ideal underlying stock, you have to do research. And once you find this ideal stock, you can sell covered calls on it month after month, quarter after quarter. Perhaps you already own one of these stocks. If so, it will save you the trouble of looking for another one.

How do you find these ideal stocks? Most brokerage firms have stock screeners that will help you find specific attributes. As you gain experience, you can also use the tools of the stock market, that is, fundamental and technical analysis, to find stocks that fit your criteria.

Perhaps you're still not sure why it's so important when using this strategy to have a flat or slightly bullish market environment and stocks that are slowly moving up. To help explain, let's first take a look at the kinds of stocks you don't want to use with a covered call strategy.

The Wrong Underlying Stock

The kinds of stocks on which you want to avoid selling covered calls are the ones that go up or down by large amounts and are too volatile. In other words, they move too quickly in one direction or the other.

For example, it is too risky to sell calls on roller-coaster technology stocks like Apple. Also, just because Apple doesn't fit our criteria for a covered call prospect has nothing to do with the worth of the company.

So what is the problem with a volatile stock? Actually, options on high-volume, high-volatility stocks like Apple have extremely high premiums. People pay more to own options in a company whose stock is volatile. But as a covered call seller, you don't want stocks that make huge percentage moves in one direction or another—the kind of stocks that may surprise you on Monday morning.

Although volatile stocks have rich premiums, for a covered call seller these kinds of stocks should generally be avoided. The reason is that the downside risk is too great. For example, if you sell calls on a wild stock like Apple (at least it was wild in the past), the stock could drop by several percentage points.

(*Note:* There is also a covered call strategy that purposely chooses volatile stocks in return for small profits. I discuss this strategy later in this chapter.)

Therefore, the biggest risk to selling covered calls is that the underlying stock drops too much, and although you keep the premium, you lose money as the stock drops. So you want to stay away from stocks that are going down in value, such as those breaking through moving averages and showing other technical weaknesses.

On the other hand, if an underlying stock like Apple moves up too quickly, you will still make money, but you will miss out on any gains past the strike price.

> *Hint:* Basically, when you are deciding whether an option is a good buy (or covered call candidate), there are many factors that must be considered, which I discuss now.

Characteristics of the Right Covered Call

You already know that to find the correct covered call, you have to search for the correct underlying stock. Let's assume that you use technical and fundamental analysis (or a stock screener) to find one of those stocks.

Next, you have to dig a little deeper and look at specific factors, including a sufficient premium, a strike price that makes sense, and where you believe the stock will be on the expiration date. All these factors must be weighed and studied before you can make the right decision, a decision that will bring you the most profit without risking too much capital or tying up your stock for too long.

The Strike Price

I've pulled up the Boeing option chain again (see Figure 5.1) to help you analyze all the characteristics you'll need to search for to find the correct covered call.

There are many factors to consider when choosing a strike price. At first, you might think of choosing the strike price with the most

Calls for BA Show Symbols | Show Analytics* ❷

Last	Change	Bid	Ask	Volume	Open Int	Action	Strike ▲
⊟ **Calls for May 18**							
4.30	+0.70	4.40	4.50	485	9,795	Select ▼	85
2.85	+0.71	2.79	2.82	1,157	14,723	Select ▼	87.5
1.60	+0.44	1.55	1.57	1,702	3,289	Select ▼	90
0.75	+0.20	0.77	0.79	27	517	Select ▼	92.5
0.36	+0.13	0.36	0.38	189	1,884	Select ▼	95
⊟ **Calls for Jun 22**							
5.15	+0.80	5.05	5.15	31	510	Select ▼	85
3.50	+0.55	3.50	3.60	72	605	Select ▼	87.5
2.31	+0.45	2.30	2.32	329	3,808	Select ▼	90
1.38	+0.29	1.40	1.42	77	114	Select ▼	92.5
⊟ **Calls for Aug 17**							
6.04	+1.14	5.95	6.05	58	8,932	Select ▼	85
4.58	+0.48	4.50	4.60	38	1,128	Select ▼	87.5
3.20	+0.40	3.25	3.35	35	3,702	Select ▼	90
2.33	+0.33	2.30	2.34	29	1,084	Select ▼	92.5
1.54	+0.24	1.55	1.58	30	1,612	Select ▼	95

Figure 5.1　Option chain: Boeing calls

Source: Fidelity Investments. © 2002 FMR LLC. All rights reserved. Used by permission.

expensive premium. As you remember, this is not necessarily the best choice.

In Figure 5.1, Boeing is still $88.10. If you want to sell a covered call on this stock, you have many strike price choices. You have to decide in advance what strike price is ideal for what you are trying to accomplish.

If you select an option that is out of the money or far out of the money, then you know that you have some room on the upside before the stock is called away (if it's ever called away). Therefore, the advantage of selecting out-of-the-money calls is that you know there is less chance that the stock will be called away (sold at the strike price) on the expiration date.

On the other hand, the higher the strike price and the farther the option is out of the money, the less premium you'll receive. For example, when we look at the Boeing option chain in Figure 5.1, we see that the out-of-the-money Boeing May 92.50 premium call has a $0.77 premium. (For many investors, that is a reasonable premium because it gives them an acceptable profit in return for the downside risk that comes with owning 100 shares.)

The Boeing May 95 call option fares worse. This is also out of the money but because it has a $95 strike price, the premium is a paltry $0.36. The chances that the stock will hit the strike price are small, and the premium reflects those odds. Only you can decide if the premium is high enough.

Note: Remember, you are not selling these calls just to collect the "free" premium. Owning stock comes with downside risk, and you want to be adequately compensated for taking that risk.

Let's see what happens if you select an option that is only slightly out of the money, for example, the Boeing May 90 call option. The premium on the May 90 call is $1.55. If Boeing actually makes it to $90 per share (or higher) at expiration, the stock will be called away. Even if Boeing goes as high as $92 or $95 per share, the stock will still be sold at the $90 per share strike price.

But what if Boeing doesn't go up but goes down? First, the value of the option contract goes down also. Fortunately, the premium you received will help reduce the pain of losing money on the underlying stock.

Nevertheless, if Boeing continues to drop, the value of the call you sold will continue to drop. *Note:* In an emergency (i.e., the stock begins to drop quickly), you could buy back the contract (this strategy is discussed in Chapter 7). Buying back the option allows you to sell the stock or sell another call.

So which strike price is best? The best strike price is the one the investor is most comfortable with. The comfort range is determined by the expiration date, premium, and volatility (discussed in Chapter 11). The strike price also depends on your outlook for the stock, the outlook for the market, and how much risk you want to take.

As you can see, choosing the correct covered call is more involved than many people realize. Many people underestimate how much thinking is involved when using this strategy. Therefore, choosing a strike price is an important decision that you shouldn't take lightly.

Advanced note: You shouldn't make a blanket statement whether it's best to sell in-, at-, or out-of-the-money calls. It's easy to make a case for each strategy, depending on whether you are bullish or bearish toward the underlying stock.

For example, some traders like the at-the-money strike price. If the stock stays in a narrow range, then the at-the-money strike price will return the highest profit. Defensive covered call writers may prefer the in-the-money strike price because it provides more premium up front. On the other hand, the stock will be called away if it's still in the money at expiration. Also, the profit might be too small. Finally, the out-of-the-money strike price may give you less premium, but it comes with more upside potential.

As you can see, you have many choices, depending on your strategy. As you gain more experience trading covered calls, you will learn which strike prices make the most sense for you.

Bottom line: Many investors consider the out-of-the-money strike price the most desirable because the option will probably expire worthless, and they keep the premium and the stock.

Premium

Although premium should not be the only factor to consider in determining which options to sell, it is definitely an important factor. After all, this is your payment. So premium must always be considered when looking at options characteristics. You are in the business of selling covered calls to make as much money as possible with the least amount of risk.

Some investors want a premium of $0.50 or more. The reason for this is simple. Let's say you sell a call with a $0.50 premium. If you are selling only one call, all you'll receive is $50. When you subtract the $10 in commissions, you gave up 20 percent of your potential profit, and there is not much left to earn. (*Note*: Only you can decide if a $0.50 premium is too low or just right. As you gain experience, you'll get a feel for what minimum premium meets your financial needs.)

If you are going to sell covered calls, you'll want to collect a premium that is high enough to provide an acceptable profit after deducting trading expenses. Anything less than "acceptable" is really not worth your effort.

Note: Keep in mind that you also want to avoid grabbing juicy premiums on falling stocks—not a recommended strategy. Why? Because it is very difficult to know when these stocks are nearing a bottom. You would collect that nice premium, but it comes with extra risk. Some stocks continue to fall (especially in bear markets).

Expiration Date

There is an old Rolling Stones song titled *Time Is on My Side*. When you sell covered calls, time *is* on your side, and that ticking clock is your friend. If the stock doesn't reach the strike price before the expiration date, the option expires and is worthless. You keep the premium *and* the stock.

When you look at the Boeing option chain in Figure 5.1, you'll notice that the May 90 is worth $1.55, the June 90 is worth $2.30, and the August 90 is worth $3.25. You can conclude that the farther out the expiration date, the higher the premium collected, but the longer your stock (and your money) is tied up in the position. All these factors have to be considered when you're searching for a good covered call.

So what is the ideal expiration date? Once again, it depends on your strategy. Many investors believe that a minimum of one month is best when selling covered calls, while three months is even better. The longer the expiration date, the more premium you'll receive. And yet, you also must be willing to let your investment dollars be tied up that long. As you gain experience (and continue reading), you will learn which expiration dates work best for you.

Conclusion: What Is the Right Covered Call?

What is the right covered call? In reality, you can choose any call. One choice is an out-of-the-money option that is one strike price away from the stock price. If you choose two strike prices away, the premium will be less and may not be desirable.

In addition, a minimum of one month for the expiration date is a good idea. A longer expiration date brings a higher premium and provides greater protection against loss. Perhaps you don't want your money restricted for that long. And finally, don't settle for less than your minimum acceptable premium, and go for more if possible.

You will eventually find a good covered call that meets your standards. It takes study and research to find good stock candidates. There are software programs that will give you ideas, but no magic answers. It's really up to you to find stocks (and options) that fit the criteria you are looking for.

Caveat: If you are a professional trader, you can find fault with what is considered the right covered call. After all, there are a number of advanced strategies that contradict these conditions. But you have to start somewhere. If you are a novice trader, start with the criteria listed above.

With more experience, you can tweak your criteria, perhaps lengthening the expiration date or choosing a strike price that is at or in the money. Once again, you want to devise your own criteria for the ideal strike price.

Carefully consider each trade, and you will be on your way to becoming a successful options trader. Your ultimate goal is independence. Then you won't have to depend on authors or instructors or other traders to tell you which options to trade and what strategy to use.

Before you put this book down and fire up your computer, remember this: There is a big difference between knowing what an ideal covered call is and finding it. Unfortunately, what you see on paper often has nothing to do with how a stock trades in the real world.

. . . .

Now that you've learned the factors you need to find the correct covered calls, you'll learn the mechanics of selling covered calls. This is the fun part!

6

Step-by-Step: Selling Covered Calls

In this chapter, we go through the actual steps of selling covered calls. Believe it or not, this is the easiest part of selling a call. The brokerage firms have spent millions of dollars to make the buying and selling of options as simple as possible—some might even say fun.

You've already signed the options agreement with your brokerage firm. I assume you already own a stock and want to sell calls on it.

Before we get started, however, let's discuss some of the risks of selling covered calls. Don't worry—I'm not trying to talk you out of trading. Although selling covered calls is considered a conservative strategy, it can also be risky. Unfortunately, no options strategy is completely fail-safe, including selling covered calls.

Any professional trader will tell you that one of the most important actions you can take before placing a trade is planning for the worst-case scenario. If you enter a trade with visions of profits dancing in your head but no clear idea of the potential risks, you could lose money. So pay close attention to all the things that could go wrong when using this strategy.

The Disadvantages of Selling Covered Calls

There are risks in selling covered calls just as there are risks in everything related to the financial markets. If you want to avoid risk completely, then put your money in a certificate of deposit (CD) or a Treasury bill. Because you are reading this book, I assume you are willing to accept some risk. Therefore, read about what could go wrong and plan accordingly. Although you can never eliminate risk completely, you can learn to manage it.

Heart-Stopping Plunges

The biggest risk with selling covered calls is that your underlying stock drops in value—a big-time drop—like what happened to a whole slew of stocks during crashes (we're talking about 70 to 80 percent drops). Even great companies like Google and Apple experience an occasional 10 percent drop on rumors or an earnings disappointment. If you had sold covered calls on any of these stocks, you wouldn't think that this strategy is so wonderful.

Advanced note: As mentioned before, there is an option strategy that allows you to buy back your option and take back control of the stock (in Chapter 7). Many beginners don't realize that they can exit their position before the expiration date by buying the call and selling the stock. If you're feeling uncomfortable about holding the underlying stock, then exit. When in doubt, get out.

Note: There is also a strategy called a *collar* that protects your account from large losses when the underlying stock misbehaves and you sold covered calls. It's so effective at reducing risk that there's an entire chapter on the strategy (Chapter 18).

Lost Opportunities

The other problem with selling covered calls is the potential loss of future profits. For example, let's say you sell a call on YYY Company at a strike price of $77.50, and it suddenly zooms from $75 per share to $85 per share or higher. You get to keep your premium and you get whatever you gained on the stock (up to $77.50), but anything higher than the strike price is not yours.

In this example, the stock will almost surely be called away at $77.50 per share on the expiration date no matter how high YYY goes. This can be very frustrating to people who don't want to be left out when a stock rallies past the strike price. Some people don't like covered calls because your profits are limited. If your goal is to make a lot of money on a fast-moving stock, do not choose this strategy. There are other option strategies you can use.

Unrealistic Expectations

Although it's possible to routinely profit by selling covered calls on a monthly or quarterly basis, there are no guarantees. Although receiving regular income from selling covered calls is a worthy goal, it can take time to find options that are appropriate to sell.

Trading Versus Investing

If you're a trader, you might not be willing to tie up your capital on a stock for a month or longer. The idea of waiting until the expiration date to sell a stock may test your patience.

Note: One idea is to sell covered calls on weekly options, which are discussed in Chapter 23. Although the premiums are smaller, the short expiration date makes this strategy desirable at times.

Ways to Reduce Risk

Many people, even after hearing about the risks, want to sell calls on all their stocks or buy stocks just to sell more calls on them. Please wait. Before you plunge into the covered call strategy, think about the following suggestions to reduce risk.

Get Organized

One of the best ways to reduce risk is to become organized. In fact, if you don't keep track of your trades, then you will never know if you're making a profit or not. Write down the strike price, the expiration date, premium received, the trade date, and days to expiration. If you are going to sell covered calls on a regular basis, you must get organized.

Create a Trading Diary

One way of getting organized is to keep a trading diary. Many professional traders have a journal or diary in which they enter their trades. After all, how do you know you've succeeded unless you know how you got there? The covered call seller enters all essential information, including what went right or wrong with every trade. If you don't write down this information, you won't learn from your mistakes.

Be Disciplined

Everyone talks about the importance of discipline, but few people know what it means. In your trading diary, you should include a set of rules that will guide you when you're buying or selling options. It's not enough to have rules. You must also have enough courage and faith in your judgment to follow your own rules. Playing it by ear, listening to tips, and trading too many option contracts are some of the worst mistakes rookies make. Your goal as an options trader is to reduce risk, even if it means giving up some profits.

Open a Practice Trading Account

Another idea is to "paper trade," or use the brokerage firm's software to practice. The CBOE and OIC have software that lets you practice. Paper trading is an excellent way to learn different options strategies.

Unfortunately, because it's a simulation, you won't experience the gut-wrenching pain of losing real money. Losing your own money in the market is one of the most effective ways to learn how to be a better trader, as long as you don't lose too much. Use the practice account to test all the worst-case scenarios and how to survive by managing risk.

Start Small

When you are first starting, begin by selling only one call, which represents 100 shares. By starting small, you'll keep your losses and emotions under control, while you're tweaking your strategies and techniques. Don't make the mistake of jumping into the options market with too much money and too little knowledge.

What to Expect from the Covered Call Strategy

One of the major criticisms of the covered call strategy is that potential losses are substantial if the stock plummets, whereas profits are limited. On the other hand, you can't have it both ways. If you are looking for slow and steady returns, then the covered call strategy might meet your needs. If you are searching for huge profits, then you'll want to read about the speculative strategies starting with Chapter 9. Only you can decide if the covered call strategy makes sense for you and what you are trying to achieve.

Let's Begin Trading!

Now that we've discussed the risks of using this strategy, it's time to learn how to trade. If you don't have a brokerage account (and even if you do), refer to the figures below to show you step-by-step how to sell covered calls.

If at first you are uncomfortable placing your own orders or want help from the brokerage firm, the representatives are willing to assist you (but they may charge a fee if they place the order). They can also discuss your covered call order and whether it is reasonable.

In the option chain, you should already know the symbol for the underlying stock, strike price, and expiration date. In fact, before you place the order, you should know well in advance exactly what call you are selling.

In this example, you have 100 shares of Boeing in your brokerage account, and now you want to sell one covered call. We'll pull

Calls for BA　Show Symbols | Show Analytics* ❷

Last	Change	Bid	Ask	Volume	Open Int	Action	Strike ▲
☐ Calls for May 18							
4.30	+0.70	4.40	4.50	485	9,795	Select ▼	85
2.85	+0.71	2.79	2.82	1,157	14,723	Select ▼	87.5
1.60	+0.44	1.55	1.57	1,702	3,289	Select ▼	90
0.75	+0.20	0.77	0.79	27	517	Select ▼	92.5
0.36	+0.13	0.36	0.38	189	1,884	Select ▼	95
☐ Calls for Jun 22							
5.15	+0.80	5.05	5.15	31	510	Select ▼	85
3.50	+0.55	3.50	3.60	72	605	Select ▼	87.5
2.31	+0.45	2.30	2.32	329	3,808	Select ▼	90
1.38	+0.29	1.40	1.42	77	114	Select ▼	92.5

Figure 6.1　Option chain: Boeing calls

up the Boeing option chain in Figure 6.1 to confirm the strike price, expiration date, and premium:

1. The current quote on Boeing is $88.10.
2. In Figure 6.1, we are interested in selling the May 90 call (the expiration date is five weeks away), an option that is out of the money.
3. The bid on the May 90 call is $1.55. You'll receive $155 in premium if you sell this covered call ($1.55 × 100 = $155).

Getting Started

Now that you are ready, you will bring up the options entry screen for covered calls (Figure 6.2). The screen at your brokerage account may look different from what is displayed here. And remember, by the time you read this book, all the options will have expired. This is true for every option in this book.

Underlying	Strategy	Last	Change	Bid	Ask
BA	Calls & Puts ▲▼	$88.26	1.0531	88.25	88.27

Figure 6.2   Option chain: Boeing calls

Source: Fidelity Investments. © 2002 FMR LLC. All rights reserved. Used by permission.

The Underlying Stock

Be sure to choose an appropriate underlying stock, and you should double-check. In the example below, we click on "BA," the stock symbol for Boeing.

Warning: If you mistakenly select an option on the wrong underlying stock (one that you don't own), you are suddenly selling an uncovered, or naked, call. This strategy is too risky. More than likely, the brokerage firm's software will prevent you from proceeding; nevertheless, be careful.

ACTION: *You enter the symbol for the underlying stock.*

After you enter a stock symbol, a blank option order entry screen should appear. It may look something like what is shown in Figure 6.3.

Before you can place your first trade, all the boxes must be filled in.

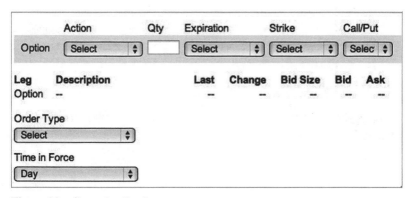

Figure 6.3   Covered call order entry

Source: Fidelity Investments. © 2002 FMR LLC. All rights reserved. Used by permission.

Sell to Open

In Figure 6.4, you need to select the correct options transaction. When you are ready to enter an order, understand what is meant by the following terms. It's essential that you know what they mean.

- *Buy to Open*: Select this when you are buying calls or puts. It's used to initiate, create, or add to a long position.
- *Sell to Close*: Select this when you are closing out or selling a call or put that you previously bought.
- *Sell to Open:* Select this when you are selling calls or puts that you do not own, and also when you are selling covered calls. (Most often used to place an order to sell a covered call.)
- *Buy to Close*: Select this when you are closing out or decreasing a call or put position that you previously sold. You also select this when you want to close a covered call position prior to expiration.

Because you are selling covered calls, we select Sell to Open, because in options terminology you have just opened or created a new position when selling a call.

ACTION: *You select Sell to Open.*

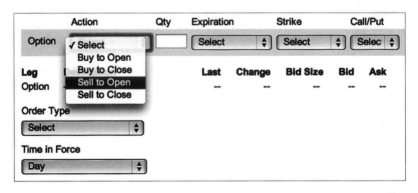

Figure 6.4   Sell to Open order entry

Source: Fidelity Investments. © 2002 FMR LLC. All rights reserved. Used by permission.

Quantity

Because you are selling one contract (representing 100 shares of the underlying stock), enter the number 1. Remember that one of the most common mistakes is entering the number of shares rather than the number of contracts. This is a mistake made by many people, even the pros on occasion (perhaps only the careless ones). For example, if you do make a mistake and enter 100, the system will hopefully prevent you from going any further (unless you happen to have 10,000 shares in your account!).

ACTION: *You enter 1 contract for 100 shares.*

Order Type: Market or Limit Order

In Figure 6.5 you must choose between a market order and a limit order.

If you are familiar with the stock market, you know that you can choose to let the market makers fill your order at prices they determine (*market order*), or you can choose your own price (*limit order*). It's generally agreed that choosing a limit order is better. Then you decide on the price at which you will buy or sell.

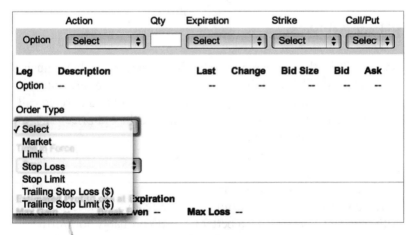

Figure 6.5 Market or limit order entry screen

Source: Fidelity Investments. © 2002 FMR LLC. All rights reserved. Used by permission.

Suggestion: Because of the way options are traded and how they change so rapidly, use limit orders only, and not market orders.

Note: Keep in mind that just because you select a limit order doesn't mean that you will be filled at the price you select. Monitor the trade closely until your order is filled. You can always change the limit price or cancel the order.

Important: It is a huge mistake to enter a market order overnight. In the morning, it's guaranteed that your order will be filled, but probably not at a desirable price. Always avoid placing market orders overnight.

ACTION: *You select limit order.*

Time

You have a choice of how long you want the order to remain open (live). You can choose "Day" or "Good-'til-Canceled." Because you are selling a covered call, you will select Day, meaning that you want the order filled by the end of the day or the order will be canceled.

Bid and Ask Price

As you fill in the screens, the option's last sale price, how much it changed for the day, and the current bid and ask prices are automatically displayed (see Figure 6.6). Because you are selling covered calls, you will focus primarily on the premium (i.e., the bid price) that you want to receive from the buyer.

We decide to sell the May 90 covered call on Boeing. At the moment, Boeing is trading at $88.25 per share.

The bid and ask price on the May 90 call option is $1.46 by $1.47, which could change by the time you are ready to place the order. Although you can try to get a better price, it's probably not worth your time to pinch pennies. One worthwhile trick is to enter a price above the bid. You can enter it, but it's unlikely you will get it filled, at least not right away. You can always try, however.

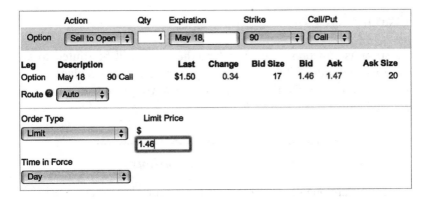

Figure 6.6   Order entry screen

Source: Fidelity Investments. © 2002 FMR LLC. All rights reserved. Used by permission.

> *Hint:* Don't pay much attention to the last sale price, because it could be from five seconds ago, five minutes ago, or five days ago.

Preview Your Order

If there is a preview button, it's always recommended that you review your order before you press the enter key. In the preview screen, the commission and the total cost of the order are usually displayed. You'd be amazed at the number of mistakes people make when entering an order. The preview button gives you one last chance to make corrections.

Broker instructions: If you called your broker and wanted to place the above order by phone, you would say, "I want to sell one covered call for Boeing May 90 at a limit price of $1.46 (or better) good for the day only."

Note: If you do decide to place a call with a broker, the recorded telephone call is proof that the order was entered at a specific time. Be sure to speak clearly and use options terminology to place the trade.

ACTION: *After you order is filled, you will receive $146 in premium, which is placed in your account the next trading day.*

Press the Enter Key

As soon as you press the enter key, the order will be routed to an options exchange. The next day, the premium will be placed into your account as a credit. Congratulations! You have sold your first covered call.

Employee Stock Options

If you are one of the 10 million employees who receives stock options, then learning more about your rights could save you a lot of aggravation. Most publicly traded corporations offer stock options, often as a reward or to enable employees to share in the success of the company. They are usually delivered on a quarterly or yearly basis. Most important, the options given to employees are not the same as those for sale on the options market (the kind discussed in this book).

When a company "grants" stock options to an employee, it gives the person the right, but not the obligation, to buy a certain number of shares in the company at a specified price, often the current market value. Unlike options traded on an exchange, however, employee stock options are issued by the company and are not transferable. More than likely, there will be other restrictions.

For example, the employee won't be able to exercise the options (i.e., convert them to stock) until the employee is *vested*. This occurs on a certain date in the future, perhaps in one or two years, maybe longer. Eventually, the employee can exercise the options and then sell stock on the open market. You should know that the company's human resources department monitors the stock options. Individuals who sell these stock options privately before the restricted date could find themselves out of a job.

Since stock options are issued without a dollar value, they are a taxable event when exercised. Nevertheless, it's essential that you consult a tax attorney or advisor to confirm the specific rules of your stock option plan. If you receive stock options, it is *your* responsibility to speak to the managers of the stock option program, as well as a tax advisor.

Find out the tax ramifications, when you should exercise, and the limitations and restrictions of the plan. Employees of companies that offer stock option programs should closely examine the restrictions of both the stock and options distribution. You want to avoid any surprises. (In the past, there were horror stories, but the IRS changed the rules to make things less confusing.)

If you are an employee receiving stock options from your employer, once again, it's essential that you find out everything you can about your rights and obligations. Consult with a tax attorney or tax advisor so a tax event that seemingly comes out of nowhere doesn't snag you.

Now that you've learned the mechanics of selling covered calls, you'll learn how to manage and maintain your covered call position.

7

Managing Your Covered Call Position

Now that you have received the premium for your first covered call, you might think that all you have to do is sit back and wait until the expiration date. This is a common but serious mistake. After you press the enter key and submit the order, the real work begins.

After all, stocks are as unpredictable as people (maybe more so), and when you are putting your money on the line, anything can happen. If you don't properly manage your position, you might let a winning option position turn into a loser.

This is why it's so important to plan for any possible scenario. Therefore, one of the most useful steps you can take is to create a trading plan, which describes what to do after you sell your first covered call.

The Importance of a Trading Plan

The purpose of a trading plan is to help you prepare for any possible market condition. You want to think of all the worst-case scenarios and plan accordingly. As you know, one of the trickiest parts of trading options is that you have so many choices. A written trading plan will help you figure out how to prepare for any what-if scenarios. A trading plan also helps you to control your emotions, one of the requirements for being a successful trader.

What Can Go Right or Wrong

And now, let's get started. To refresh your memory, Boeing was trading at $88.25 per share. Earlier, you had sold 1 Boeing May 90 call at a bid price of $1.46.

Following are the three possible outcomes for Boeing.

The Underlying Stock Moves Up

> *Outcome*: The stock price moves above the strike price. In this example, Boeing rises above $90 per share.
>
> *Analysis*: This is what you wanted to happen. If Boeing rises above the strike price and is in the money on the expiration date, you should anticipate that the stock will be called away.
>
> *Hint:* The more the stock price is above the strike price, the more likely the stock will be called away. Even if the underlying stock is above the strike price by as little as $0.01, the stock will almost certainly be called away at expiration, but seldom earlier.

For example, if Boeing moves past the $90 strike price to $95, a buyer will exercise the option, and you will sell your shares at the $90 strike price. You, as the option seller, are required to deliver 100 shares of stock to the buyer and get paid the strike price per share (don't worry; the transactions are done automatically by computers).

Although you have made money by receiving the premium, you won't receive any profits on your stock above $90 per share (no matter how high Boeing goes). Nevertheless, you benefit in three ways if the underlying stock is above the strike price (and in the money).

1. You earn capital gains.
2. You collect dividends from owning the stock (if the stock pays dividends) on the ex-dividend date.

3. You keep the $146 premium, and it becomes part of the sale price for the stock.

Note: Keep in mind that if you are using the covered call strategy, you have to prepare for the possibility of the stock being called away. If you can't bear to sell your stock, for either emotional or tax reasons, then you shouldn't be selling calls on it.

The Underlying Stock Remains At or Near the Strike Price

> *Outcome*: The stock price stays at or near the strike price of the option you sold. In this example, Boeing stays at or near $90 per share.
>
> *Analysis:* This is not a terrible outcome. If the stock is near the strike price and is not far out of the money, the option will expire worthless and the stock will *not* be called away.

This outcome is what many covered call writers consider the ideal scenario. If the underlying stock is below the strike price at expiration, you get to keep the premium, and at the end of the expiration period you can sell another call.

When you hear people say they repeatedly sell calls, this is what they mean. For example, if Boeing stays at or near $90 per share, that's actually a profitable outcome. The stock won't get called away, and you can sell another covered call for the following month (or another expiration date).

Some people sell covered calls, month after month, on the same stocks. However, before you start counting your money, remember that you can't always count on the strategy working.

The Underlying Stock Is Below the Strike Price

> *Outcome*: The stock is below the strike price when expiration arrives. In this example, Boeing falls below the $90 strike price.
>
> *Analysis*: The stock will remain in your account until the expiration date. If the stock stays below the strike price, you keep the premium and can write another call for the next month.

Unfortunately, the major risk of selling calls is that the underlying stock price drops too much. For example, if Boeing drops far below the current price of $88.25 per share, you will lose money on the falling stock price even though you keep the premium. Although the pain of a sudden drop is somewhat buffered by the premium, you still don't want to be trapped in a losing position. This is why it's essential for you to monitor your option position.

If you believe the underlying stock will bounce back, then you don't have to take action. However, once the stock falls below *breakeven* (see below), you might have to consider emergency actions to get out of your option position.

Calculating Breakeven

There is a calculation you can do to determine when you have to take emergency action:

$88.25 Boeing stock price
–1.46 premium
———————————
$86.79 breakeven

Explanation: Take the credit you received from the covered call—in this example, $1.46—and subtract it from the price of the underlying stock, $88.25. Breakeven is $86.79. If the stock drops below this price, you are losing more on the underlying stock than the amount you received as premium.

How to Buy Back Your Call Option

If your stock falls, you have two choices. You could watch the stock drop and hope it recovers. Your second choice is to buy back the calls you sold, allowing you to unwind the stock position.

This is not a strategy you will use often, but you should be aware of how it works. To buy back an option, enter the option symbol on your brokerage order entry screen, and select Buy to Close. You may enter the current ask price, but you can try to get a lower price. After you buy back your option, you are free from the terms of the contract, and you are in control of your stock. You can still continue to own the stock, or you can sell it at any price you can get.

Note: Another choice is to write another call option, bringing in additional cash. This alternative is advisable only when you still want to own the stock. Do not feel "married" to a losing position.

Advanced Covered Call Strategies

Now that you've been introduced to the basics of selling covered calls, let's take a look at more advanced covered call strategies.

Another Buy-Back Strategy

In the previous example, we discuss how to buy back your option in an emergency. What you might not realize is that many covered call traders purposely use a strategy in which they buy back options.

For example, let's say you sell a covered call for $1.00. When you look at the option quotes, you see that the premium is now only $0.10 with only a couple of weeks left until expiration. Obviously, the combination of time erosion and a falling stock has reduced the premium. So you could consider buying the option for $0.10, pocketing a $0.90 profit ($1.00 premium received minus $0.10 cost to buy the option back = $0.90 profit).

Once the stock is under your control again, you are free to sell another call for the next month (or any other expiration date). You may elect to do nothing until expiration, but with this strategy, you buy back the option (select Buy to Close on your brokerage order entry screen) and sell another call (Sell to Open) when the premium is attractive. This strategy is designed to manage risk.

Rolling Options Up, Over, or Out

When you roll options up, over, or out, it means that you are closing the covered call contract you are currently holding and opening a position with a different strike price and later expiration date. People roll options for various reasons.

Roll Up

Traders will *roll up* options when they don't want the stock to be called away. When you roll up an option, it means you close the current position and roll it up to a higher strike price. Your new option position may have the same expiration date, but it will have a higher strike price. This way, your option is once again out of the money and will probably not be called away at expiration. You spent some cash, but gave yourself a little breathing room.

For example, let's say you sold 10 YYY February 68 calls. When YYY hits $67.50 per share, you fear that the stock will continue to rally and that it may be called away from you. So you close the option position by buying back the calls at the current ask price or less. (Once again, select Buy to Close on your brokerage order entry screen.) Then you sell 10 calls, maybe the February 70 strike price. This gives the stock more room to move higher, and the stock won't get called away.

Note: People who use this strategy are attempting to earn even more than the maximum profit that was available from their original position. It's not wrong to want more money, but when selling covered calls, you must accept reality: sometimes the stock may be called away.

Roll Out or Roll Forward

A *roll out* is also known as a *roll forward*. For example, let's say you are still holding 10 YYY Feb 68 calls. You are certain that YYY will not reach $68 per share before the expiration date. In this case, you want to keep selling calls on the same stock. So you roll the 10 options over to the *March* 68 call. (Basically, you close the February contract and simultaneously open the March contract.) The strike price may remain the same, or you may choose a different strike. Only the expiration month changes.

If you find the right underlying stock, you could do well rolling options over and over again, month after month.

Roll Up and Out

Some investors will roll up and out in one transaction. Let's say you sold a one-month Mar 50 covered call on YYY, and the stock zoomed up to $51. If you believe that the stock is going to continue to make a nice run, you could close out the current contract and sell an April contract at the 55 strike price.

The Buy-Write Strategy

Although the buy-write strategy is listed under advanced strategies, a buy-write is actually very simple. It works like this: When you simultaneously buy a stock and write (sell) a covered call, it's called a buy-write. Nearly all brokerage firms allow you to simultaneously buy the stock and sell the call, and most have a convenient drop-down menu for making that selection.

Another buy-write strategy is to look for stocks just so you can sell calls on them. The idea is to buy a stock that you'd love to have in your portfolio, and that also provides a reasonable premium.

For example, one of my trader acquaintances bought Tyco International just so he could sell its covered call. He bought 1,000 shares of Tyco at $26.70 and simultaneously wrote (or sold) 10 of the $27.50 calls. The premium was $0.50 with one week left until expiration (not a bad premium with a week left to expiration).

Tyco made it to $27.50 before the expiration date, just as he expected, and his stock was sold. The profits were very favorable. He first made $500 from the premium he received by selling the calls ($0.50 times 10 calls, or 1,000 shares = $500). He also made an $800 profit from the stock (it went from $26.70 to $27.50 for a profit of $0.80, or $0.80 per share on 1,000 shares, or $800.) So in one week he made a total of $1,300.

Using the Options Market to Sell Your Stock

A very clever approach to the options market is to use it to sell stocks that you own and make a few extra bucks in the meantime. The idea is to use the options market to sell your stock.

For example, let's say you own 100 shares of Home Depot at $70 per share. You had been thinking of selling this stock at a target price of $72.50 per share. So instead of selling the stock immediately, you look up the premium and sell the Home Depot $72.50 call (at the money) and choose an expiration date. You can choose a one-month expiration because you want to sell the stock, and don't want to wait too long.

If everything goes as planned, you will receive at least a dollar in premium (in this example), and assuming the stock moves up more than 2 points, it would be called away at the strike price of $72.50. In other words, you are using the options market to sell your stock at $72.50, which is what you wanted. (Typically, you will sell an out-of-the-money call.)

The good news is that you receive a little extra income from the sale. This works best if you were thinking of selling the stock anyway. In the worst-case scenario, although you receive and keep the premium, the stock might fall in price (which is always the risk with covered calls).

Note: I like this strategy. When a stock I bought is a point or two below my target price, if the premium is attractive, I'll sell a covered call. My target price is my strike price. I receive the premium, and if my strategy works, the stock gets called away and sold at the strike price. Once again, this strategy wouldn't be wise if there was a market decline and you needed to sell the stock immediately.

Half and Half

If you are not sure how many covered calls to sell on your stock, you can sell calls on a portion of the position. For example, if you own 1,000 shares of Home Depot, you could sell two, five, or eight calls. The only problem with splitting positions is you have to keep detailed records, and it can get confusing for some investors, especially at tax time.

Who Are Market Makers?

Market makers are individuals or firms that are obligated to make bids to buy and offers (ask prices) to sell listed options during the trading day. It is a market maker's job to provide liquidity in the marketplace. The main job of the market maker is to keep the market moving or flowing in order to maintain a "fair and orderly market."

The market makers who trade options on the floor of the CBOE in Chicago were once called *floor traders*. They yelled and screamed the bid and ask prices (the open outcry method). They wanted to be heard so that the broker who represented the customer orders could see and hear them. Today, almost all options are traded on the same trading floor, but market makers are using computers to display their bid and ask prices. Computers automatically match buyers and sellers.

As is the case with any trade, there must be someone on the other side, either to buy or sell. If you buy an option, someone is the seller. That someone is probably, but not always, the market maker. If you want to sell an option, the market maker will buy it from you. By bidding and asking, they are literally "making a market" for the option.

Market makers have to make a market in the options of every underlying stock that they trade. So, if everyone's selling, they have to post a bid price. Keep in mind that although market makers are obliged to maintain liquidity in the market, they are not required to take a loss. In other words, if there are too many options for sale, expect the prices to decline.

The market makers are also not obligated to take everything that everyone wants to sell. When a transaction isn't immediately profitable, market makers hedge their positions. To compensate for the risk that they are taking, market makers maintain a bid-ask *spread* on each option that they cover.

For example, market makers might buy 10 IBM call contracts from you for $1.00 (the bid price) and then "offer" to sell them to another buyer for $1.05 (the ask price). The market makers keep the $0.05 difference *if* they can quickly find a $1.05 buyer. If they can't find a buyer immediately, they'll offset their position with another stock or another option. When you add up the millions of contracts that are traded each day, the potential profits can really add up (but so can the risks).

Market makers almost never hold options until expiration. In fact, they rarely hold options longer than a few *minutes*. They'll buy a covered call from you and plan to immediately turn around and sell it to someone else or sell stock. When there are no buyers, the market makers find a hedge. One such hedge is the sale of stock.

There is a lot you can learn from market makers. First, market makers have no preconceived opinion of the market. They follow the volume and direction of the market but don't try to predict which direction the market is going. Second, they pay attention to the market all day long. Even if they go to lunch, they are usually watching their position.

In the next chapter, we're going to take a closer look at the nuances of exercise and assignment.

8

Assignment: Your Obligation to Sell

Many beginners are confused by assignment, which is why I wrote this chapter. With each option strategy in which an option is sold, there is a possibility that you will receive an assignment notice, so it's important to learn how it works.

Because assignment has caused so much unnecessary anxiety and confusion, the term "assignment anxiety" explains the phenomenon. To help ease any concerns (and because I remember my own confusion when I first learned about options), I go into more detail about this procedure. (Some of the main points will seem like a review.)

When you sell covered calls (or uncovered calls, which we'll discuss later), before the stock can be called away (i.e., assigned), the call buyer must exercise his rights. The buyer does not have to exercise, but has the right to exercise. It is a choice. If any buyer does exercise the call option, and if that exercise notice is assigned to your account, you are required to deliver shares of the stock on which the calls were sold. Don't worry—the OCC and your broker do it all automatically so you don't actually have to do anything.

From the covered call seller's perspective, which is your perspective, the stock you own is taken from your account and sold at the strike price. You also get paid for selling the stock at the strike price.

To review, at what price does the exerciser get to buy your shares? If you said at the strike price, then you are correct. If the buyer decides to exercise the option, the stock transaction is always at the strike price. This is according to the rules of the option contract.

In summary, you could wake up on the Monday after the expiration date and discover that the stock on which you sold calls is no longer in your account because it was called away at the strike price. This is because the buyer decided to exercise his or her right to buy the stock. You could always buy back the stock immediately and sell calls on it for the next month. Some people do this every month.

It's important to remember that you are obligated to deliver the shares of stock to the call buyer. You do not have a choice. When you sell any call, you become obligated to sell stock at the strike price (but only when you are assigned an exercise notice).

Let's see what happens behind the scenes. When the buyer decides to exercise the option at the strike price, his brokerage firm notifies the Options Clearing Corporation (OCC). After the OCC takes over, it randomly selects a brokerage firm with a matching short position in that option. As a result, his stock was sold at the strike price and called away. The transaction took place overnight. It will look like any other sell transaction except it may have the word *assignment* next to it.

In summary, exercise and assignment are a two-part process. First, the option is exercised. Next, the option seller is assigned (i.e., the seller of the call option is assigned an exercise notice, and the stock is sold). You can't have one without the other. It's really that simple, and yet it can sometimes be confusing.

Note: If you have questions, be sure to call your brokerage firm because each firm may have a different procedure for notifying you whether you got assigned.

Note: Remember that you have no control over whether the stock is called away. This is completely up to the buyer.

Important note: Although your stock can be called away at any time until expiration, it's almost always done on the expiration date (with few exceptions).

Assignment is not something to be feared if you are selling covered calls. When selling covered calls, you will welcome assignment because it means your strategy worked. The stock was sold at the strike price. You received premium, and you sold stock at a price that you thought was acceptable.

The Unexercised Option

What happens if the stock is below the strike price at expiration? This happens a lot more often than you might think. Although there is some controversy over the exact numbers, it has been reported that most options expire unexercised by the expiration date. No one agrees on the exact percentage.

Nevertheless, if the option doesn't get exercised, you get to "pocket the premium" and keep the stock. You also get to sell another call on the same stock if you wish. Some would say this is the perfect outcome. Perhaps that's why many sellers secretly hope the stock never makes it to the strike price (and expires worthless).

When Do Buyers Exercise Their Options?

Do you want to know when a buyer will exercise an option? This is actually a fascinating question, one that is the key to understanding covered calls. The answer is that this will only happen when the stock price is above the strike price and usually when expiration has arrived.

That's right. Usually the buyer will wait until the last minute to exercise the option. So when you sell a covered call, you must be prepared to wait until the very last day before the stock is called away from you.

Of course, there are exceptions. On rare occasions, a stock will be called away from you before the expiration date. And it's extremely rare, almost unheard of, for someone to exercise an option that is not in the money because they would pay more for a stock than he or she has to. If the strike price is higher than the stock price, it would be silly to buy the stock at the strike price when it is available for a better price. (Nevertheless, people do make mistakes, so it is possible an option that is *not* in the money could be exercised.)

As you remember, if at the end of the expiration period, the stock price is above the strike price, even by $0.01, your stock will automatically be called away at expiration. So if you are going to sell covered calls, you have to expect your stock to be called away on the expiration date, that is, the third Friday of the month, if the option is in the money.

You (the covered call seller) don't have to do anything to sell your stock. You usually find out the Monday after expiration if your stock was called away.

Early Assignment

Most of the anxiety about assignment occurs when you don't expect the stock to be called away. If you are selling covered calls, you expect assignment on the expiration date. Most of the time this is when the stock will be called away. But on occasion, the stock can be called away *before* the expiration date. It's relatively rare, but it does happen.

Even if the option is deep in the money before the expiration date, the chances for early assignment are remote. Why? Because as long as there is some *time value* (also known as *time premium*) left, the call buyer will not exercise early. If he or she did, it would be throwing away money. This will make more sense when you learn about option pricing. Most important, it's highly unlikely your stock will get called away before the expiration date. And if it is, consider it a gift.

There is one exception: On occasion, a trader will want to capture an impending dividend on the underlying stock. To capture that dividend in time, the trader must exercise early (one day before the stock goes ex-dividend). If that happens, your stock will be called away before the expiration date, and you will not get the dividend. My advice: Prepare for the possibility of early assignment, especially as the expiration date approaches.

Note: To review, early assignment is not that common (although it does happen), and if it does occur, it will usually be very close to the expiration date. If your stock is called away early, it's a good outcome (if you are selling covered calls).

Avoiding Assignment

For a variety of reasons, some people try to avoid assignment. If you're selling covered calls, you expect and plan for assignment. When your stock is called away, your strategy is working. You initiated the covered call strategy knowing in advance that your stock could be taken out of your account and sold at the strike price.

On the other hand, if you absolutely don't want your stock called away and sold (perhaps for tax reasons or because you think the stock is going to explode higher), you probably shouldn't be writing covered calls. However, you can avoid assignment by buying back the option. You might have a loss on the position, but you gain back control of your stock.

Warning: On occasion, some novice traders assume that there was no assignment and their stock was not called away. Rather than checking their account, they initiate a new covered call position on the underlying stock. But there's one problem: They no longer own the stock.

If you inadvertently sell a call option on a stock you no longer own, you'll be exposed to an uncovered, or naked, position. More than likely, your brokerage firm will stop the transaction from proceeding (because you need permission to use Level 4 strategies). It's still a good idea to check your account position on Monday following the expiration date.

Important: The best advice I can give is that if you are holding an option position, do not wait until the expiration date to decide what to do. Many of the complications and confusion about exercise and assignment (especially with advanced strategies) could be avoided if investors planned ahead.

Assignment Summary

Let's review what you've learned about assignment:

1. If you sell covered calls, you are obligated to sell your underlying stock if the call buyer exercises.

2. As a covered call seller, be prepared to have the stock called away (assigned) at any time, but assignment almost always occurs on the expiration date.
3. Your stock will automatically be called away if it is in the money, even by a penny, on the expiration date.
4. If you are selling covered calls, assignment is a positive outcome.
5. An assignment notice will appear in your brokerage statement, and the stock will have been sold at the strike price.
6. Early assignment is relatively rare, but it can happen.
7. After your stock is called away, you can immediately buy it back by purchasing shares in the stock market.

Now that you've been introduced to the covered call strategy, you're going to learn how to buy calls, a strategy used by option speculators. Whether you are interested in speculating or not, it's essential that you understand the strategy.

· ·

You might want to take a break before moving to Part 3. After all, there's a big difference between being a seller of options and being a buyer of options. Instead of receiving premium, you will be paying premium to the seller.

PART THREE

HOW TO BUY CALLS

9

Introduction to Call Strategies

If you are reading this book because you want to leverage your money to make more money, this is the chapter you've been waiting for. *Buying calls* (you can also say you are *long calls*) is the preferred strategy of speculators, and there is a good reason why. For a fraction of what it costs to buy stocks, you can leverage your money with a possibility to double, triple, or quadruple your initial investment.

At first glance, buying options seems a lot less complicated than selling them. As you'll see later, the mechanics of buying calls is a breeze. The hard part, as usual, is making a profit.

Many traders agree that it can be tough to make a consistent living as a call buyer (I discuss some of the risks in Chapter 12). On the other hand, if you occasionally speculate by buying call options, it is possible to overcome the odds and make money.

As you'll see when you read this chapter, finding the correct call option takes skill, knowledge, and an understanding of how options are priced. Professional options traders take their work very seriously. If you don't have discipline and think trading options is a way to make easy money, you will be disappointed.

So take the time to read this section thoroughly. You will want to know how to buy calls when you learn about the intermediate option strategies introduced later in this book. Learning how to buy calls is deceptively easy, but also an essential skill.

What It Means to Buy a Call

In simple terms, when you buy calls, you will profit if the underlying stock goes up, and you may lose money if it goes down. And because you don't own the stock, buying calls is a lot cheaper than buying stock, which is why speculators like it. Let's take a closer look at this strategy.

The official definition of a call, from the Options Industry Council (OIC), is, "An option contract that gives the owner the right to buy the underlying security at a specified price (its strike price) for a certain, fixed period of time (until its expiration)." That sums it up quite well.

My explanation is similar. When you buy a call, you have the right to *buy* the underlying stock at a specified price on or before the expiration date. You are not required to buy the stock, but you can if you wish. Once again, the buyer is sometimes referred to as the *holder*.

In other words, you have the right, but are not required, to buy the underlying stock at the price listed in the option contract (the strike price). Just like the option you bought on the house or the option you bought on snow shovels (see Chapter 1), you are temporarily acting as the potential owner of the underlying stock. You have the right to buy the underlying stock but are under no obligation to do so.

For the right to potentially own this stock, you have to pay money (the *premium*) to the seller. And in return for this payment, you control the stock and hope to participate in its rising value. Don't forget. When you buy call options, you are in control of the stock.

Note: If you do earn a profit when the stock rises, you will want to sell the call at a profit. As a speculator, you take profits and do not want to be a stockholder. We discuss the reasons why in this chapter.

Why People Buy Calls

Buying calls is an option strategy primarily used by speculators. When you buy a call, it means that you are bullish on the stock market, the index, or the underlying stock. This strategy works best when, after you buy the call, a particular stock makes an explosive move upward in a relatively short time period. Like most options strategies, you can leverage a relatively small amount of money into a large amount of money, assuming your trade is successful.

As a call buyer, you believe that the underlying stock is going to go up in price. If it does, you could make money. If it doesn't, then the most you could lose is what you paid for the option.

Call options are linked to an underlying stock. If the underlying stock goes up in price, so does the option (usually, but not always, which I'll discuss later). When you buy a call option, you are basically long the underlying stock. You are speculating that the underlying stock (and your option) will go up in price before the expiration date.

There are a number of plays that you can make with call options:

1. First, after buying the call, you can eventually sell the option for a profit (assuming that the price increases). In fact, most of the people who buy calls have no interest in owning the stock. They are interested in selling the more valuable call option for a price higher than they paid for it.
2. Second, you can buy the call with a plan to eventually buy the underlying stock (as you know, this is called exercising your option). This strategy is not for speculators.
3. Finally, if the stock play doesn't work out, you can allow the option to expire worthless or sell it for a loss.

The Advantages of Buying Calls

Even if you don't think you'll ever buy calls, it is essential that you learn how to do it. As mentioned earlier, all options strategies are based on buying or selling calls and puts. So no matter what options strategies you eventually use, it's likely that you'll need to know how to buy calls.

Low Cost

Perhaps the most attractive part of buying calls is the low cost, For instance, a stock might be selling for $25 per share, but the call contract is only $1.00. You basically get to participate in the movement of the stock for a limited time without having to purchase it.

There are other reasons to buy call options. For example, let's say your neighbor tells you about a "once-in-a-lifetime" stock that is going to take off in the next two weeks. Although you know you should never buy stocks based on tips, you are tempted to sink thousands of dollars into the stock. (Imagine how you'd feel if your neighbor was actually right!)

Basically, you don't want to risk too much money, but you still want to participate. So instead of tying up thousands of dollars in a stock purchase, you buy a call option. More than likely, the neighbor's stock will go nowhere. But instead of potentially losing thousands of dollars, you might only lose a few hundred. (Of course, there is always the remote chance that your neighbor is right.)

Another advantage is that buying calls allows you to buy stocks that are too expensive. For example, let's say you want to buy XYZ Company when it is over $300 per share. It is well beyond the financial means of many people to buy 100 shares when the cost is more than $30,000. But for a fraction of the cost, you can buy call options on XYZ and other expensive stocks and participate as they climb higher (at least you hope so).

In real life, how many people can afford 1,000 shares of Google or Apple, or even 100 shares? With call options, you can own the rights to the shares of these stocks for thousands of dollars less.

How many people knew that Google was going to zoom up because of its popular search engine but did nothing about it? And how many people knew that Apple was going to go up because of the iPad and iPhone? These stocks, and hundreds more like them, would have been ideal option plays (and good investments). Some people do both: buy stock in the company and supplement the purchase with call options.

And finally, some people buy options because they don't have a lot of money or don't want to tie up capital. You need thousands of dollars to get started in the stock market, but only a few hundred to buy call options.

Note: Because of mini-contracts, you also have the right to buy call options on only 10 shares of certain high-priced stocks rather than on 100 shares. This is explained more fully in Chapter 23.

Leverage

The number one reason that speculators are attracted to buying calls can be summed up in one word: *leverage*. For a fraction of the cost, you are able to control many times more than you invested. For example, for only $500 you can potentially "control" $10,000 or more in stock. Many call buyers are willing to take the chance, knowing that they can make many times over their investment through leverage.

Call buyers profit when the stock goes up, and they do not have to buy the stock outright. If they are successful, they use a small amount of money to make a profit.

Less Risk

I'm sure you've heard how risky options are, but the truth is that many options strategies can be less risky than owning stocks if they are used properly. First of all, when trading options, you know in advance how much you can potentially lose. Therefore, you have controlled your risk. When you buy calls, although you can still lose 100 percent of your money, it may be less than the amount you would have invested in stocks.

The advantages of buying calls were clear many years ago when many bank stocks (and stocks of other financial companies) dropped by 80 or 90 percent in a few months. If you owned their stocks, the losses were catastrophic. Had you bought 100 shares of Lehman Brothers at $100 per share, for example, it would have cost you approximately $10,000. After Lehman blew up, you could have lost approximately $9,500 or more. If you were holding a call option on Lehman, the most you would have lost was perhaps $500, the total cost of the call.

The Right and Wrong Underlying Stocks

When you sold covered calls, you wanted a rather tame market and stocks that were going nowhere. Not so with buying calls. The ideal environment for buying calls is a bull market. The higher and stronger the market rallies, the better it is for call buyers.

During a bull market, call buyers may do very well when stocks zoom higher than anyone anticipated. As you probably guessed, call buyers look for stocks that have the potential to explode to the upside within a short period of time.

The worst market for call buyers is a flat or falling market. Nevertheless, even if the market goes down, your underlying stock could go up. It takes skill to find stocks that are not following the market trend.

You might wonder where you can find these ideal stocks. As with covered calls, you should use technical or fundamental analysis to find stocks that are either breaking through resistance levels or are leaders in their sector. Underlying stocks that have broken above the 50-day, 100-day, or 200-day moving average are often good candidates for going long. You can also be on the lookout for stocks by reading or listening to the news or by using your brokerage firm's software to scan for prospects.

> *Hint:* Speaking from experience, I urge you not to buy stocks or
> options based on tips. Do your own research to find good
> underlying stocks. You can also read my book *Understanding*
> *Stocks*, which shows you how to use technical and
> fundamental analysis to look for underlying stocks that have
> the potential to take off.

What Is Open Interest?

When you look at an option chain, you will see a column for "Open Interest," a useful indicator that is updated daily. *Open interest* shows the total number of open option contracts that are available to be exercised and that haven't yet been closed out.

Every day, the OCC determines the number of option contracts that remain open, and that is the open interest. For example, if you bought five Boeing calls as an opening position from a seller who was also opening a position, five call contracts would be added to open interest. And if you sold the five calls that you bought to someone who was also closing his or her positions, open interest would be reduced by five calls.

Just as with any marketplace, supply and demand play a large role in dictating prices. For example, let's say that the open interest for some YYY calls is 10,000 for the February 30, 5,000 for the February 35, and 10 for the February 40. What is the market telling us? It's telling us that the 40 strike price is far enough out of the money that the option attracted neither buyers nor sellers.

It also gives a clue that almost no one believes the stock might go above the 40 strike price. Perhaps the stock will land somewhere between the February 30 and February 35 strike price (although there is no guarantee this will happen). The most likely explanation is that the at-the-money options usually attract the most traders.

In Figure 9.1, the May 87.50 call has 14,723 open interest call contracts, while the May 92.50 has open interest of only 517. You can assume that there isn't a lot of interest in the March 92.50 call and that it is currently out of the money. On the other hand, the May 87.50 call has attracted more attention, and, therefore, is more liquid. When you have a liquid option, the bid-ask spread could also be tighter.

You can also compare the open interest from one day to the next by looking for unusual spikes in activity. If one day there are 10,000 open interest contracts and the next day there are 14,000 contracts, it appears that some investors believe the underlying stock is going one way or the other.

Calls for BA Show Symbols | Show Analytics* ❷

Last	Change	Bid	Ask	Volume	Open Int	Action	Strike ▲
⊟ Calls for May 18							
4.40	+0.80	4.35	4.45	559	9,795	Select ▼	85
2.77	+0.63	2.74	2.76	1,544	14,723	Select ▼	87.5
1.49	+0.33	1.51	1.53	1,780	3,289	Select ▼	90
0.75	+0.20	0.73	0.75	149	517	Select ▼	92.5
0.35	+0.12	0.34	0.35	195	1,884	Select ▼	95

Figure 9.1   Open interest

Source: Fidelity Investments. © 2002 FMR LLC. All rights reserved. Used by permission.

Another observation: Let's say that the 30 call has an open interest of 10,000 contracts, and open interest for the corresponding put is 9,000. You could deduce that the bears and bulls are split down the middle.

But if the open interest is 10,000 for the *calls* and 1,000 for the *puts*, you might take an educated guess that 10 times more open interest volume is leaning toward the more bullish call position. (Just because members of the public are interested in that strike price doesn't mean they are right. Nevertheless, options with high open interest will have more liquidity.)

Note: Next to the Open Interest column is Volume. Volume indicates how many contracts were traded that day. When you are trading stocks, volume is an extremely important indicator. When trading options, however, open interest is much more useful.

Now that you've been introduced to the buying calls strategy, you'll learn what factors you need to look for to choose options that lead to a successful trade.

10

How to Choose the Right Call Option

There are many factors that will help you find the correct call option. The key to success is not getting distracted from your goals: price and profit. Nevertheless, there are some important concepts introduced in this chapter that you should learn. By the end of this chapter, you'll have a much better idea of the attributes to look for when choosing call options.

How Much Will It Cost?

The first question most people ask is, how much do options cost? Perhaps they should really be asking how much they are worth. When you were a call seller, you wanted to receive the highest possible premium. But as a call buyer, you are looking for a good deal. At first, you might think that you should simply buy the cheapest option you can find. You'll learn that this is almost never a wise choice.

Before we go any further, let's take a look at your ultimate goal and determine how to make a profit. Now that you are the call buyer, your criteria will be different from those of the call seller. Do you remember these terms from the last section: out of the money, at the money, and in the money? These are so important that we do a quick review.

Review: Out-of-the-Money, At-the-Money, or In-the-Money Options

Unlike the call seller, who wants premium, call buyers are looking for a bargain, that is, a call that is priced fairly or even undervalued. They are willing to pay that premium for an opportunity to earn a good return when the underlying stock rallies. They want to buy an option that will rise in price as the underlying stock price rises.

The option must match your expectations for the stock. In other words, if you believe a $73 stock may move as high as $77 or $78, don't buy a call with an 85 strike price, even if it seems like a bargain. Some options fail to perform as expected, which is why you need to make good choices.

To help you understand which option to select, look at the chart below. Assume that YYY Manufacturing Company is trading for $60 per share one month before expiration. You choose which option to buy, and there are good reasons for each choice.

YYY Manufacturing Company

Stock Price	Strike Price	Call Option	Premium
$60	$70	Far out of the money	$0.10
$60	$65	Out of the money	$0.38
$60	$62	Near out of the money	$1.10
$60	$60	At the money	$1.75
$60	$58	Near in the money	$2.75
$60	$55	In the money	$5.10
$60	$52	Deep in the money	$8.00

In the chart, we can see that YYY is trading for $60 per share. Let's say you choose the 58 call, which is in the money. It will cost $2.75 per contract to buy. Because the 58 call is already in the money, the probability is good that it will still be in the money when expiration arrives. It doesn't mean 100 percent, but it is well over a 50 percent probability. Hint: YYY must continue rising for this trade to be profitable at expiration. If it does rise, your call option will increase in value. And meanwhile, the clock is ticking and your option loses some of its *time value* as the days pass.

On the other hand, if you wanted to take a chance, you could buy the inexpensive 65 call. What are the chances that YYY will rise from $60 to above $65 before the option expires? The chances are not great, which is why the 65 call costs so much less ($0.38). However, surprises do happen in the stock market, which is why people keep buying cheap options.

Note: I recommend avoiding cheap options. Imagine how you would feel if your stock pick moves slowly from $60 to $64 and you lose 100 percent of your investment dollars. When you buy an in-the-money call, at least the option has value, that is, it has *intrinsic value* in addition to time value. The 65 call option has only time value, and with each passing day, that time value will decrease.

Quick Review

1. A call option is in the money when the stock is above its strike price.
2. A call option is out of the money when the stock is below its strike price.
3. Any option is at the money when the stock is at its strike price.

Logging into Your Account

Now that you remember these important terms, let's sign onto our brokerage account and enter the symbol of the underlying stock, Boeing. Then select the option chain for Boeing. An assortment of strike prices and expiration dates will appear on your screen.

The option chain for Boeing is shown in Figure 10.1. It's April 10, and the current price of Boeing is $88.25 per share.

Calls for BA Show Symbols | Show Analytics* ❷

Last	Change	Bid	Ask	Volume	Open Int	Action	Strike ▲
⊟ Calls for May 18							
4.40	+0.80	4.45	4.50	561	9,795	Select ▼	85
2.77	+0.63	2.79	2.81	1,545	14,723	Select ▼	87.5
1.49	+0.33	1.54	1.56	1,780	3,289	Select ▼	90
0.75	+0.20	0.75	0.77	149	517	Select ▼	92.5
0.35	+0.12	0.34	0.36	195	1,884	Select ▼	95
⊟ Calls for Jun 22							
5.05	+0.70	5.10	5.15	63	510	Select ▼	85
3.40	+0.45	3.50	3.60	115	605	Select ▼	87.5
2.26	+0.40	2.30	2.32	340	3,808	Select ▼	90
1.40	+0.31	1.39	1.42	128	114	Select ▼	92.5

Figure 10.1   Option chain: Boeing calls

Source: Fidelity Investments. © 2002 FMR LLC. All rights reserved. Used by permission.

For now, we're going to select the May 87.50 call, which is in the money by almost a dollar. It is trading for $2.81 per share, which is the ask price. Perhaps you noticed that when we sold covered calls, we selected an out-of-the-money call. Now that you are buying calls, we selected a slightly in-the-money call. By the end of this chapter, you'll understand why.

Let's determine how much it will cost to buy one call contract.

How Much Does a Call Cost?

Let's see how much a call costs:

$2.81 per share (May 87.50 call)
× 100 shares of Boeing stock per contract

Total: $281

Explanation: To buy 1 May 87.50 call will cost a total of $281. To buy 2 March 87.50 calls will cost $562. Five calls will cost $1,405. Ten calls will cost $2,810. Although buying 10 calls at this price may seem expensive, if you bought 1,000 shares of this stock, they would cost approximately $88,000.

How Do You Calculate Breakeven?

After you calculate how much the option costs, do a breakeven calculation to determine at what point the option trade becomes profitable (if held to expiration). Often, option buyers think that they are making more money than they really are earning. But because an option's price depends on a number of factors, especially time erosion and *implied volatility* (which I discuss later), you may end up making less than anticipated.

The breakeven calculation below will help you determine when your option is profitable. The formula for calculating breakeven is as follows:

The call strike price + the premium paid = breakeven

$87.50 strike price
+ 2.81 premium paid

Total: $90.31 breakeven

Explanation: In this example, the underlying stock, Boeing, has to rise from $88.25 to $90.31 per share for you to break even (if the option is held until expiration). Anything above $90.31 is profit. If the stock rises high enough over the strike price, the option could follow the exact movement of the underlying stock, and they will trade in unison.

As you probably guessed, by the time the underlying stock has reached this point, the stock is well above the strike price (and the option is deep in the money), and expiration is probably very near.

Now that we have finished our review, let's take a closer look at what factors are important when buying a call option.

The Right Strike Price

As you know from our earlier discussions, understanding strike prices is important. If you choose the wrong strike price, you could lose money, even if you're right about the direction and timing of the stock. So before you choose a strike price, you must take the time to think about the many factors that will lead you to the correct call option.

Out-of-the-Money (OTM) Strike Price

Note that the calls that are out of the money are the cheapest. For example, looking at the option chain in Figure 10.1, it will only cost you $0.77 to buy the May 92.50 call. The May 95 is even cheaper—$0.36. If you bought 10 contracts representing 1,000 shares of this far out-of-the-money option, it would cost you only $360.

Before you run out and load up on call options, think about this: What are the chances that Boeing is going to rise from $88.25 to $95 per share by May 18, five weeks away? That is the bet you'll make if you buy the May 95 call. Keep this in mind: many (perhaps most) out-of-the-money calls expire worthless.

Many people love buying out-of-the-money calls because they are not only cheaper but can also provide a greater percentage of return on their investment if the underlying stock explodes higher. Since trading options is a game of probabilities, you could say that the probability of an out-of-the-money call becoming profitable by the expiration date depends on how far out of the money it is. However, when buying those "cheap" options, the chances are slim, but not impossible. It's true that people hit home runs on occasion, but don't confuse this with a trading strategy.

In-the-Money (ITM) Strike Price

When you look at the ask price of the deep in-the-money May 80 call (not shown), it is $8.30. The near in-the-money May 87.50, however, is priced more reasonably at $2.81 (but whether it's a good value is another discussion). If you go out another month, to June 87.50, the ask price is $3.60. As you remember, the farther away the expiration date, the more the option costs. Notice that the August options cost more.

As an option buyer, you have to weigh all these factors before committing your money to the purchase of a specific option. In general, you'll probably want to start with in-the-money options, but not too far in the money. The reason involves several factors, all of which we explore next.

If your stock is $72 per share, you may consider buying a call option with a $70 strike price. If your stock is $75 per share, perhaps aim for the $72.50 strike price. The reason is this. When buying call options, in-the-money options won't erode as quickly as out-of-the-money or at-the-money options (because their premium contains less *time value*, a term you will learn in Chapter 11). On the other hand, you probably don't want to buy too deep in-the-money calls because they are expensive and you could lose too much money if the stock goes down. You must become skilled at the art of compromise to select suitable options.

Nevertheless, when buying in-the-money calls, the option may cost more, but you are paying less for "hope" and more for real value (*intrinsic value*). Remember the old saying, "You get what you pay for." Too many traders are lured into buying out-of-the-money calls because they are cheaper. Although $0.25 and $0.40 options are tempting, they are cheap for a reason: lower probability of leading to a profitable trade.

On the other hand, if you are speculating, you can buy many more of the cheap options for the same total dollars with an opportunity to double and triple your initial investment (and also a good chance to lose 100 percent of your investment!).

Advanced note: Another advantage of choosing an in-the-money call is that a moderate move in the underlying stock is more likely to bring you profits than out-of-the-money calls. There is a way to estimate how much an option's price will change if the stock does make such a move. It's called *delta*, which is discussed in Chapter 22.

One rule of thumb: Don't let price alone determine which calls to buy. This allows me to bring up one of my favorite quotes, paraphrased from Oscar Wilde: "Many people know the price of everything but the value of nothing."

Here is something else to think about. If you are buying calls for the first time, I encourage you to start by buying slightly in-the-money calls. As with everything else, as you gain experience, you will learn on your own which calls will bring you the most profits.

Ticktock: The Expiration Date

Unlike for call sellers, time works against the call buyer. That ticktock sound you hear is the sound of your option losing value. Call buyers are always concerned with how much time is left to expiration.

As soon as you press the enter key and buy the call, the clock is running. This is why it's essential that you pay close attention to the expiration date.

Options have a funny way of expiring before your option play had time to develop. Even if you are right about the direction of the underlying stock, you have to beat the strike price (plus the premium) or you won't make a dime.

Reminder: When buying call options, you also have to be a good market timer, a difficult task. You have to be right about the time and the direction of the change in the price of the underlying stock, which is one of the reasons that buying calls (or puts) is so challenging.

So what expiration date should you choose? As you know, the farther away the expiration date, the more expensive the option. That makes sense. You are paying more money for the privilege of having more time for the underlying stock to rise in value.

To review, when you look at the option chain for Boeing in Figure 10.1, you see that the May 87.50 call may cost as much as $2.81 (one month away), while the June 87.50 call is $3.60 each (two months away), and the August 87.50 is $4.65 (three months away).

In general, you'll want to avoid buying calls with the current month's expiration date because the time span is so short. Most traders believe it's worthwhile to pay a bit more for an extra month's breathing room. The only exception would be if you believe something explosive is going to happen to the underlying stock soon; then short-term options should be suitable.

In general, if you are going to buy calls, it's probably best to buy a call with an expiration date at least one month out. If it's November, then trade the December or January contracts. This gives you a balance between a reasonable price and enough time for the stock to make a move. Once again, as you gain confidence in your ability to time the market, you may choose other time frames.

Note: When you sold covered calls, time was on your side. Now that you're buying calls, time is your enemy. Every day closer to the expiration date means less time value, which makes the option less valuable. You'll need the underlying stock to move higher, and quickly, so it can rise above the breakeven point.

Important note: The closer the call option gets to the expiration date, the faster it loses time value. This is why an option is called a wasting asset (think of how an ice cube melts in the sun).

What Is the Right Call Option?

Ultimately, finding the correct (or at least, a suitable) call requires skill. But finding the right stock and the right time to buy the call is far more important. By studying the underlying stock and the option chain, you will eventually develop your own criteria.

If you are a novice trader, you may want to choose slightly in-the-money calls. Far out-of-the-money calls are cheap for a reason and are less likely to be profitable. To be on the safe side, however, you should practice trading options by buying only one or two call contracts at a time. This will help you learn how to profit from rising stocks.

· ·

Now that you know how to choose call options, you will be introduced to one of the most fascinating but complex concepts in options trading: volatility and options pricing. You will not learn about volatility in one day, but only with time, practice, and experience. Nevertheless, understanding how options are priced is an essential skill, as you'll soon learn.

11

Volatility and Options Pricing

Even though I've told you that buying calls is relatively easy, I'm going to contradict myself and look under the hood of the car and see how the engine works, to use a popular analogy. It won't be long before you understand why options trading has a reputation for being challenging. (Some say this really is rocket science!) Many consider option pricing the most complex area of finance.

Although volatility and options pricing can be baffling at times, I try to make these concepts understandable. This chapter is so important, and also so theoretical, that you may have to read it more than once.

If you are serious about trading call options, it's essential for you to understand volatility and options pricing. For professional traders, their livelihood depends on understanding these concepts. The good news is that once you have learned these concepts, you can apply them to all the options strategies in this book. This will help make you a better trader and give you additional insights into the inner workings of the options market.

If you still don't know how options are priced after reading this chapter, you can gain additional knowledge from my interview with options expert Sheldon Natenberg in Chapter 25.

What Factors Affect the Premium?

You shouldn't underestimate the importance of premium when you are buying or selling calls. In fact, it takes time to understand the factors that affect option premium. [*Reminder:* The premium is how much you will pay for an option (if buying) or how much you will receive (if selling).] Although I touched on these factors when discussing covered calls, let's take a closer look.

There are seven major factors that directly affect options premiums. These include:

1. A change in the price of the underlying stock
2. The strike price
3. The option type: call or put
4. How much time is left until expiration
5. Interest rates
6. Dividends
7. Volatility of the underlying stock

I previously discussed the importance of the strike price, the expiration date, the option type, and the underlying stock. Obviously, these four factors directly affect the option premium.

In addition, although interest rates and dividends affect the price of an option, they are not as important, which is why I won't discuss them in more depth.

Before I discuss the seventh factor on the list, volatility, let's take a look at option pricing. It's not enough to simply know the price of an option. You also must have a decent idea of what an option is really worth. This is one way of determining if you are getting a fair deal. As you'll see later in this chapter, option traders use a variety of methods to determine whether they are paying a reasonable price.

What Is an Option Worth?

The option premium is the price of an option. But traders also want to know the true value of the option. After all, they don't want to overpay. To help explain further, let's look at the following formula:

Option price (premium) = intrinsic value + time value

$5.50 $5.00 $0.50

You just learned that the option premium consists of two factors, *intrinsic value* and *time value* (also known as *time premium*). The time premium concerns not only how much time remains before the option expires, but it also includes the effect of volatility. Volatility is discussed later in this chapter. For now, I explain intrinsic value and time value in more detail.

What Is Intrinsic Value?

When you look at an option price, the portion of the premium that is in the money is its intrinsic value. In other words, it's how much the option is worth. To be precise, intrinsic value is the cash you would have if you exercised the call option and then immediately sold the stock at its current price. It is also the portion of the option that won't lose value because of the passage of time. In fact, intrinsic value is immune to the passage of time.

It's easy to calculate intrinsic value. For example, if Home Depot is currently $71 per share, then the intrinsic value of the $70 call option is $1. It's simply the difference between the underlying stock price and the strike price. Here is a formula to help you remember:

Stock price − strike price = intrinsic value

$71 $70 $1

To give you another example, if a stock is trading at $33 and the strike price is $30, the intrinsic value of the call is $3. It has an intrinsic value of $3 no matter when it expires.

Therefore, when you hear traders say that their options have intrinsic value, it simply means their options are in the money (i.e., they are worth something tangible).

Fact: An option that is in the money will be worth at least its intrinsic value. At-the-money and out-of-the-money options have no intrinsic value. They have only time value.

What Is Time Value?

You already know that as soon as you buy an option, time becomes your enemy. As the option nears the expiration date, the option price begins to deteriorate rather rapidly because of a very important concept: time value.

Time value is simply what is left over after you subtract intrinsic value from the premium. It is calculated based on several factors, one of which is how much time is left until expiration (the other is volatility, which we discuss later).

For example, if the Home Depot call option costs $1.20 and the intrinsic value of the option is $1.00, then the time value is $0.20.

An at-the-money option that expires in four months will have a certain time value, but an at-the-money option due in one month will have one-half as much time value as the four-month option. The more time left until expiration, the greater the time value. During the last day before the market closes on expiration Friday, there is hardly any time value left.

Remember when you learned about selling covered calls in Chapter 4? With covered calls, time was on your side. It favored you, which is one of the advantages of being a seller. But as a call buyer, time works against you. As soon as you buy the call, the clock is ticking. As the expiration date approaches, the time value of the option deteriorates, and the option price drops in value.

Why is this? As the option approaches expiration, the underlying stock has less and less time to move in the right direction and less time for any option to increase in value. There are fewer opportunities for the stock to move above the strike price as the expiration date approaches.

The last 30 days of an option is when time value becomes more noticeable. For example, if you compare owning a February option contract with one that expires in March or April, you will see that the February option loses value more rapidly. On the other hand, if you bought an option with three months until expiration, it will still erode but not as quickly.

If there is only a month or less left, the time value of that option is less because it offers fewer trading days (and that means fewer opportunities) for something good to happen to the stock price. With only days left, the time value will decrease even more quickly, and soon there will be no time value remaining because when expiration arrives, all of your chances to see the stock rally have been used up.

One reason traders lose money is that they fail to appreciate the value of each passing day. Options are wasting assets, and the rate at which they lose time value is not linear (i.e., not a fixed amount every day). Instead, the rate of time decay increases each day until it disappears altogether.

Time value can vanish under two conditions: expiration has arrived, or the option is so far out of the money that it is worthless. Therefore, on the close of business on the expiration date, an option has zero time value. Zero.

The Mystery of Option Pricing

Now we get to the fun part. You are ready to buy a call option and calculate that the intrinsic value of your Home Depot option is $2 ($72 stock price − $70 strike price = $2 intrinsic value). There is a month left to expiration, so we'll estimate a time value of $0.90. When you look up the price of the option, we are assuming it will cost approximately $2.90.

Guess what? Instead of the $2.90 you thought you'd pay, you're surprised when the cost is $3.50. Why is it so expensive? Because there are several other variables included in the option price—especially a very important and somewhat mysterious concept called *volatility*. Therefore, the option price is based on a number of factors. Remember that some of the premium represents intrinsic value, some is time value, and some of that time value is based on the volatility of the underlying stock.

To accurately calculate volatility, you need an advanced degree in calculus, an understanding of options pricing models, or a good options calculator (I chose the calculator). In fact, you could say that volatility is one of the most misunderstood but most important variables when pricing options.

I can explain volatility with a short answer or a long answer. The short answer uses Apple as an example. A stock like Apple is very volatile because it moves up and down like a yo-yo.

In reality, volatility describes how much a stock changes on a day-to-day basis. When the stock is very volatile, call buyers will pay more for its options, knowing that there is a good chance the option will reach the strike price (and beyond) before expiration.

Therefore, call buyers willingly pay more for options of a volatile stock like Apple, and the price of its options can be costly. On the other hand, a stock like Johnson & Johnson isn't volatile at all. Therefore, traders do not pay as much for its options.

That was the short answer.

Volatility: The X Factor

Now I'll give you the long answer.

When pricing options, volatility is one of the most important factors (many believe it is *the* most important factor). Unfortunately, although many traders mention volatility, few understand what it represents.

At the most basic level, *volatility* means movement, as in how much the underlying stock moves within a certain amount of time. From that movement, we calculate just how volatile that stock has been in the past. That's simple enough. But using the measurement of volatility to price options is complex and confusing, relying on complicated formulas. (Luckily, all you have to do is plug numbers into an options pricing calculator to determine that volatility.)

Volatility is that elusive factor that causes traders to lose money even when correctly predicting stock direction and timing. Why? One possibility is that you overpaid for the options. Because of volatility, you may have paid so much for the pumped-up option premium that you ended up losing money, even when the stock price moves higher.

There are two main types of volatility: *historical* and *implied*. The other type of volatility, *future* (or *expected*), is difficult to quantify because the future can only be estimated. (For your information, expected or forecast volatility is the amount that the stock price is expected to fluctuate during the lifetime of the option.)

Many retail traders use future volatility to estimate the price of an option. Traders plug their estimate for the future volatility (along with other factors that determine the value of an option) into the calculator to determine the value of that option.

Historical Volatility

Historical volatility, displayed as a percentage, measures how much a stock has moved on a daily basis over a certain period in the past. For example, let's say that the average daily range for a $50 stock over the last six months is approximately $0.10 (or 0.2 percent). The greater the daily range of the stock price, the greater the volatility.

If a stock moves no more than 2 or 3 percent within six months or a year, it has a low historical volatility. A stock that moves 20 or 30 percent in a year has higher historical volatility.

How does this information help you? Be aware that some stocks deserve higher option prices and some do not. It should also make you question whether to pay the going rate (i.e., the market price) of any option. Option prices are higher when the underlying stock is more volatile. Also, remember that the higher the volatility, the greater the risk that the stock will fall (resulting in losses for call buyers), as well as the greater the potential profits on stocks that rise.

People often make decisions based on historical data even though they don't realize that this is what they are doing. When you are trying to predict the future, the first thing you do is look at the recent past. Why? Because many of us believe that the recent past repeats itself, or at least represents the best guess for the future.

Understanding Implied Volatility

Understanding *implied volatility* is not easy, so don't worry if you don't get it the first time. I certainly didn't. To demonstrate how difficult it is to define, I'd like you to answer a question. Can you define gravity? It's not too easy to explain, is it? If you are a scientist, the most precise way to define gravity is through complicated scientific formulas. You could also explain implied volatility with complicated formulas using standard deviation.

Without getting too scientific, implied volatility, displayed as a percentage, is simply based on what the market believes (or implies) the option is worth. Unlike historical volatility, which can be measured exactly, implied volatility is more like a real-time indicator of how much the market is willing to pay for the option. Using a calculator and the actual market price, we can calculate implied volatility.

Another way to think of implied volatility is the feeling of urgency that traders have about options. Because of this urgency, you'll see higher implied volatility on options that are in the greatest demand. Lots of buying pushes option prices higher. By definition, when option prices increase and the stock price remains virtually unchanged, the volatility estimate will be higher. It's the urgency, or expectation, that the stock price might undergo a big change that drives traders to bid-up the options (forcing both the premium and implied volatility higher).

Generally, stocks like Priceline and Apple had very high implied volatility—and might today. You can sense the urgency to own options before an earnings release or some other important news announcement. Guess what? Priceline options were expensive because of its high implied volatility. On the other hand, the lack of urgency of options on stocks like GE typically means there is no urgency, and no pressure on the premium. Therefore, the implied volatility does not increase. For stocks whose options have a lower implied volatility, option prices are lower (for equally priced stocks). There isn't the same demand for these options.

Market makers always know the implied volatility because their computers generate that number, based on all the factors that go into pricing an option. They set option prices, and at times, supply and demand force the market makers to raise and lower prices.

Therefore, if the implied volatility of a call or put is too high, then the option would be viewed as overpriced. Option buyers end up paying much more than the option is worth, and there is no profit in doing that.

Don't worry if you don't know where to find implied volatility. Fortunately, your brokerage firm has software that gives you the implied volatility figures. This software is based on the once-revolutionary options pricing model, *Black-Scholes* or *Cox-Ross-Rubenstein*.

To use the pricing model, enter a number of parameters (for example, stock price, strike price, interest rate, dividends, expiration date, option type, and the actual price of the option) into the model, and it will calculate implied volatility.

Note: Options with higher implied volatility sometimes have a wider bid-ask spread. The spread on a stock option like the GE April 15 call might be $0.10 whereas the spread on an option with high implied volatility will be wider, for example, $0.30 or $0.40. It is much more difficult to make money when your trades must pass through the wider spread.

Bottom line: If you are buying calls, you are looking for underlying stocks that will rise in price and soon. A stock like GE is an ideal candidate for a covered call, but perhaps not for speculative call buying. And with options that have a higher implied volatility, you could be paying extra. The key is to be sure that the stock has been volatile enough in the past, or is expected to be volatile enough in the future, to justify higher option prices. This comes with trading experience.

How Traders Overpay for Options

Let's say that over the weekend you read about a small biopharmaceutical company with a promising drug that treats central nervous system disorders. The company, XYZ Corporation (not its real name), was mentioned on a financial program because the U.S. Food and Drug Administration (FDA) might approve its latest experimental drug. You are thinking of buying call options on XYZ.

When the market opens on Monday morning, you enter the stock symbol on your brokerage firm's screen. XYZ is currently trading for $10 per share, up by a whopping $3. You look up the implied volatility of the XYZ options.

What do you see? The XYZ May 10 at-the-money call option has implied volatility of 128 percent (see Figure 11.1), which is well above average.

In fact, all the May call and put options have extreme implied volatilities. This tells you that these options are priced for a huge move, either up or down, before the expiration date.

How does it help to know the implied volatility? First, the XYZ May 10 call option is theoretically overpriced based on the past volatility of the stock. It is pumped up and has an extremely high implied volatility. In fact, all the May options have extreme implied volatility. This tells you that a big move is expected, and that is very

Strike ▲	Bid	Ask	Volume	Open Int	Imp Vol
Calls for May 18					
5	5.00	5.60	0	297	178.03 %
6	3.90	4.80	50	974	149.78 %
7	3.20	3.80	0	829	137.65 %
8	2.65	2.95	0	1,130	136.04 %
9	2.10	2.35	0	976	136.35 %
10	1.55	1.75	0	624	128.12 %
11	1.15	1.35	26	2,634	126.98 %
12	0.80	1.05	80	4,688	125.06 %

Figure 11.1   Implied volatility

likely because an FDA decision can make or break the company. It's anyone's guess how far the stock will move.

Fifty percent or lower implied volatility is more reasonable based on history, while 100 percent is rather high. In XYZ's case, an implied volatility ranging from 125 percent to 178 percent is off the charts. However, the high implied volatility means that the market is anticipating a big price swing when the news is announced. That move could be either negative or positive, and the high implied volatility reflects that anticipation. Implied volatility is high (and deserves to be high in this example).

Nevertheless, it didn't stop options traders from scooping up the XYZ May 11 and May 12 out-of-the-money call options. Figure 11.1 shows the open interest in these call options. As you can see, there is a lot of interest. Buyers obviously believe these options are a bargain for a little over a dollar each.

More than likely, uninformed traders heard about the positive news and loaded up on these call options, hoping for a big score. Instead, they probably overpaid. Note that the spread between the bid and ask prices is extremely wide, which is another red flag. Not only are you potentially overpaying when buying calls with these strike prices, but you are already 6 or 7 percent behind if you pay the ask price to buy your options.

Note: Whether an option is expensive or cheap has nothing to do with its price. It depends on the implied volatility. In other words, a $5 option (like the one in this example) could be expensive while an $8 option could be a bargain.

Should you buy these calls? Let's keep analyzing.

Comparing Historical Volatility

In normal circumstances, you would study the historical volatility of XYZ for clues (see Figure 11.2). By comparing the historical volatility of the stock with the implied volatility of its options, you have another way of determining if the option is overpriced. A week ago, the historical volatility of XYZ was only 32.15 percent.

Historical Volatility ❷

Term	HV	1 Week ago	1 Month ago
10 Days	33.72%	32.15%	74.14%
20 Days	31.88%	38.02%	61.56%
30 Days	49.17%	49.94%	57.35%
60 Days	59.31%	59.35%	60.49%
90 Days	54.50%	54.29%	54.91%
120 Days	50.73%	51.55%	51.60%
150 Days	49.63%	49.53%	50.05%
180 Days	50.81%	50.71%	53.01%

Figure 11.2   Historical volatility

Source: Fidelity Investments. © 2002 FMR LLC. All rights reserved. Used by permission.

Note: Implied volatility tells you how the underlying stock is predicted to move in the future. Historical volatility, however, tells you how a stock actually did move in the past. In this case, we expect a big move, dwarfing the historical numbers. There is a good reason for that. The outlook for the future of this company will change significantly after the news, so in this example it is correct to ignore historical volatility.

Implied Volatility Strategies

There are several option plays you can make using this information. First, you can decide not to trade, knowing you are probably overpaying for that higher implied volatility. (That might be the wisest decision.)

Second, you could speculate by purchasing what appears to be a high price for the May call options. Maybe you think the underlying stock has room to move on the upside if the FDA approves the drug. It's a bit of a gamble because you know that the stock could go in either direction, up or down. Generally, buying options with extreme implied volatility is not recommended.

In fact, one way that many option traders get hurt is by overpaying for a call option on a stock that has already made a move. Even if the underlying stock continues to move higher, the option premium could collapse.

The name of this phenomenon is *volatility crush* (defined as the deflation of option premium after an expected event), and you can avoid problems by looking at implied volatility *before* buying or selling. It's great to get on the bandwagon for a momentum-driven stock, but those who get on last are going to lose money.

Here's what happened to XYZ. The next day, XYZ fell by 20 percent so every single XYZ call option got squashed, some falling by almost 100 percent. People who bought those pumped up call options probably lost their entire investment.

Why did this happen? After the negative FDA report (the drug did not perform as hoped), there was no chance that the stock could reach the strike prices, and the options were almost worthless.

Advanced note: There is another strategy you can use, one favored by experienced traders. They call it *buying volatility*. This means that they buy a market neutral option position based on the implied volatility of the options and not based on predicting direction.

To learn how to make this play, you'll have to wait until Chapter 20, where I discuss *straddles*, an intermediate options strategy. Ideally, you want to *buy* options when volatility is low and about to go higher. You want to *sell* options when volatility is high and about to go lower. Obviously, that's not easy to predict.

Don't Ignore Implied Volatility

Knowing what an option is worth provides a big edge. However, the value of an option depends on also knowing the future volatility. So the best you can do is make a good estimate. But in the end, it's the marketplace that determines the true value of that option. Unfortunately, sometimes it's only after the fact that we know whether the option was over- or underpriced.

In the real world, because of pending news or extreme events, the most sophisticated option formula may not work. During these unanticipated events, supply and demand will push option prices up or down. During normal times, however, these formulas are very helpful.

Option pricing is based on equations that predict future volatility. In fact, all option buyers and sellers determine an option's price (and thus, its implied volatility) by driving the option premium to its current level. Also, human emotions affect buying and selling decisions and therefore affect option premium.

It's not easy to fully appreciate how implied volatility affects premiums, but it's worth making the effort. Unfortunately, many investors don't understand implied volatility, which is why I spend so much time explaining it to you. It is something you should continue to study.

· ·

Now that you have been introduced to the concepts of volatility and pricing, you're ready to learn the mechanics of buying call options. Guess what? That's the easy part!

12

Step-by-Step: Buying Calls

If you got through the last chapter without too much difficulty, you're doing great. Learning how to price options and determine the chances of profitability are extremely challenging concepts, even for the experts. As you gain more experience, you'll pay more attention to option pricing before taking on a position. Nevertheless, try to learn the concepts before you place your first trade.

And now, the most exciting part is actually signing on to the brokerage firm's website and buying call options. As I've said before, brokerage firms have invested millions of dollars in making it easy to buy and sell options.

Before we get to the mechanics of buying calls, however, I discuss some of the risks. Once again, I'm not trying to talk you out of this strategy; I only want to make you aware of the potential pitfalls. By being aware of the potential risks of using any options strategy, you will know exactly how to protect yourself in worst-case scenarios.

The Risks of Buying Calls

There are actually a number of risks when buying calls, which is why it's considered a speculative strategy. As I mention before, most option contracts expire unexercised by the expiration date. Although the exact figure is hard to estimate, many speculators lose money. Of course, some traders have scored big in the options market, but many have not.

Perhaps you bought this book because you're looking for quick money without too much risk. That is how many people get lured into the options market (or any market, for that matter).

I've been to options seminars where the instructors incorrectly said that buying calls allows you to make "consistent income." First, there is nothing consistent about buying calls. And second, you should know that the odds are against you from the beginning.

Nevertheless, as long as you are fully aware of the risks, there is nothing wrong with speculating on occasion. As always, knowledge (and discipline) can help you avoid making mistakes and losing money. What is the biggest risk to trading calls? The answer is simple. You could lose the entire amount you paid for the contract (100 percent of your investment). At least you won't lose more than you paid, and perhaps less than if you had bought stock. Still, this shouldn't be taken lightly.

Although the mechanics of buying calls is simple, many people underestimate the skill it takes to be successful. Unfortunately, people don't always take the time to research. They are looking for the quick score, and the truth is that occasionally people do get lucky. As an options trader, however, you cannot depend on luck to be successful.

In addition, some people make huge paper gains but fail to realize how quickly profits can disappear. Once again, the problem is they aren't fully aware of the speculative nature of call options. In the options market, if you don't move quickly, you could lose your entire investment.

Another problem with buying calls is that you have to be right on three counts: the timing, the direction, and paying a reasonable price. That is, if the underlying stock moves in the right direction but does not move before the expiration date, you will lose money. And if the stock doesn't move in the right direction, you could lose your entire investment (although it's a fraction of the cost of a stock investment).

And finally, because the pros at the exchanges or in their home offices have the best software and make a career from trading, you are at a disadvantage (although you can still make money). Yes, it's possible to make a profitable living buying and selling options, but it's not easy. As I said before, some people think that buying calls is similar to buying a lottery ticket. And others think that the right software will help them find a winning option.

Rule: You should not use the options market (or any market) as a substitute for gambling, although some people do. Compulsive gamblers are drawn to this market because of the action. More often than not, they lose money, usually because the options expire before they were proved correct (or so they say). If you follow the advice in my book, you'll have a better chance of success (but no guarantees) than the gamblers.

Now that you are aware of the risks of buying calls, I introduce you to a word you learned in the previous chapter: the *spread*. Understanding spreads is essential. Otherwise, your trading costs could be so high that your chances of success become slim.

The Power of the Spread

The *spread*, the difference between the bid and ask prices, directly affects the price at which you transact business. If you buy options, you want to pay a fair price for the option. So what is a fair price? Probably somewhere in between the bid price and ask price. Although measured in pennies, being forced to pay a higher price (when buying) takes money out of your pocket.

When trading *stocks*, the spread is often small enough (on a percentage basis) to be ignored. When trading *options*, however, the spreads can be rather significant.

Because of the spread, you immediately begin with a loss when you make any options trade. For example, if the bid price is $1.00 and the ask price is $1.10, you are probably going to pay $1.10 (perhaps $1.05 if you're fortunate). If you turned around to sell it for $1.00, you would be looking at a 9 percent loss. That is the power of the spread, which is the dime the market maker would like to collect. Obviously, you are hoping that the value of the option moves high enough to overcome this immediate loss.

Although $0.10 doesn't sound like much, in percentage terms it's substantial. So how do you manage a 9 or 10 percent loss right from the beginning? Although most call buyers have extremely positive attitudes, you'll have to work hard to overcome this disadvantage.

When the spread is small, there is nothing wrong with paying the ask price. However, when the market is wide, bid a little more than halfway between the bid and ask prices.

Example: If the bid is $1.50 and the ask is $1.75, bid $1.65. The bid can be raised to $1.70 if no one sells to you at your first bid. Trading is an auction process, and you do not want to pay the highest possible price unless you are forced to do so.

Note: One of the threats to your trading profits is a loss to the spread (called *slippage*), which is why you need to pay close attention to the constantly changing bid-ask market.

Bottom line: Pay close attention to the spread before buying calls or puts.

Before You Place Your First Trade

Despite all these risks and caveats, knowing how to buy and sell individual options is important. It can be part of your risk-management program and also plays a role when you are trading more advanced strategies. The main advantage of buying calls is that profit potential is unlimited, whereas losses are limited. Only you can decide if this strategy makes sense for you and your financial goals.

Now that you are aware of the advantages and disadvantages of using this strategy, let's get started. The following screens will give you step-by-step instructions on how to buy calls.

In the option chain, you have already looked up the underlying stock, all the options, and the expiration dates. As you look at the chain, it is very possible that you will make your final decision as to which option to buy.

If you're uncomfortable placing your own trade at first, you can ask the brokerage representatives for help (but remember that they charge extra if they place the trade). Once again, the most common mistake in trading is carelessness: entering the wrong information.

Let's Begin Trading!

Before you begin, you must know the symbol for the underlying stock. In addition, choose a strike price and an expiration date. Figure 12.1 is the call option chain for Boeing. Here are some observations:

1. The current price of Boeing is $88.16.
2. The call option we want to buy is the May 87.50 call, an option that is in the money by almost a dollar ($0.66).
3. The expiration date is one month away.

Calls for BA Show Symbols | Show Analytics* ❷

Last	Change	Bid	Ask	Volume	Open Int	Action	Strike ▲
☐ **Calls for May 18**							
4.40	+0.80	4.45	4.50	561	9,795	Select ▼	85
2.77	+0.63	2.79	2.81	1,545	14,723	Select ▼	87.5
1.49	+0.33	1.54	1.56	1,780	3,289	Select ▼	90
0.75	+0.20	0.75	0.77	149	517	Select ▼	92.5
0.35	+0.12	0.34	0.36	195	1,884	Select ▼	95
☐ **Calls for Jun 22**							
5.05	+0.70	5.10	5.15	63	510	Select ▼	85
3.40	+0.45	3.50	3.60	115	605	Select ▼	87.5
2.26	+0.40	2.30	2.32	340	3,808	Select ▼	90
1.40	+0.31	1.39	1.42	128	114	Select ▼	92.5

Figure 12.1   Option chain: Boeing calls

4. The ask price is $2.81. You should also notice that the spread is $0.02, the difference between the $2.79 bid price and the $2.81 ask price. (In this example, the spread is so narrow that it's not wrong to pay the ask price.)

Note: For $281, you are controlling approximately $8,800 worth (100 shares) of Boeing stock. This is the power of leverage that I mentioned earlier—and the reason people like buying calls.

To make a profit, the underlying stock, Boeing, will have to move well past the strike price of $87.50 before the expiration date. In this example, you have one month for that to happen, and this fact has to play a big part in your decision of whether to buy this call.

Note: Instead of the May 87.50 call, we could have bought the June 87.50 for $3.60, which will give us an extra month of time but will cost $0.79 more. These are the kinds of decisions that call buyers have to make all the time.

Now that you are ready, you will bring up the call option entry screen. The screen on your brokerage account might look different from what is displayed here.

The Underlying Stock

Once again, double-check the stock symbol. In Figure 12.2, we enter "BA," the stock symbol for Boeing. (Your brokerage firm may have different requirements for entering the symbol.)

ACTION: *Enter the symbol for the underlying stock.*

Underlying	Strategy	Last	Change	Bid	Ask
BA	Calls & Puts ⬍	$88.16	0.95	88.15	88.16

Figure 12.2   Option chain: Boeing calls

Source: Fidelity Investments. © 2002 FMR LLC. All rights reserved. Used by permission.

Buy to Open

Let's review the choices when you are buying or selling options. You must become very familiar with these before you can successfully trade options.

- *Buy to open*: Select this when buying calls or puts. It's used to initiate or create a long position.
- *Sell to close*: Select this when you are closing out or selling a call or put that you have previously bought.
- *Sell to open*: Select this when you are selling calls or puts, including selling covered calls. (Most often used to initiate a covered call position.)
- *Buy to close*: Select this when you are covering or decreasing a call or put position that you previously sold. Select this when closing a covered call position prior to expiration.

Because you are buying calls, you will select buy to open, because in option terminology you plan to open, or create a new position (you want to go long the call)

ACTION: *Select buy to open* (see Figure 12.3).

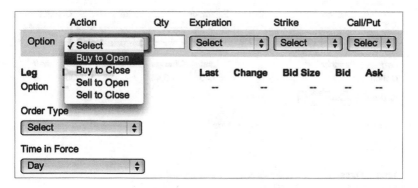

Figure 12.3   Buy-to-open order entry

Source: Fidelity Investments. © 2002 FMR LLC. All rights reserved. Used by Permission.

Quantity

Because you are buying one contract (representing 100 shares of the underlying stock), you enter the number 1. Once again, a common mistake is entering the number of shares instead of the number of contracts.

For example, if you enter 100 contracts, it will be similar to buying options on 10,000 shares of the underlying stock. Obviously, you don't want to make that mistake!

ACTION: *Enter one contract for 100 shares.* (Most beginners never enter more than 10 contracts at one time.)

Order Type: Market or Limit Order

In Figure 12.4, you need to choose between a market order and a limit order. When trading options, it's recommended that you select limit order, meaning that you select the price at which you are willing to buy the call. You let the brokerage firm's computer work the order to get you the best price.

If you select market order, on the other hand, you are letting the market determine your price. That's not a good idea. The only

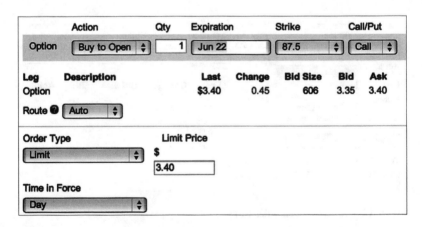

Figure 12.4 Buy call order entry

Source: Fidelity Investments. © 2002 FMR LLC. All rights reserved. Used by permission.

advantage of a market order is in the speed of the fill, although you might not get the price you anticipate.

ACTION: *Select limit order.*

Time

Select "day," which means that the order must be filled by the end of the day or it is canceled. More than likely, the order will be filled in a timely manner.

You can see what we've entered so far in Figure 12.4.

Bid and Ask Prices

After you fill in the screens, the option's last sale price, how much it changed, and the current bid and ask prices automatically appear on the screen. Because you are buying calls, you will focus primarily on the ask price, which is the maximum you could pay for the option.

We decide to buy the Boeing June 87.50 call (because we want that extra month). Boeing is currently trading at $88.16 per share. The bid price is $3.35 and the ask price is $3.40,. You may have noticed that the bid and ask prices changed before we placed the order. This is very common.

If you do enter the current ask price as your limit price, you will probably be filled quickly.

ACTION: *Enter the current ask price of $3.40.*

The brokerage firm's computer will seek a price of $3.40 per share or better. When the order is filled, a $340 net debit (plus commission) will show up in your account. This is the total cost of buying one contract.

Preview Your Order

If there is a preview button, double-check your order before pressing the enter key. In the preview screen, the commission and the total cost of the order are usually displayed. This is your last chance to make any changes before the order is entered.

Broker instructions: If you called your broker and wanted to place the above order by phone, you would say, "I want to buy one Boeing June 87.50 call for a limit price of $3.40 (or better) good for the day only."

Note: If you do decide to place a call with a broker, the recorded telephone call is proof that the order was placed. Be sure to speak clearly and use options terminology to place the trade.

ACTION: *After the order is filled, $340 is taken out of your account.*

Press the Enter Key

When you press the enter key, the order will be routed to one of the options exchanges. A seller will be matched to your buy order. Congratulations! You have bought your first call. You can't relax, however, because you need to monitor your option position.

Now that time is your enemy, it is a good idea to have a profit target in mind and be ready to sell your option. It is also important to have a plan to cut your losses. You may want to establish a maximum loss you will accept before selling the option. Or you may change your opinion about the stock. When you no longer expect the stock to rally, there is no reason to own the call. Important: Do not plan to hold until the option expires.

Advanced note: Before considering any option, you should be aware of *splits, mergers, acquisitions, special dividends,* and other corporate actions and adjustments that can do odd things to options contracts. If the option you want to trade has a strange symbol, it is best to avoid that option and find one with the "correct" symbol.

A Trading Disaster

As mentioned earlier in the book, one of my acquaintances, Daniel (not his real name), made $130,000 in three days, trading options. His roller-coaster ride started a week earlier when he received a tip from his stockbroker about a small California drug company whose stock was rumored to move much higher.

According to the broker, the company, Hollis-Eden Pharmaceuticals (Symbol: HEPH), was going to receive a multi-million-dose order of its newly developed antiradiation drug from the

U.S. government. The government was supposed to announce its intentions soon.

After doing some basic fundamental research on the company, Daniel believed that his broker was right. Daniel was looking for a home run, and a play like this didn't come along very often. At the time, the stock was trading for almost $7.50 per share. Daniel's initial target price was $10 per share with a possible target of $30 per share (or so he hoped).

So with the broker's blessing, Daniel bought approximately 500 call contracts (controlling roughly 50,000 shares of stock) with multiple expiration dates and strike prices. The cheapest out-of-the-money calls were about $0.50 each.

By any standard, this was a huge bet on one stock. As it turned out, the broker was right. The stock went up over 34 percent before the anticipated announcement date. The call contract went from $0.50 to more than $2.80 on the expectation that the government would purchase a large quantity of the new drug.

I saw Daniel at the local coffee shop when he told me he was up over $130,000 in paper profits. He was giving high fives to his friends. This was the best one-day gain he had ever made in his life. This is the home run that all call buyers dream about.

Although I was glad to hear about his good fortune, I did ask him one question: "Did you sell?"

He looked at me with a slightly annoyed look. "I thought about it," he said. "But the announcement is coming out on Friday." You could see that look in his eye. "And the news is going to be good!" In his mind, it would be crazy to sell after such a large gain when a bigger gain was around the corner.

The next day, Thursday, September 29, Daniel had second thoughts about his huge gains. He thought about selling his profitable calls to finance buying new calls. He even discussed it with his broker but never placed or confirmed the order.

Friday morning, the announcement was made on HEPH. Unfortunately for my friend, the government decided to buy only 100,000 doses of the drug, not nearly enough for the company to make a substantial profit. Not surprisingly, HEPH plunged on the news.

A picture is worth a thousand words, and Figure 12.5 tells it all. When the stock crumbled, so did all of Daniel's profits.

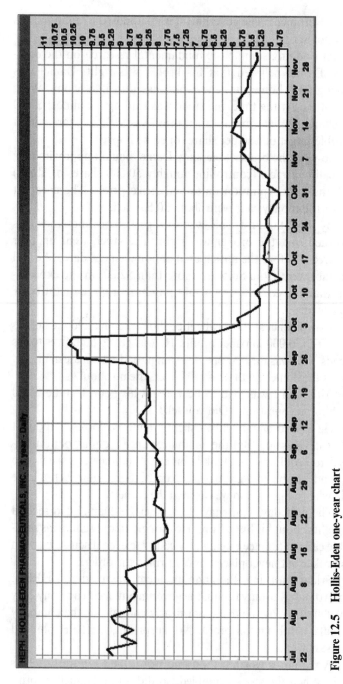

Figure 12.5　Hollis-Eden one-year chart

134

In retrospect, Daniel learned several lessons: First, he vowed never to get so greedy (always easier said than done). He also vowed to take control of his buying and selling decisions and not leave them completely with the stockbroker. Ultimately, it's the responsibility of the client to tell the broker when and what to buy or sell.

By the way, when I ran into Daniel a few weeks later, he had just placed another order with his broker to buy more call options on HEPH (although not as many as before). This is quite common; some traders, after losing money on a stock or option, take it personally and want revenge. Once you get emotional about a stock, the market will probably beat you, which is exactly what happened to Daniel after he placed his second order. For the next three months, HEPH never went higher than $6 per share. For the second time, his call options expired worthless.

Follow-up: Another company eventually bought out Hollis-Eden Pharmaceuticals, which had become a penny stock.

Now that you've learned the mechanics of buying calls (and hopefully a lesson about greed), you will next learn how to manage and maintain your call position.

13

Managing Your Call Position

The easy part about buying calls is placing the order. In this chapter, you will do the hard part—manage your call position. After you place your order, you feel the most hopeful. Perhaps you have already calculated how much money you are going to make (always a bad sign). There are many choices of what you can do, which is why you have to keep close track of the underlying stock as well as the option.

As you remember in Chapter 7, I discussed why it is essential that you create a trading plan before and after any trade. A trading plan is a road map that helps you to determine when to enter or exit an option position.

What Can Go Right or Wrong

As the call buyer, you are in control of the right to buy the stock until the expiration date. This is why you need to monitor the position closely. Once you own the option, the underlying stock has only three ways to move: up, down, or sideways.

Note: The underlying stock will help determine the direction of the call option. When you own calls, when the underlying stock rises, that is good because your call option will increase in value. When the underlying stock falls, your call option will decrease in value. (On occasion, there are exceptions.)

· ·

To refresh your memory, the current quote on Boeing is $88.16. You bought call options on the Boeing June 87.50 call option. The premium was $3.40.

· ·

The Underlying Stock Moves Down

What should you do if the underlying stock price moves down?

> *Outcome*: The stock falls below the strike price. In our example, Boeing drops below the 87.50 strike price.
>
> *Analysis*: This is not what you wanted. As the underlying stock falls, watch as the option price deteriorates. As the stock falls, the option will lose value. The time value of the option deteriorates rapidly with only weeks left until expiration.

As the clock counts down, your option will expire worthless on the expiration date. If a stock moves in the wrong direction, you have a number of choices. First, if there is still time left and you don't think the stock will make a dramatic turnaround, you could try to salvage what is left of the contract by selling the option position.

Remember that it's hard for options whose underlying stocks are trading below the strike price to become profitable. By the time one week is left, you might as well hold onto your nearly worthless call option (but that is a decision only you can make).

At this point, you have little to lose by holding the position until the expiration date, while hoping for a miracle. Occasionally, a few days before expiration, positive news about the underlying stock is released and once worthless call options suddenly become valuable. By the way, if the option does expire worthless, you don't have to do anything. You already paid for the option, so the cash balance in your account doesn't change. Actually, the only thing that happens in your account is that the option disappears.

To Sell (or Close) Your Position

If you do decide to sell at a loss, the procedure is the same as when you sell at a profit. Go to the brokerage screen and select *sell to close*. This means you are selling to close the position. You mark it as a bad trade, and you may have learned some lessons.

Broker instructions: If you called your broker and wanted to place the above order by phone, you would say, "I want to sell to close all Boeing May 87.5 calls at the current bid price or better."

The Underlying Stock Stays the Same

What should you do if the underlying stock price stays the same?

> *Outcome*: The stock stays at or near the strike price. In our example, Boeing remains between $85 and $88 per share.
> *Analysis*: This is not a good situation. The option has already lost time value, and things can only get worse in the days ahead. If the underlying stock doesn't move a lot higher, and soon (expiration is near), this trade will be a loser.
> *Hint*: This is when you might think of salvaging the remaining premium. You can sell the call option and cut your losses before you lose everything. On the other hand, if the stock makes a dramatic move higher, you will wish you hadn't sold. There are always difficult decisions to make, but make them on something other than hope.

Note: Holding all your option positions into expiration is not a good plan.

The Underlying Stock Moves Up

What should you do if the underlying stock price moves up?

> *Outcome*: The stock remains above the strike price. In our example, Boeing moves well above the 87.50 strike price to $91 per share.

Analysis: This is exactly what you wanted. As the underlying stock price moves up, watch as the option price climbs. The higher the stock moves above the strike price, the more valuable the call option becomes.

You have a number of choices when the underlying stock is higher than the strike price. It's much easier psychologically to manage a winning position than a losing position, but this is no time to be careless.

Because of the fickle nature of the options market, it's always a good idea to take money off the table and book profits. Just be aware that if you are too quick to take profits and too slow to cut losses, you may not make much money.

On the other hand, if the underlying stock moves up a lot and your profits are so high that you are giving high fives to your friends and family, sell immediately. Too many option traders let winning options turn into losers because of greed. Don't let that happen to you. If you hit a home run with a call option, take the money and run. (If you establish a profit target when making the trade, the exit decision is much easier.)

Therefore, if the stock is above the strike price (and your call option is in the money), you can sell the call when you no longer want to own it and book the profits (if any).

To close out the option position, select *sell to close* on your brokerage screen. If your call option is in the money at expiration, you have another choice. You have the right to *exercise* the call option. This is so important to understand that I created a chapter devoted to helping you understand this procedure. Hint: You'll learn later than it makes more sense to sell your option rather than exercise.

Before you read about exercise, however, let's look at these four advanced call strategies.

Advanced Call Strategies

Some of the strategies described below will give you other ideas about using options to increase returns.

Buying Options on ETFs

Instead of buying calls on individual stocks, you can also buy calls on ETFs such as SPY (S&P 500), QQQ (Nasdaq 100), DIA (Dow Jones Industrial Average), and IWM (Russell 2000). Buying options on ETFs is discussed in Chapter 23.

Roll Up to a Higher Strike Price

We discuss rolling up in the covered call section. You can do the same with call options that you own. To review, rolling up a call means that you close out your current position and move the position to one with a higher strike price.

For example, let's say you paid a dollar ($1) for a call for an underlying stock selling at $20 per share. The stock is now at $23 per share at expiration, and the call is worth $3. Instead of exercising the option, you sell the option for $3 (a $2 profit), and replace it by buying the next month's call. You are basically continuing to own a call option on this stock.

Note: this strategy works best when a stock is "on a roll."

Roll Over to a Later Expiration Date

When you roll over an option (also known as a *roll forward* or *roll out*), it means that you exchange the option for one with a later expiration date. The strike price may or may not remain the same, but the expiration date changes. For example, you close the March contract and open an April contract.

· ·

And now, in Chapter 14, I go into more detail about the call buyer's right to exercise.

14

Exercise: Your Right to Buy

The good news about exercise is that once you understand the rules and procedures, it is not a mystery. In fact, it is very straightforward. In this chapter, I do my best to help you understand exercise and what actions you can take before the expiration date.

What It Means to Exercise

When you sold covered calls, the stock was called away from you when the call buyer exercised the option. As the call seller, if the stock was called away, you had only one obligation—to deliver the stock. Now that you have traded places and are the call owner, you are the one who gets to do the exercising.

To review, the call buyer (which is now you) has the right to exercise the call option. When the buyer exercises a call option, he or she buys the underlying stock. Do you remember at what price the buyer exercises the option? The answer is at the strike price.

There are several reasons why you, as the call buyer, would want to exercise the option to buy the underlying stock. For example, you may want to own shares of stock. This is your choice, but it's not required.

When you exercise a call option, it simply means that you are exchanging your in-the-money call option for 100 shares of stock. You are not obligated to exercise, but you have the right to do so at any time before the option expires.

Important note: You should know that most option investors *do not exercise* the call option. Instead, they will sell the call and close the position before the expiration date.

What to Do Before the Expiration Date

As the expiration date approaches, option activity tends to increase. Buyers and sellers are making important decisions. If your call option is in the money, should you sell, or should you exercise?

Here are the four actions you can take:

1. You can sell the option.
2. You can exercise the option.
3. You can do nothing, allowing the out-of-the-money option to expire and become worthless.
4. You can roll the option up or out to the following month (introduced in the previous chapter).

Let's explore the first three choices.

First, before the expiration date, you should have a plan in place. The last thing you want to do is wait until the last day to make a decision.

Choice 1: Sell the Option

Most investors sell the option if it's in the money. You can sell the option at any time. However, if you decide to wait until expiration day, make your trade before the market closes at 4:00 p.m. ET. You don't want to be holding an in-the-money option after the market closes on the last day. If you do, it will be automatically exercised and you will take possession of the shares of stock.

Choice 2: Exercise the Option

Let's look at your second choice: exercise the option. Many beginners do not realize that they don't have to exercise. It's a choice, not an obligation.

If you decide to exercise, you almost always do it on the expiration date and not earlier. Why not? As long as there is some time value left in the option premium before the expiration date, you will lose money (the time value) if you exercise early. (There is one exception, which I discuss later.)

There is seldom any good reason to exercise, but if you want to do so before the last day, then you must notify your broker of your intent. The cutoff time is shortly before the market closes on the day you want to exercise. Most brokers prefer a phone call.

Once you notify your broker, the decision is irrevocable, and you can't change your mind. Your brokerage firm notifies the OCC of your intention to exercise, and the OCC issues an exercise notice, which is assigned to a randomly chosen account. The shares of stock are automatically taken out of the call seller's account and delivered to your account overnight, where they will appear the next morning. Your account will be debited for the amount of the stock purchase.

For example, if you exercised 1 Boeing May 87.5 call option, you now own 100 shares of Boeing stock, having paid $8,750. If you owned 5 Boeing call options, and exercised all five, you now own 500 shares of Boeing stock.

Fortunately, if you have buyer's remorse on Monday and no longer want the stock, you can turn around and sell your shares in the stock market.

> *Question from a reader:* Can you exercise an option that is out of the money?
>
> *Answer:* Yes, you can if you want to, but you would lose money. If you exercise an out-of-the money call, you are overpaying for the stock. It makes no economic sense to do that.

Hint: Once again, few call buyers exercise. If you really want the stock, however, then go ahead and exercise at expiration (but not earlier).

Choice 3: Do Nothing

Doing nothing is your worst choice. Sometimes beginners forget that they even bought a call option. Imagine their surprise when they discover they now own a stock they didn't want or cannot afford.

Important reminder: If your option is in the money by a penny ($0.01) or more on the expiration date, the OCC will automatically exercise your option. The "automatic exercise" rule that was created by the options industry has caused some people grief. After you buy a call option, never forget that you own it. Mark the expiration date on your calendar and monitor the position.

Technically, you have until shortly after 4:00 p.m. ET on the Friday expiration date to exercise your option. Nevertheless, some firms automatically force traders who do not have enough cash in their account to close their option *before* the end of the day if it's in the money on the expiration date. Call your brokerage and find out its exact rules regarding exercise.

Question from a reader: Can an option that is out of the money be automatically exercised?

Answer: No.

Early Exercise

As you know, exercise is almost always done on the expiration date. However, there's one time when you might consider exercising before the expiration date. This one time occurs when a stock pays a dividend.

Question from a reader: Do you have to exercise to capture the dividend?

Answer: Yes. Only the stockholder gets the dividend. The call owner does not get the dividend.

Note: The Do-Not-Exercise Notice

Here's a rule few people know about. You can notify your brokerage firm that you do not want an option that you own exercised if it's in the money. The problem here is that if your option is in the money at expiration and you do not exercise, you just threw away any remaining cash value.

If you don't want to buy the stock at the strike price, you must tell your broker of your intentions before the cutoff time. Note: You can avoid all these complications by selling the option before it expires.

Finally, let's review the most important exercise guidelines:

1. Most people buy calls to make a profit, not to own stock. Therefore, they have no intention of exercising the option. Other people buy calls because they are truly interested in owning the underlying stock at a later date. The consensus: Do not exercise. Instead, sell the option before the expiration date.
2. If you do decide to exercise any option, do it at the end of the day (i.e., notify your broker and submit an exercise notice).
3. If you instruct your brokerage firm to exercise, it is irrevocable. You have already purchased the stock.
4. Exercising early usually doesn't make financial sense.
5. American-style options, the ones discussed in this book, can be exercised at any time after the option is bought, as long as it is on or before the expiration date. European-style options, however, can be exercised *only* on the expiration date.

• •

Now that you've been introduced to buying calls, you're going to learn how to buy puts, another speculative strategy. Once again, it's essential that you learn this strategy even if you never decide to use it. For your information, buying puts is a mirror image of buying calls (although the reason for buying or selling is different).

PART FOUR

HOW TO BUY PUTS

15

How to Choose the Right Put Option

If you believe that the market or your stock is going to drop in value, you have several choices. First, if you are long a stock, you can sell it to avoid future losses. Another choice is to *sell stocks short*. And your third choice is to *buy puts*. (You can also say you are *long puts*.)

When buying puts, you often profit when the underlying stock price goes down. For example, many years ago, housing stocks weakened after doubling or tripling in price. Instead of selling the housing stocks short, you could have bought puts on them. As the housing stocks continued to fall, your puts would have become more valuable.

Sometimes you get the feeling that put buyers get no respect. Maybe it's because most investors have been programmed to go long and stay long. Generally, the public has shied away from shorting strategies. After all, shorting means that you are thinking negatively about stocks. Or perhaps it's because so few people understand how and why anyone would want to short stocks.

Note: If you don't know how to sell stocks short, you can read about this intriguing strategy in my book *Understanding Stocks.*

In my opinion, if you are taking only one side of the market, the long side, you are cutting yourself out of a very lucrative share of the market. By trading both sides of the market, you can be flexible. When stocks are flat, you can sell covered calls. When stocks are bullish, you can buy calls. And when stocks are bearish, you can buy puts.

In reality, the mechanics of buying puts is the same as buying calls. However, the reason for buying puts is completely different from the reason for buying calls. In fact, if you can understand the reasons why you would buy puts, you will have an edge over many traders. It is well worth your time to understand how to use this strategy.

In addition, when you learn intermediate and advanced strategies such as *spreads*, you will often buy and sell puts. As you will learn in Chapter 17, puts are also used to protect your stock portfolio. In fact, this is one of the best reasons to buy puts.

What It Means to Buy a Put

When you buy a put, you plan to profit when the underlying stock declines in price. The faster and farther the stock declines, the more valuable the put option becomes. During a prolonged bear market, when stocks seem to be going down, buying puts is a strategy that makes sense.

When you bought calls, you typically did not own the underlying security. Similarly, put buyers do not have to own the underlying stock. In simple terms, when you buy puts, you will profit if the underlying stock goes *down* far enough and quickly enough. Conversely, you will lose your initial investment if the stock goes *up*. And because you aren't shorting the stock, buying puts places less money at risk (which is why speculators like it).

Traders at the CBOE remind each other, "Puts are your friend." Some retail investors ignore put strategies, which is a mistake. Here are the two main reasons why you'd buy puts.

1. Speculation

If you are speculating, the goal is to make money in as short a time as possible. When buying puts, you are hoping that the underlying stock or index moves down. Buying puts does limit losses, but it's always possible you could lose all, or most, of your investment.

Buying puts is less risky than shorting stock. When you buy puts, you know in advance how much you can lose. When shorting stocks, there is no limit, unless you have a stop loss order. Compared to shorting, you use less cash when you buy puts (although puts can be expensive).

2. Insurance or Hedging Risk

One effective way to use puts is to buy them as an insurance policy—to protect a portfolio from a disaster in the stock market (which is why some call them "disaster insurance"). If you believe that your portfolio or an individual stock is at risk, you can buy puts on part of or on your entire portfolio.

Although puts can reduce loss, they don't provide 100 percent protection. Nevertheless, put protection is one of the best ways to help you sleep at night during volatile markets (although you can also sell your stocks rather than buy puts).

Many investors also buy puts to hedge against their long stock portfolios. For example, if you own mutual funds and stocks that invest in market indexes such as the S&P 500, you can hedge against downside risk by buying options on an index or index ETFs. In Chapter 23, I explain this in more depth.

Finally, another use of the options market is for tax management. Perhaps you are worried about the short-term prospects of the market, but for tax reasons you don't want to sell your stocks. So by buying puts, you can leave your stocks intact while protecting their value in case of a disaster. Be sure to consult a tax attorney or accountant before buying puts for tax management.

Buying Puts: Selecting the Right Environment and Stock

If you're looking for the ideal market environment to buy puts, then you have to think like a short seller. The market often goes down faster than it goes up. It could take weeks or months for the market to build itself up, and in a single day lose all its gains in one dramatic plunge.

The ideal underlying stocks for buying puts are those that are about to fall fast. To help discover such stocks, some traders use a combination of technical and fundamental analysis. At times, stocks that are trading below their 50-, 100-, or 200-day moving averages are good candidates for put buying. You can also use a stock screener to identify potentially weak stocks.

When Bad News Hits Good Companies

Almost every day, a number of stocks get hit with bad news. Even great companies like Apple or Google temporarily disappoint investors with an earnings release, and the stock will be brutally punished by 10 or 15 percent in one day. If you happened to own puts when the bad news hits, you could earn a lot of money, perhaps many times your investment. While the stock might fall only 7 to 8 percent, the put option could rise by 200 to 1,000 percent. (This also happens to call options, but during rallies.)

If you are buying puts for speculation, first look at the overall market environment. Negative economic reports can send the entire market plummeting, especially if the news catches the market off guard. Bear markets occur every few years and can last months or years. During a bear market, puts really are your friend.

Even stocks in good companies go down in a bear market. Look for stocks that have risen too far and too fast. It doesn't take much for investors' moods to change from optimism to fear. Once fear floods the market, investors will head for the exits. That's when you'll be glad you learned how to buy puts.

Understanding Puts

In buying puts, the objective is to make money when the underlying stock goes lower, not higher. Therefore, when choosing strike prices for the put to buy, the list of available options may appear to be upside down. It is not. The out-of-the-money put options have strike prices that are *below* the stock price.

The chart below should help you understand whether a put option is in the money, out of the money, or at the money.

Buying Puts: Out-of-the-Money, At-the-Money, and In-the-Money Options

Assume that the underlying stock is currently trading at $30 per share with a month until expiration. You choose whether you want an in-, out-of-, or at-the-money put option. There are good reasons for each choice. Remember that you are looking for a good deal, that is, an inexpensive (based on value rather than cost) put that rises in price as the underlying stock drops.

YYY Manufacturing Company is trading for $30 per share with a month until expiration:

Stock Price	Strike Price	Put Option	Premium
$30	$40	Deep in the money	$10.10
$30	$35	In the money	$ 5.20
$30	$32	Near in the money	$ 3.25
$30	$30	At the money	$ 1.50
$30	$28	Out of the money	$ 0.70
$30	$25	Out of the money	$ 0.20
$30	$20	Far out of the money	$ 0.01

To make sense of this chart, you have to think in reverse: the lower the strike price, the less expensive the option. Looking at the chart, YYY is trading for $30 per share. Let's say that you choose an in-the-money put option, one with a $32 strike price. It will cost you $3.25 per share to buy. The chances are pretty good that YYY, which is trading at $30, will still be *below* the $32 strike price when the market closes on the expiration date. (Note: Later in this chapter you'll learn about the breakeven price, which will help you to know how low the stock has to go before you earn a profit.)

On the other hand, if you wanted to take a chance, you could buy the cheap put option with a $25 strike price. What are the chances that YYY will fall from $30 to below $25 before the option expires? That is a 17 percent decline in one month. The chances are not good, which is why the $25 put is only $0.20 per share contract.

Note: When you buy an in-the-money put, the option has value, that is, it has intrinsic value, but it also has time value. The only value the $25 put has is time value, and with each passing day, the time value decreases. The time value of an option represents "hope," and to have a successful trade, that hope (your prediction for the stock price) has to come true before the option expires.

Quick Review

1. A put option whose underlying stock is *below* the strike price is in the money.
2. A put option whose underlying stock is *above* the strike price is out of the money.
3. A put option whose underlying stock is the same as the strike price is at the money.

Logging into Your Account

Let's sign onto our brokerage account and enter the symbol for the underlying stock, Boeing (BA). Select the option chain and study the assortment of strike prices and expiration dates. We begin by calculating the cost of one put contract.

How Much Does a Put Cost?

You calculate the cost of a put the same way you calculate a call. To help refresh your memory, look at the option chain in Figure 15.1. We will buy the Boeing May 90 put with an ask price of $3.80. Boeing is currently trading at $88.10.

Buy 1 May 90 put for $3.80 per share contract
× 100 shares of Boeing stock

Total: $380 cost

Puts for BA Show Symbols | Show Analytics* ❷

Strike ▲	Action	Last	Change	Bid	Ask	Volume	Open Int
⊟ Puts for May 18							
80	Select ▼	0.53	+0.03	0.52	0.54	78	3,257
82.5	Select ▼	0.89	+0.06	0.87	0.89	70	5,843
85	Select ▼	1.41	+0.08	1.45	1.46	59	2,548
87.5	Select ▼	2.36	+0.12	2.37	2.39	134	1,192
90	Select ▼	3.75	+0.25	3.70	3.80	39	298
⊟ Puts for Jun 22							
80	Select ▼	0.97	+0.10	1.02	1.04	58	2,581
82.5	Select ▼	1.55	+0.14	1.52	1.55	12	321
85	Select ▼	2.11	+0.02	2.24	2.26	45	482
87.5	Select ▼	3.10	0.00	3.20	3.30	1	371
90	Select ▼	4.20	-0.10	4.50	4.60	2	372

Figure 15.1   Option chain: Boeing puts

Source: Fidelity Investments. © 2002 FMR LLC. All rights reserved. Used by permission.

Explanation: Because the ask price is $3.80 per contract, and 1 contract equals 100 shares of stock, the highest price you expect to pay for buying this option will be $380. If you bought 2 contracts, you would pay $760. If you bought 5 contracts, you would pay $1,900. If you bought 10 contracts, you would pay $3,800.

Remember: If you had shorted 1,000 shares of the stock instead of buying puts, you would have to put up margin of approximately $44,000.

How to Calculate Breakeven

The key to your success as an options trader is your ability to calculate risk-reward, and knowing your breakeven point is an important part of this process. To calculate breakeven for buying puts, let's take a look at our formula.

Put strike price − premium paid = breakeven
$90.00 strike price
−$3.80 premium paid

Total: $86.20 breakeven

Explanation: In this example, the underlying stock, Boeing, has to drop to $86.20 per share for breakeven when you hold the option until expiration. Anything *below* $86.20 is profit. If the stock falls far enough below the strike price, the option could follow the exact movement of the underlying stock and trade in unison. By the time the underlying stock has reached this point, the stock is well below the strike price (and the put option is deep in the money).

The Factors That Influence Puts

The same factors that influence the price of calls also influence puts, such as the strike price, the expiration date, the price of the underlying stock, volatility, dividends, and interest rates.

To help you understand the put option more clearly, let's look at the Boeing option chain in Figure 15.1. Only put options are displayed.

Strike Prices

If you are buying puts for speculation, you have choices. Some traders suggest buying in-the-money puts because they have intrinsic value. In other words, an in-the-money put is worth something tangible. Others disagree, and suggest that you buy out-of-the-money puts. I suggest buying the kind of options that works best with your skills and ability. As you gain experience, you will choose strike prices that best suit your personal needs.

For example, in Figure 15.1, Boeing is $88.10. Therefore, the May 90 put is in the money by almost 2 points. You might want to know whether $3.80 per share is a fair price for this put option, but it's not that easy to determine. Note that the ask price of the June 90 put is $4.60, only $0.80 more. For $0.80 more, you gain another month of time.

Note: It's probably not a brilliant strategy to buy expensive deep in-the-money puts because the high cost means you can lose a lot of money if the stock rallies (despite your expectations). After all, the whole idea of buying options is to use less money. Perhaps you will be comfortable buying near-term in-the-money puts because they give you some intrinsic value as well as a relatively reasonable price. More importantly, the stock doesn't have to move as far to generate a profitable trade.

On the other hand, if you buy the cheaper out-of-the-money puts, you would be buying all time value. For example, the May 85 is 3 points out of the money, so Boeing would have to drop well below $85 per share for you to make a profit if you hold to expiration. The May 80 seems like a bargain at $0.54 but it's like a mini lottery ticket. Boeing would have to plunge by 8 points within a month for you to make a profit. It's possible but unlikely.

Inexperienced investors who hope for miracles tend to gravitate toward cheap out-of-the-money puts. And miracles do happen, but usually not often enough to make this strategy a success. Just don't confuse this with a trading strategy. Nevertheless, all these factors have to be considered when you are buying options.

Here is something else to consider: If you are speculating, start by buying in-the-money puts. Then take time to examine your trade history and determine which put-buying strategy works best for you and provides the highest profits. Your results depend on what you bring to the table. If you have no skills in predicting which stocks will decline, do not expect to make money by buying puts (until you gain that skill). On the other hand, if you do have a decent history, then it should be easy to determine which options will provide the best results.

Expiration Dates

Although you might consider buying puts with one or two months to expiration, you have to experiment and learn how accurate your market guesses are. If your predictions come true quickly, shorter-term options (one month) should be the most efficient. If most of your successful predictions take a while to develop, then buy options with enough time remaining for the strategy to be profitable.

Obviously, the longer the time before the option expires, the more expensive it is. If you choose an option with a month or less to expiration, although cheaper in dollar terms, it does decay more rapidly, and it might not give you enough time for the strategy to play out.

To balance a reasonable time period and cost, think about buying options with at least a month to expiration. Never forget that time is not on your side when buying puts (or calls). The main reason that speculators lose money is that time runs out and the option expires. In addition, they have no idea how much to pay for an option or which option to buy. In reality, market-timing skills are more important than deciding which option to buy.

What Is the Right Put Option?

The correct put option is one that leads to a profitable trade. For example, one of the biggest advantages of choosing an in-the-money put is that a moderate move in the underlying stock can bring you profits. On the other hand, out-of-the-money puts offer the chance for larger percentage gains for less cash, but with reduced odds of making any money. The chance that the underlying stock will drop far enough to be profitable is a long shot. Ideally, you are trading based on skill and probabilities, not long shots.

If you're a beginner, you should practice trading options by buying only one or two put contracts at a time. This will help you learn how to profit from falling stocks. By all means, experiment with various strike prices and expiration dates. As I said before, your long-term goal is to devise your own criteria for what is a winning put.

. . . .

Now that you have a few ideas of how to choose the right put option, you will next learn how to manage your put position.

Note: The step-by-step procedure for buying a put is exactly the same as it is for buying a call.

16

Managing Your Put Position

In this chapter, I discuss ways to manage your put position and some of the decisions you have to make. Since you already know how to buy calls, this chapter should be relatively easy. After all, managing a put position is similar to managing a call position. The hard part, as always, is exiting the position with profits, which is why it's essential that you have a trading plan.

And now let's review some of the risks you take when you are buying puts for speculation.

The Risks of Buying Puts

The advantage of buying puts is that losses are limited while your profit potential is substantial. However, as I said before, the risk of buying puts is the same as that for buying calls: the stock will not move in your favor, and options will lose value and expire worthless. In fact, the biggest risk in buying any option is the loss of your entire investment.

As you already know, many speculators lose money when trading options. So if your only reason for buying puts is for speculation, then the odds are against your making a profit, although it's still possible to succeed.

When you buy puts (or calls) for speculation, it's easy to forget that profits, like options, are fleeting. For some reason, many option buyers tend to believe that stocks will continue to go down (or up) forever.

I encourage you to establish a profit target when buying options and to take your profits when that target is reached. That is an important part of your trading plan. Put option profits are often short-lived because markets trend higher more often than lower. Therefore, if you make a profit when you are buying puts, it's suggested that you sell the option for a gain without waiting for expiration (as I've repeatedly said).

Buying puts (and calls) is difficult because you have to be correct on the direction as well as on the timing of the underlying stock. Unless you are a talented stock picker, the stock may end up close to where it started, turning your trade into a money loser. It is also possible to lose your entire investment (if you don't sell the option before it expires worthless).

Buying puts is simple to execute, but earning profits is much harder. Only you can decide if this strategy makes sense for you and your financial goals. (Unfortunately, most speculators pay too much for the wrong options, and this leads to losses or lower-than-expected profits.)

Even with these risks, buying puts is a useful strategy that you will want to use during bear markets (or if you identify a weak stock in any market).

Buying Puts: Step-by-Step

Now for the good news: It's easy to buy puts (the order screen is identical to the screen for buying calls). For example, let's say you wanted to buy the Boeing May 90 put, as shown in Figure 16.1. Boeing is trading at $88.10.

Step 1: After entering the underlying stock symbol, check the bid-ask market for the May 90 put. It is $3.70 to $3.80.

Step 2: You select *buy to open* and enter a limit price of $3.75 or $3.80 "good for the day only." In options terminology, you entered a day order to buy a put.

Step 3: Before you place the order, preview it. Be certain you made no typos and checked the correct boxes. This prevents any unnecessary and possibly costly mistakes.

Puts for BA Show Symbols | Show Analytics* ❷

Strike ▲	Action	Last	Change	Bid	Ask	Volume	Open Int
⊟ **Puts for May 18**							
80	Select ▼	0.53	+0.03	0.52	0.54	78	3,257
82.5	Select ▼	0.89	+0.06	0.87	0.89	70	5,843
85	Select ▼	1.41	+0.08	1.45	1.46	59	2,548
87.5	Select ▼	2.36	+0.12	2.37	2.39	134	1,192
90	Select ▼	3.75	+0.25	3.70	3.80	39	298
⊟ **Puts for Jun 22**							
80	Select ▼	0.97	+0.10	1.02	1.04	58	2,581
82.5	Select ▼	1.55	+0.14	1.52	1.55	12	321
85	Select ▼	2.11	+0.02	2.24	2.26	45	482
87.5	Select ▼	3.10	0.00	3.20	3.30	1	371
90	Select ▼	4.20	-0.10	4.50	4.60	2	372

Figure 16.1   Option chain: Boeing puts

Source: Fidelity Investments. © 2002 FMR LLC. All rights reserved. Used by permission.

Step 4: Press the enter key and send in the order. In this example, your account will be debited for the price you pay for the option, or $380 (possibly $375), if the order is filled.

Broker instructions: If you call your broker to place the order, you would say, "I want to buy one Boeing May 90 put for a limit price of $3.80 (or better) good for the day."

Note: If you do decide to place a call with a broker, the recorded telephone call is proof of an order entry. Be sure to speak clearly and use options terminology when placing the trade.

What Can Go Right or Wrong

If there is anything you've learned in this book, it's that buying an option is the easiest part of trading. The hard work begins as soon as your order is filled. Decide what you will do under various conditions before placing your order. Have a profit target and a maximum loss in mind, and act when either is reached.

As you know, the underlying stock can move in only three directions: up, down, or sideways. Let's analyze how you would react under each scenario.

Note: You must not forget that you own the position. Keep track of the underlying stock and the price of your put option. You don't want to miss an opportunity to take your desired profit. Nor do you want that option to expire worthless because you weren't paying attention. If you are going to trade, realize that it takes time to monitor the position.

The underlying stock price helps determine the price of the put. When buying puts, if the underlying stock falls, your put option will increase in value (most of the time). When the underlying stock rises, your put option will decrease in value. (Occasionally, there are exceptions.)

• •

To refresh your memory, Boeing is at $88.10 per share. We bought the Boeing May 90 put (which is in the money) for $3.80.

• •

The Underlying Stock Moves Up

What happens if the underlying stock moves up?

> *Outcome*: Instead of falling, Boeing moves above the 90 strike price.
>
> *Analysis*: This is not what you wanted. (Remember, these are puts, not calls.) As the underlying stock moves higher than the strike price, all intrinsic value is gone from the option. The option price declines and eventually becomes worthless (unless Boeing suddenly retreats below the strike price). In this example, you will lose 100 percent of your investment.

If the stock goes in the wrong direction (up), you can sell part of your position (assuming you bought more than one put) to minimize losses. You can also hold longer if you expect that the stock will drop in value.

If you do decide to hold on, you must weigh many factors, including how much time is left until expiration, volatility, and whether there is a chance the stock will reverse direction. Most important: You must still have a good reason for believing that the stock price will fall. If you no longer believe this, don't own the put.

Managing a put option position requires skill and discipline, especially when it goes against you. This is what separates the pros from the novices. It's hard enough to manage your winners, but it takes a tremendous amount of skill and discipline to manage losers. Any time you place a directional trade (such as buying puts), taking action to avoid that maximum loss is a skill that you must learn.

The Underlying Stock Stays the Same

What happens if the underlying stock stays the same?

> *Outcome*: Boeing stays at or near $88. In our example, Boeing drifts between $88 and $90 per share.
>
> *Analysis:* This is not an ideal situation. If the underlying stock is stuck in neutral, the option will lose value, especially as the expiration date nears and the time premium deteriorates. Because there is still some intrinsic value left in the option, you can either sell for a loss and recover part of the premium paid, or you can wait a bit longer, hoping for a turnaround.

As you know, hope is not a practical investment strategy. Only you can decide whether to cut your losses by selling or wait for a sudden bearish move in the stock price. More than likely, the stock won't make a miraculous turnaround as expiration approaches.

The Underlying Stock Moves Down

What happens if the underlying stock moves down?

> *Outcome*: Boeing suddenly plunges, dropping well *below* the May 90 strike price. In our example, Boeing falls to $84 per share.
>
> *Analysis:* As a put buyer, this is exactly what you want and expect. The more the underlying stock falls below the strike price, the more valuable the option becomes.

When the stock falls, it makes sense to take profits when you earn your profit target. As you already know, there is no reason to wait for expiration. Stocks often rebound, and that would place your profit in jeopardy.

If the stock is below the strike price (the option is in the money), consider selling the put to book the profits. You select *sell to close* on your brokerage screen to close out the option position.

Important: If your put option is in the money at expiration, you have another choice: You have the right to exercise. The process is exactly the same as when you exercise a call, but with a different result. It's important to learn how to exercise a put, even if you never do it.

Note: Although you have the right to exercise the put, more than likely, you won't. If you do exercise, you will end up with a short stock position. Almost all option investors (and especially speculators) who buy puts sell the put before it expires, thus avoiding exercise.

Why Would You Exercise a Put?

To review, after you buy a put, you have three choices on or before expiration. First, you can sell the put, hopefully for a profit. Just as with calls, selling the put before expiration is recommended. Second, you can do nothing, which is not recommended. Nevertheless, if the put is out of the money at expiration, it will expire worthless.

Your third choice is to exercise, but only when the put is in the money.

As a call buyer, you have the right to exercise the option and *buy* the underlying stock. As a put buyer, you have the right to exercise the option and *sell* the underlying stock.

When exercising a put, you convert your put option into a short stock position. You are not required to exercise the option, but you can if you wish to.

Why would you exercise a put option? Perhaps you believe that the stock will keep going *down*. By exercising, you can continue to profit if the stock price moves lower. That is a high-risk play (because losses become unlimited if the stock suddenly rallies). It is less risky to sell your put and buy another (with a later expiration date).

For example, let's say that YYY is currently trading at $85 per share. Since your put option is in the money by 5 points, you decide to exercise 1 YYY put and thereby sell stock at $90 (the strike price). As soon as you exercise, your put is converted to a short stock position. Your brokerage firm lends you 100 shares of YYY (and the shares are sold at the strike price). You are now short 100 shares of YYY at $90 per share. Since YYY is trading at $85 per share, after exercising the option at the 90 strike price, you will already have 5 points of value in the position.

Advanced note: You can also roll out the put option instead of exercising.

> *Question from a reader:* Do I have to exercise the put option?
>
> *Answer:* No; in fact, most people do not exercise. Most put contracts are sold before the expiration date. Just be certain to sell the put before expiration, and don't wait until the last day. Remember, if the option is in the money and expiration arrives, the put option is automatically exercised, and you will own a short stock position.

How to Exercise a Put Option

The chain of events for exercising a put option is the same as that for exercising a call option. Prior to expiration, you *must* notify your brokerage firm (ask your broker for the preferred notification method) that you plan to exercise your option. You must let him or her know before the brokerage firm's cutoff time on the day you want to exercise. Wait until the close of trading when you are sure that you still want to exercise.

Once you notify your brokerage firm that you want to exercise, it notifies the OCC, which issues an exercise notice to some random person who is short that option. The exercise is irrevocable.

As the put owner, when you exercise a put, you usually have no stock shares to deliver to the put seller. Because you have no stock to deliver (your brokerage firm lends you the shares that are sold), you now have a short position. You will see that position in your account the next business day.

If you planned on shorting the underlying stock, then this exercise will be welcomed. If you didn't expect to exercise and do not want the short position, you will have to cover your short position by buying back (covering) the borrowed shares.

Although you have the right to exercise the put before the expiration date, there is no economic value in exercising a put early. As long as there is some time premium left in the option, even pennies, it doesn't make sense to exercise early. It's like throwing money (time value) away. With calls, you might consider exercising early to capture a dividend, but not with puts.

Remember, if your put is in the money by a penny ($.01) or more at expiration, it will be automatically exercised (unless you instruct your broker not to exercise).

Some brokerage firms may automatically force you to sell your option on the final day of trading (typically, the third Friday) when it's in the money and your account does not have enough cash to pay for the shares. Each firm has its own rules and procedures regarding exercise. Just ask. They will be happy to let you know.

Note: If your option is *not* in the money at expiration, it will expire worthless.

The Futures Market

Although the options market was created based on the successful platform of the futures market, they are completely different markets. This is an account of how the futures market was created and what often happens behind the scenes.

History
The futures market can be traced back to Japan during the Middle Ages where commodities like silk and rice were traded in advance

of a certain date (although informal trading of futures contracts was recorded in England as early as the thirteenth century). In the U.S., however, the futures market was created in Chicago to help farmers sell their grain in advance of the harvest so they could receive money and lock in the price. Then they didn't have to gamble on the price after harvest.

As a result, in 1848, Midwestern grain traders, along with wealthy Chicago businessmen, created the Chicago Board of Trade (CBOT). They wanted a central location for the buying and selling of agricultural futures contracts.

In 1865, the Chicago Board of Trade created standardized contracts, called *futures contracts* (or *forward contracts*), for buying grain from Chicago area farmers. Trading of grain and other agricultural products was conducted on the trading floor of the exchange, affectionately called *the pit*. This is the place where members disclosed their bid and ask prices, often by screaming and shouting at each other. This is referred to as *open outcry*. Using hand gestures as well as outcry, they signaled the price and quantity of contracts with the person taking the other side of the trade. Each commodity had its own designated pit.

In 1919, the Chicago Butter and Egg Board, an offshoot of the Chicago Board of Trade, changed its name to the Chicago Mercantile Exchange (CME, or "the Merc"). In 2007, the Merc and Chicago Board of Trade merged to form CME Group. Although it is guaranteed there will be more mergers and acquisitions, CBOT and CME will be fondly remembered in Chicago as the world's two largest futures exchanges. In recent years, the futures exchanges have moved to electronic trading.

The terminology of the futures market is quite similar to that of the options market. For example, a futures contract is a *derivative*, which means its value is derived from an underlying asset such as corn, soybeans, or currency.

In the futures market, people buy and sell contracts whose underlying assets are commodities like agricultural items (sugar, corn, coffee), currencies (dollar, euro, yen), precious metals (gold, silver), petroleum products (heating oil, gasoline), interest-rate products (Treasuries), and stock indexes (Nikkei, DAX, Dow).

The two types of traders who primarily use the futures market are speculators and hedgers. Hedgers use the futures market as an insurance policy, to protect their product or lock in a price. For example, a company like Starbucks will use the futures market to lock in the price of coffee and will obviously take delivery of the product.

Speculators, on the other hand, use the futures market to increase income and make profits, just as they do in the equity markets. They have no desire to take physical delivery of the commodity. For example, unless you really want to take delivery of 1000 pounds of coffee, you must sell the contracts before the settlement date.

The futures market uses a form of accounting called *mark to market*. If a futures contract is worth $1,000 and the contract drops by $500, the $500 loss is deducted from your account at the end of the day. In addition to mark-to-market rules, futures trades are also *cash-secured*, meaning your account must be paid off in cash or settled by the end of the day. The mark-to-market rule has ruined many unsuspecting futures traders who were forced by the rules to pay for their losses immediately.

The bottom line is that the futures market, although a useful and necessary trading platform, is not recommended for rookies. At a minimum, you should master the options market before even thinking about speculating in futures.

Now that you know how to manage a put position, let's look at other ways of using puts. Instead of speculating with puts, you will be using them for protection.

17

Protective and Married Puts

The put strategies you learned about earlier were for speculators who want to make money on weak underlying stocks. The advantage of buying puts is that you can make a profit without having to sell short the stock.

There are other ways to use a put. One strategy is to buy a put on a stock that you already own. Why would you do that? For protection, which is why it's called a *protective put*. The cost of the protective put is similar to the premium you pay on an insurance policy.

The main disadvantage to buying puts for protection is the relatively high cost. Like any insurance, protective puts eat into your profits, which is something you must consider. Also, the most volatile stocks cost the most to insure. Nevertheless, if there were a stock disaster, you'd be glad you bought puts. If nothing happens, however, you may wonder why you gave up some gains for unused protection.

The Protective Put: Disaster Insurance

Buying protective puts makes sense if you have reason to fear that your stock may plunge. The protective put strategy works when something unexpected happens (i.e., a market correction or an earnings miss). This strategy works even better when the stock soars so much the profits exceed the cost of owning the put.

Usually, people who buy protective puts will buy a number of puts that equal the number of shares they have in their account. For example, if you own 1,000 shares of IBM and believe that the stock might go down in the short term, you can buy 10 put contracts. If you own 100 shares, you would buy one put contract.

Although buying protective puts sounds like a wise idea, you don't want to throw away your money. If you are so concerned that your stock might plunge, perhaps you should think of selling your stock rather than paying for protection.

Bottom line: Only you can decide if the amount you pay for puts is worth the security.

> *Alternative investment*: Instead of buying a protective put on an underlying stock, you can hedge your position by buying puts on an ETF such as SPY (S&P 500), QQQ (Nasdaq 100), DIA (Dow Jones Industrial Average), or IWM (Russell 2000). This strategy is introduced in Chapter 23.
>
> *Hint:* In my opinion, using puts to protect a stock or index fund is an excellent strategy, although the cost can be high. In addition, it's difficult for most retail investors (and pros) to time the market, so those unused protective puts can be expensive.

On the other hand, if you time it correctly, the high cost of the puts will be forgotten if the strategy works. Nevertheless, this is a decision that only you can make. It's still important that you learn the strategy in case you decide to use it one day.

A Protective Put Trade

Following is an example of a protective put trade.

Example: In March, you buy 100 shares of XYZ at $45 per share. After a month, XYZ drops to $44, and you're worried it will keep falling. Instead of selling the stock for a small loss, you buy a XYZ May 42 put. Note that this is an out-of-the-money put, which is a little cheaper. When buying puts for protection, you will typically buy out-of-the-money puts.

In this example, the cost of the put is $2.00, or $200. For $200, you are protecting $4,200 in stock ($42 strike price × 100 = $4,200).

Note: The put protects the downside for anything below the 42 strike price. You are not protected from $44 to $42.

If your stock goes higher, not lower, your put will expire worthless, which may be a good outcome (depending on the stock price when the put expires). You want XYZ to go up so you can earn money on the rising stock. The protective put was not designed to be profitable, only to protect you from disasters. The most this protection can cost is the amount you paid for the put, or $200. It is similar to an unused insurance policy, and just because the option expired worthless doesn't mean you wasted money.

If your stock falls below the strike price, the value of the put rises and protects your portfolio against losing money. In the above example, if XYZ fell to $35 per share, although you would lose 9 points on the stock ($44−$35 = $9), the value of the put would rise substantially.

In this example, if the stock is at $35 per share and the put is deep in the money, you have to make a decision as expiration approaches. Let's briefly look at your choices:

1. You can exercise the put, thereby selling your long stock position.
2. You can sell the valuable put to offset most of the loss from the stock.
3. You can do nothing, allowing the put to be automatically exercised.

No matter what your choice, before the expiration date, decide what action you plan to take. Don't wait until the last day to make a decision.

Let's examine each of your choices in more detail.

1. If the stock is below the strike price (the put is in the money), you have the right to exercise. When you exercise an in-the-money put on a stock you own, you are instructing your brokerage to *sell* your underlying stock at the strike price. Choose this option when you don't want to own the stock.

    In this example, in one transaction your put is exercised and YYY is sold at the strike price.

    Note: If you exercise the put, you'd almost always do it on the expiration date and not earlier. It usually makes no economic sense to exercise a put early, even if you wanted the stock sold.

2. You can always sell the protective put if it's in the money. If you're no longer bearish about the underlying stock, sell the put and keep the stock in your account.
3. If you do nothing, and the protective put is in the money by even a penny, it will be exercised and the underlying stock will be sold at the strike price. If you wanted the stock sold, then this is a good outcome.

Note: On the other hand, if the put is out of the money at expiration, it will expire worthless, and you will still own the stock. If you want to continue owning the stock, then this is also a good outcome.

Next decision: If you still own the stock and still want insurance, you must buy another put. I hope that you can see why this can be expensive.

Using the Put as a Stop Loss

Following is an example of using a put as a stop loss.

Example: In March, you bought YYY for $60 per share, and it quickly rose to $66. You decide to lock in some of your gain in case YYY reverses direction. Although you could sell the entire position for a $600 profit (not a bad choice), you may believe that the stock is moving higher, or there may be tax reasons. You decide that a traditional stop loss is not suitable.

In this example, you buy an out-of-the-money April 64 put. The cost of the put is $2.50, or $250, but it's protecting $6,400 of your investment. If YYY drops below the $64 strike price, you are guaranteed the right to sell your shares at $64.

Note: That protective put gives you the right to sell YYY at $64. However, the put will not protect you from $66 to $64.

The tighter the stop loss, the more the protection costs. Think of it as an insurance policy with a smaller deductible. In the above example, the April 65 put costs more than the April 64 put and offers extra protection. On the other hand, if you had selected a far out-of-the-money April 60 put, it would cost much less, but you would risk losing your entire gain.

In addition, the farther out the expiration date, the more the put costs. A put with a two-month expiration date costs more than the one-month put. Three months cost even more.

There is one negative about using a put as a stop loss, however. Stop loss orders are free, while protective puts cost money. Only you can decide how much you're willing to pay for protection.

The Married Put

The term *married put* comes from an old IRS ruling. The term has lingered for years even though the IRS no longer recognizes it. The strategy refers to *simultaneously* buying the underlying stock and the put option. Identical to the protective put, the married put is a hedging strategy designed to protect your assets from a decline in the price of the underlying stock. The difference is that with a protective put, you buy the put *after* you buy the stock. With the married put, you buy the put at the same time.

Note: Since a protective put and a married put are really the same strategy, most people call it a protective put. It acts as a hedge against potential losses.

   Hopefully, you now have a better idea of the benefits and disadvantages of put protection. On one hand, the put protects you in a worst-case scenario. On the other hand, the put costs money, and with some stocks or indexes, protection is expensive.

· ·

   Next, you will learn about an options strategy, the collar, which helps protect covered call positions.

18

The Collar

As you know, the main risk when selling covered calls is that the underlying stock could fall in price. If you own a covered call position on a stock that plunges, the premium you received from selling the covered call will not offset much of your loss.

Fortunately, there is a strategy called a *collar* that can protect the value of underlying stock when you are selling covered calls. If, after selling a covered call, you believe that the underlying stock might tumble, and you want protection against a large loss, you can initiate a collar. Perhaps the stock has had a nice upward run, and using the collar strategy is one way to protect your gains. (Don't forget that you can also sell the stock outright to lock in those gains.)

Creating a collar is relatively simple. First, you buy stock. Next, you sell a covered call. Finally, you buy a protective put. Buying the put creates a collar. You can construct a collar on an existing covered call position, or you can initiate a new collar position.

Defensive investors who primarily want to preserve capital rather than make huge profits may appreciate the collar. Basically, you are exchanging some of the possible profits for protection, but it's still possible to earn decent profits with this strategy. Consider the strategy as an "insured covered call position."

Why Not Initiate a Collar?

One of the disadvantages of putting a collar, or limit, around a stock is that you significantly limit your gains. Then again, it also limits potential losses. This strategy is not designed to make a lot of money, but it can be designed so there is decent upside potential for each trade. It sacrifices profit potential for safety.

While the collar limits losses, it does not eliminate them. After all, options trading, and especially the collar strategy, makes investing less risky, but not riskless. For example, investors can lose money on the collar when the stock declines. Without the collar, however, stock losses could be excessive. Although you may lose money on occasion, the collar prevents you from getting hurt badly.

Like insurance, the collar buys peace of mind and is a decent strategy for conservative investors or people who are more concerned with capital preservation than with earning additional wealth.

> *Hint:* Typically, you will construct the collar so that both the call and put are out of the money.
>
> *Hint:* By initiating a collar, you reduce risk. The nice feature of the collar is that you can construct a collar so that the premium received from the call pays for the put. This is called a *zero-cost collar*, as you'll see below.

Let's go through a few examples of the collar.

Your First Collar

In August, you buy 100 shares of YYY at $52 per share. You *sell* one YYY September 55 call (it's a covered call) and receive $2.20, or $220 ($2.20 × 100), in premium. You want to initiate a collar because you cannot afford to lose much money on this stock, and would like to be protected in case of a temporary pullback.

You *buy* 1 September 50 put for a cost of $2.00, or $200 ($2.00 × 100), which completes the collar. Your put protects the value of your YYY shares in case the stock moves below $50 per share.

Hint: Use out-of-the-money strike prices for both the call and
the put.

Note on zero-cost collars: You collect more from the sale of the
call option ($220) than you paid for the put ($200). The difference may
be small (it is only $20 in this example), but it means that it cost zero
cash out of pocket to own the collar, which is why it's a "zero-cost
collar." That is a good thing because when expiration arrives and
nothing special happens to the price of YYY, the protection didn't
cost any cash.

Note: Depending on the strike prices chosen, in the real world, the
put may cost more than the call, which means that you will pay out of
pocket for protection.

A Collar Trade

Let's a take a look at what could go right, or wrong, with the collar.

*Example 1: The underlying stock, YYY, rises and is $57
when the market closes on the expiration day.*

If YYY remains above the $55 strike price at expiration, the stock will
be called away (i.e., it will be sold at the $55 strike price). The put por-
tion of the collar expires worthless.

You received a credit of $20 on the collar ($220 − $200 = $20), and
also made a 3-point gain, or $300, on the underlying stock (you bought
stock at $52 and sold it at $55). Total gain: $320. In this example, the put
acts as unused insurance protection. This trade earned the maximum
possible profit for the collar position.

Note: For anyone who is concerned that there is too little gain from
the collar, this example shows otherwise.

Example 2: The underlying stock, YYY, falls to $45 on the expiration date.

The put is in the money and the call expires worthless. That put eliminates all losses below the 50 put strike price. Because of the collar, the stock plunge is not a catastrophe for the collar owner.

If YYY falls even more, it does not make a difference to you, the collar owner. Your put increases in value at the same rate that the stock loses value. If you want to keep the stock at expiration, sell the put. If you prefer to rid your portfolio of this stock, then exercise the put.

Note: The collar's primary function is to provide protection, not profits, if the underlying stock falls. Instead of taking a $700 loss on the stock, you lost only $180 ($200 loss on the stock and $20 gain on the options trade) in this example. This is the maximum possible loss for this position.

Example 3: YYY rises to $53 per share on the expiration date.

If YYY moves between the strike prices of the call ($55) and put ($50), and is $53 at expiration, both options expire worthless, and you keep YYY. You also keep the $20 premium collected earlier. At expiration, no action has to be taken. Although the put expires worthless, consider the premium you paid as unused insurance protection.

Note: Without the collar, your profit would have been $20 less.

Risks: Although this strategy sounds attractive on paper, in reality it limits upside profits. This is the main reason that it is not used more often. It also limits downside losses, and that is the trade-off. This strategy is for the very conservative investor (or a temporarily worried investor). Also, if the underlying stock does fall, you will never offset the total loss from the stock.

Now, let's take a closer look at the LEAPS option.

Introducing LEAPS

Long-term equity anticipation securities (LEAPS) are long-term option contracts with expiration dates from seven months to three years. In a way, buying a LEAPS option is similar to leasing a car for up to three years, except that you are leasing the right to buy stocks, not cars. Just like a leasing agreement, you benefit from using the stock, but you don't own it.

Most important, LEAPS are identical to traditional options except for the longer time period. To make record keeping easier, LEAPS have different symbols. To be precise, when LEAPS come within seven to nine months of expiration, they are no longer classified as LEAPS but change their symbol to that of a standard option.

Many experienced investors like LEAPS because they can use their favorite options strategies but for longer time periods. They can save on commissions by trading less often. However, more active traders prefer shorter-dated options. Some jokingly call LEAPS the "poor person's stock," because people who can't afford stock sometimes buy LEAPS.

Note: LEAPS are always less expensive than buying stock but cost more than ordinary options.

Disadvantages of LEAPS

There are also disadvantages to investing in LEAPS. First, buying calls (or puts) is still a speculative strategy, so you can lose money when buying LEAPS if the underlying stock doesn't move far enough in the right direction before the expiration date.

In addition, the bid-ask spreads on LEAPS are a bit wider than are spreads with traditional options. This could be a problem if you must immediately exit the position. If you are going to buy a LEAPS call option, you should do it on an underlying stock you really want to own.

Because LEAPS are very sensitive to changes in volatility, you'll also need a good understanding of how volatility affects option pricing. If you're new to options, first understand standard options before even thinking about LEAPS.

The question you should ask yourself is: Are you trading or investing? LEAPS are not for traders. And second, do you need the extra time that a LEAPS option provides? If so, it may justify spending money on a financial instrument with expiration dates up to three years in the future.

A LEAPS Trade

Here's a brief example of how to buy a LEAPS call. In January, YYY is trading for $92 per share. You are interested in YYY for a buy and hold investment. If you bought 100 shares of stock, it would cost you $9,200 plus commission.

Instead, you decide to buy a deep in-the-money January 85 call that expires in 12 months. The cost of the contract is $9.00, so the most you can lose on this trade is $900. Because the call is deep in the money, it provides adequate upside participation and comes with good protection against a downturn. In this example, you are buying a YYY LEAPS call option as an alternative to buying stock.

Advanced note: Whenever you own LEAPS, the day-to-day time loss is small (at first). After the first six months, approximately 15 percent of the time premium will be gone (assuming you buy an at-the-money LEAPS option with 24 months until expiration). In addition, if the underlying stock moves down and the call option moves out of the money, you could lose most of your investment (just as with any other call option). And if the stock stagnates, you would lose all or part of the $200 time premium in this LEAPS option because of the ticking time clock.

Conversely, if YYY moves up in price, you could make a significant profit. Some people buy LEAPS as a long-term investment. However, remember that these are still options, and it is usually best to sell, rather than exercise them on or before the expiration date.

Congratulations! You are now familiar with the basic option strategies. You might want to take a break before moving on. After all, even the most basic option strategies can take a while to understand.

Suggestion: If you feel like you need a break, you might want to skip over to Part 6, one of my favorite sections. You can always go back and read Part 5, which includes intermediate and advanced strategies.

••••••••••••••••••••••••••••••

On the other hand, if you are comfortable with the basic option strategies and are ready to move on, Part 5 is waiting for you. I do my best to explain these strategies in understandable language.

PART FIVE

INTERMEDIATE AND ADVANCED STRATEGIES

19

Credit and Debit Spreads

Some of you have waited a long time to learn about the intermediate and advanced option strategies. Perhaps you took an expensive seminar or class and need a quick review. Or perhaps you are planning on taking a class (or the Series 7 exam) and want to know what to expect. Nevertheless, the strategies included in Part 5 are the playground of the experienced investor. Many of these strategies, such as spreads, are quite intriguing and flexible.

It makes sense to understand these strategies. After all, your ultimate goal is to gain an edge over other traders. By learning all the strategies in this book, you will be one step closer to that goal.

In Part 5, you will be introduced to credit and debit spreads, straddles and strangles, selling cash-secured and naked puts, the Greeks, iron condors, calendar spreads, the butterfly, trading options on ETFs, indexes, weekly options, and mini-option contracts. It's a lot of information, which is why this chapter is the longest in the book.

And now, let's start with credit and debit spreads, which are like having your cake and eating it, too.

What Are Spreads?

Basically, a spread is a position with a long option and a short option. To be exact, you are simultaneously buying one call (or put) and selling another call (or put). It's really that simple. Although there are tons of fancy names for different spreads, never forget that all the strategies are based on the buying and selling of calls and puts. Spreads do not require owning the underlying stock, and this is good because it makes them easier to trade.

Note: The major difference from what you have learned so far is that the two trades are made simultaneously.

More important, spreads are risk-reducing strategies (i.e., hedges). Some strategies are directional so their success depends on the movement of the underlying stock (as well as its volatility). Others are market-neutral and depend on the passage of time to generate profits.

Successful option traders prefer spreads because they are designed to reduce risk. As long as you don't trade too many spreads at one time, potential losses are limited, but so are the profits. For many, the returns are very acceptable, especially when you don't have too much money at risk.

A huge advantage is that you can construct spreads that use less capital but have the potential to make higher percentage returns on your investment. This is another reason why spreads are so popular with investors.

Spreads also appeal to experienced investors because the full power and flexibility of options are revealed when you trade spreads. In fact, there is a spread for nearly every market opinion, no matter how bullish, bearish, or neutral you might be.

Nevertheless, spreads are not risk-free, and it's essential to fully understand the risks as well as the potential rewards before initiating any spread.

Understanding the Differences

Before we get started, let's review the vocabulary. First, there are many types of spreads, but most fall into only three categories: Vertical, horizontal, and diagonal spreads. The spreads we discuss in this chapter are *vertical spreads*. For now, we limit our discussion to two vertical spreads—credit and debit. (By the way, they are referred to as vertical spreads because the expiration date is the same.)

With a *credit spread*, premium is collected. This means that the option sold has a higher premium than the option purchased. With credit spreads, the plan is for time to run out so that the cash collected becomes your profit.

With a *debit spread*, you spend cash to make the trade, and the option bought costs more than the option sold. You'll profit if the underlying stock moves in the right direction before the expiration date. This will make more sense later.

You'll discover that the four *vertical spreads* have similar names: *bull put, bull call, bear call*, and *bear put*.

Don't worry if you mix up by the strategy names. You should remember, however, that there are only two types of vertical spreads: credit and debit. And these spreads use either calls or puts. Don't waste your time memorizing the strategy names because they will become obvious to you later.

Which is better, credit or debit spreads? Truthfully, there is no right answer. Generally, investors like credit spreads because they bring in cash (not necessarily profits, but cash is collected when the trade is made). Others like debit spreads because they increase in value when the trade is working. As you learn more about spreads, you can decide for yourself which strategy meets your needs.

Here is something you may find interesting: When you initiate either a credit or a debit spread, an additional goal is to *reduce risk*. When you initiate a debit spread, your goal is to *reduce cost*.

Remember this: It's essential that you know the risk and the rewards of trading spreads (or any strategy, for that matter). Even though spreads are designed to reduce risk, there are still risks. If you don't understand that risk, spread positions can be unpleasant (primarily because of the traps that lie in wait for the unwary). Fortunately, I warn you of potential pitfalls, beginning now.

The Risks of Trading Spreads

Spreads are a very powerful tool. If used properly, the tool can help build a beautiful house that provides income and security. If not used properly, that tool can cause the whole house to collapse into rubble.

When trading spreads, be aware of worst-case scenarios. Sometimes people believe that trading with less risk means no risk. Be aware of the difference. Also, don't be afraid to ask questions if you don't fully understand the concepts. It can take a while to fully understand them. (Don't forget to call the toll-free number if you have questions.)

When you first hear about spreads, it seems that you have found the path to easy money. Unfortunately, in the real world, the underlying stock and options often don't behave as you expected. With spreads, exercise and assignment are particularly important, and if you don't fully understand what can go wrong, you could be holding an unwanted stock position. Most of the time, the problem is easily fixed, but not always, which is why it's best to prevent problems before they occur.

Note: Because spreads are a Level 3 trading strategy, almost all brokerage firms require you to fill out a margin agreement before they allow you to initiate a spread. At some brokerage firms, you will be allowed to trade spreads in your 401(k) or IRA using the cash in your account as collateral. Check with your brokerage for the exact rules.

Now that you have a general idea that risk is always present, let's get started learning about spreads. To make it easier for you, I discuss *credit spreads* first, and then *debit spreads*.

> *Hint:* Even though a spread consists of different options, think of a spread as one position.

Good luck and welcome to the world of spread trading!

Credit Spread: Bull Put

I'm delighted to introduce you to the popular *bull put spread* (also referred to as a *put credit spread*). Because it's a credit spread, you'll be receiving cash when you initiate this trade. Your goal is to keep as much of the cash as possible. Why? The cash is your maximum possible profit for this strategy.

You will typically use a bull put spread if you are slightly bullish about the underlying stock. With this strategy, you sell one *put* option (short put) while simultaneously buying another *put* option (long put). The expiration dates of both puts are the same (and that is why it is a vertical spread), but the strike prices are different.

The interesting part of this spread is that the long put acts as a protective put, preventing large losses from the put you sold. To be certain the whole trade does not result in a loss, trade an appropriate number of spreads. In addition, when you buy that protective put, it reduces your gains. That is how a spread works. If this is hard to understand, it will make sense when you study the examples in this chapter.

Risks and Rewards of the Bull Put Spread

One benefit of the bull put spread (and other option strategies) is that you can easily calculate how much can be earned or lost on the trade. In options terminology, your risk is defined (limited). Investors like the bull put spread because they collect cash up front.

The bull put spread can work like a charm if everything goes right (as with any options strategy), but things can also go terribly wrong. I'll do my best to help you avoid surprises.

Characteristics of a Bull Put Spread

Before you even consider initiating your first bull put spread, let's look at the following criteria:

- *Underlying stock*: Before you place your first spread, think about your forecast for the underlying stock. This is a bullish strategy, and you are moderately bullish about the stock. You'll need to do research to find stocks that meet your criteria. (Hopefully you will get stock ideas if you keep reading.)
- *Strike price:* When using this strategy, the key to success is choosing the correct stock and strike prices. In particular, you will need to bring in enough premium (the credit) to make the strategy

worth doing. Choosing the correct strike prices is a balancing act between risk and reward, and it becomes easier as you gain trading experience.

· ·

Short put: Typically, the strike price for the short put (the put you sold) is out of the money.

Long put: Typically, the strike price for the long put (the put you bought) is even more out of the money.

· ·

Generally, to have good odds of owning a winning bull put spread, you'll want to start with out-of-the-money puts and hope that both puts expire worthless. You can choose an at-the-money strike price for the short put and collect more premium, but this increases the odds of your losing money. At-the-money spreads are for traders who are confident that the stock price will not decline.

Remember: With this strategy, you do *not* want the puts to be in the money at any time, but especially at expiration.

Caveat: If you are an experienced trader, you might disagree with these guidelines. But if you are a beginner, you have to start somewhere, so I suggest starting with the criteria provided above. As you gain experience, you may find different criteria for the options you choose—ones that match your goals and expectations for the underlying stock. Hopefully this will bring you more profits.

Rule: Generally, the larger the distance between strike prices, the more bullish (and more risky) your position. For example, if you sell the 60 put and buy the 55 put, that 5-point difference is bullish. If you sell the 60 put and buy the 50 put, that 10-point spread is more bullish. The underlying stock has to rise (or remain) above the higher strike price in order for you to achieve the maximum profit.

Expiration date: With a bull put spread, you'll probably want to choose short time frames such as 30 to 45 days. After all, time decay works in your favor. By the expiration date, you want time to run out, both puts to end above the strike price (out of the money), and expire worthless. Then you can keep the entire credit you received from selling the put (that is your profit). Therefore, a short time frame increases that probability. Although this may give you less profit, it also increases the chances that you earn the credit received.

Think about this: You already received a credit for selling the spread. The long put that you bought is protecting your short position. If you didn't have the long put, you would not have made the trade, or you would have the potential for unlimited losses. With this strategy, when the long put expires worthless, it shouldn't bother you. It was bought only for protection.

If the spread suddenly gains value, it means that the underlying stock is falling. That is not what you want. Do not think of the long option that you bought as something that you want to see increase in value. You want it, along with the put sold, to *decrease* in value. You want your insurance option (the long put) to lose value and become unneeded by the expiration date.

Implied volatility: When implied volatility is high, premium is high. That is ideal if you are selling options. After all, high premium means more cash, which is obviously what you want. Therefore, when you sell a bull put spread, high implied volatility also means higher premium, but it also means that the stock is likely to be more volatile, thus increasing the chances of your losing money.

Ideally, you hope that implied volatility is high and about to drop. Unfortunately, knowing when implied volatility is about to top out and decline is easier said than done, similar to "buy low and sell high." Instead, high premium and the stock moving in the right direction before the expiration date are the best way to bring quick and good-sized profits.

How Much Money Can You Lose (or Make)?

Maximum risk: When using the bull put spread, the maximum risk is the difference between the strike prices and the premium received for the spread. Therefore, the larger the distance between strike prices, the more premium collected, but also the more money you could lose. A 10-point spread is more aggressive than a 5-point spread. In other words, the 10-point spread gives the trader more cash, but increases the potential loss.

Let's look at specific examples, which should help you understand the risks and rewards of the bull put spread. The first spread you do is always the hardest. After you gain experience, spreads are a lot easier to manage!

Your First Bull Put Spread

In October, you believe that YYY Manufacturing Company, which is currently $43 per share, will rise to $45 per share or higher over the next month or two. Because you are bullish about the prospects for this stock and you also want to limit risk, you consider initiating a bull put spread.

You sell 1 YYY November 42 put for a limit price of $3.60, receiving $360 ($3.60 × 100). At the same time, you buy 1 YYY November 40 put for a limit price of $2.70, paying $270 ($2.70 × 100). Net credit is $90.

Instructions to your broker: If you placed a bull put spread with your brokerage firm, you might say, "I would like to sell one YYY March 40/42 put spread for a credit of $0.90 or better."

Note: You don't need to mention specific prices for individual options.

Reminder: In this example, both puts are out of the money. The November 42 put is out of the money. The November 40 put is even farther out of the money. The trade begins with out-of-the-money options, thus increasing the odds that both options will finish out of the money. If both puts expire worthless at expiration, you earn the initial premium as your profit.

Maximum profit: In this example, the premium, or credit, that you receive is $90 ($360 cash received minus $270 paid = $90) less commission. This is your credit and the most you can earn on this trade.

Note: No matter what happens, you keep that $90 cash, and your goal is to retain as much of it as possible.

Note: As a realistic trader, don't count on making the maximum profit on any trade. You never know when an unforeseen event will appear out of nowhere to ruin your trading plans. Also, don't forget that you can always exit a trade before expiration in order to lock in a profit and eliminate risk.

Maximum loss: In this example, the maximum loss for the trade is $110, or the difference between the two strike prices minus the premium received ($200 difference in prices minus $90 premium received = $110) plus commission.

Note: Before initiating a spread, always calculate the maximum profit and maximum risk, and write them in your trading plan.

Right or Wrong?

Let's see what can go right, or wrong, when you initiate a bull put spread.

• •

   To review, YYY is currently at $43 per share. You sell 1 YYY November 42/40 put spread for a credit of $90 (the maximum possible gain). Your maximum loss is $110.

• •

Example 1: The underlying stock, YYY, is above the November 42 put strike price on the expiration date.

This is exactly what you hoped would happen. As the underlying stock moves up in price, both puts lose value. As long as the underlying stock stays above the strike price, you can keep the premium you received.

   If YYY is above $42 when the market closes on the expiration date, both puts expire worthless. (Note that when the stock is above the strike price *before* expiration, the puts are not yet worthless.) In this example, three weeks after you initiated the position, the long put might fall to $0.50 and the short put to $1.00. The spread is still worth $0.50 at that time, but ideally, both puts will be worthless at expiration.

Closing a Winning Trade

Before the expiration date, you have several choices in managing a winning trade. First, you could wait until the expiration date and try to achieve the maximum profit. In this case, if both puts expire worthless on the expiration date, you earn the maximum, $90.

To make this easier to understand, you already have the $90 in the bank. However, if the options do not expire worthless, you must spend some cash to exit the trade. When you spend less than $90, you have a profit. If you spend more, you have a loss.

Second, you can close both legs before expiration and take the profits. Using the above example, you might be able to pay $0.50 to exit the spread. This is not a bad outcome. Although achieving maximum profit is ideal, waiting for that to happen involves risk. In a worst-case scenario, you might be forced to exit the trade by paying as much as $200 at expiration (this occurs when the stock is below the lower strike price, or $40).

To avoid complications, all traders should close both legs of the spread no later than the expiration date (or earlier, if your target exit price has been reached). Traders who attempt to squeeze out every penny from a trade often end up losing all their profits. No matter what you decide to do, monitor your position closely and be certain that you are not holding positions that are too risky.

Example 2: The underlying stock, YYY, drops below the November 42 strike price before the expiration date.

This is not what you wanted to happen. In the real world, option trades don't always work out as you hoped. If the underlying stock goes down, not up, you could lose money with the bull put spread. Sometimes your expectations for the stock are wrong.

In this example, if YYY drops below $42 (the strike price), the value of the spread will increase. The short put moves in the money and increases in value more rapidly than the put you bought.

Your goal was to keep as much of the $90 premium that you originally received as possible. In this example, when the long November 40 put is also in the money at expiration, the spread is worth $200 and you lose the maximum amount, or $110.

If the stock is priced between the strike prices, then your long put expires worthless and you must be careful to cover the November 42 put. Failure to buy that put (to close) will result in your being long 100 shares after you are assigned an exercise notice. (It will cost between $1 and $199 to cover that put, depending on the stock price.)

The most important concept is that the long put is your protection, and without it, you'd be exposed to the possibility of a large loss. For example, if the stock plunged to $30, you would have to pay $1,200 (the option's intrinsic value) to cover the November 42 put. Because you have a 2-point spread, the maximum cost to close is only $200, or the difference between the strike prices.

Closing a Losing Trade

If you are in the middle of a losing trade, you have a number of choices, including cutting your losses (buying the put spread to close the position) and moving on. Closing both put options is usually the most effective action you can take.

In this example, if you decide to close both legs of the spread before expiration (recommended to manage risk), you will buy back (buy to close) the put that you sold, and sell (sell to close) the option that you own. You might pay $160 to close the spread, resulting in a $70 loss. Under no circumstances should you pay as much as $200 for a 2-point spread (and never pay more) to get out of the position. The worst possible scenario is paying $200 at expiration (so there is no need to pay that much earlier).

In real life, the loss could be greater or smaller than $70 in this example, but not more than the maximum. This is why it's so important to close both legs of the spread at the same time.

Unfortunately, some option traders will hold onto a losing position, hoping for a miracle. Sadly, miracles don't happen very often.

Doing Nothing

You have a third choice and that is doing nothing and waiting for expiration to arrive. This is not recommended because wise traders manage risk and do not let the chips fall where they may.

Typically, if both puts are in the money at expiration, the long put will be automatically exercised. Simultaneously, the short put is more than 2 points in the money (in this example) and will be exercised auto-matically (guaranteed to be exercised). An exercise notice will be assigned (i.e., assignment) to you. In this example, the exercise and assignment cancel each other, and you will have to buy the stock at $42 and sell it at $40, losing $200 per spread. That results in the maximum loss.

Example 3: The underlying stock, YYY, falls to $41 on the expiration date (between the 40 and 42 strike prices).

When the underlying stock lands between strike prices, your attention to detail is required. In a best-case scenario, both put options will expire worthless and you keep the credit originally received. But there is also a chance that the put you own expires worthless while you get assigned on the short put. That is a mild inconvenience, so don't panic. Solution: Cover the short put option before the market closes on expiration day (if not sooner) to prevent being assigned. Then the position and the risk are eliminated.

If it is expiration day, eliminate the problem by buying to close the November 42 put. That solves the problem, because there is no longer any chance of getting assigned. Your November 40 put will expire worthless when the day ends. In this example, the cash required to make the suggested trade is $100. The loss is only $10 plus commission ($100 to exit minus the $90 original premium collected).

Without a doubt, exercise and assignment cause the most confu-sion among beginners. One of the risks of a credit spread occurs when the trader is careless. When the long leg is sold and the short leg is left open, the risk is high and problems can and do occur. Fortunately, brokers do not allow novice traders to take this action.

For this reason, take this advice: Always trade the two options as a spread. Do not close one leg without closing the other. If an option is converted to stock (via assignment), close the stock position and sell your long option.

Assignment Risk

If you aren't aware of the intricacies of exercise and assignment, you could find yourself holding an unwanted stock position. As men-tioned previously, the long put and short put work together as a team. If you are holding a winning (out-of-the-money) position on the expi-ration date, both put options will expire worthless.

If you are holding a position with both options in the money, you have the worst-case scenario and the maximum loss. The long put will automatically be exercised, and the short put will be assigned. The exercise and assignment cancel the stock positions, and you no longer own the spread. But you do lose the maximum.

The problem occurs if the long put is sold or expires worthless, and you are left holding the short put. As I've said before, close the entire position. (*Rule:* Do not sell your long put without covering the short put.)

If you don't follow my advice to cover the in-the-money short put, on Monday morning following expiration you'll be holding a long position on a stock that has been falling. That was not the plan when trading the bull put spread. Please don't allow this to happen. Although you can immediately turn around and sell a stock position, it's better to avoid being assigned.

Note: This is the first time in the book that you have encountered assignment on a short put. To repeat, if you are assigned on a short put, you are obligated to *buy* shares of the underlying stock at the strike price. Avoid all these problems by covering the position no later than expiration Friday.

If you have a winning position, one choice is to close both legs of the spread before expiration and take less than the maximum profit. If you have a losing position, you may elect to close both legs of the spread before expiration and salvage what you can by taking a loss that is less than the maximum.

Just be aware that waiting involves risk. You can choose to wait until Friday by holding onto the position, but you would be in a situation where the value of the spread may change significantly in a very short time. I encourage you to exit when the risk becomes uncomfortable.

Early Assignment

Most people don't think they will be assigned early (for good reason), but it occasionally happens. It's not a problem, so stay calm. Sell the long stock and sell the put that you own. This closes the position. If you are assigned early, call your brokerage firm to make sure there is no margin call (where you would be forced to put up more cash or close the position). But you already know how to unwind: Sell the stock and sell your long put.

Final Notes

Here is a summary of the most important points about the bull put spread:

1. With the bull put spread (and all vertical spreads), you typically want to avoid assignment.
2. Do not make the mistake of selling only the long put because you are exposing yourself to unnecessary risk. The long put is designed to protect the position against major losses, so *don't* sell it.
3. Even more painful, some investors don't close out a profitable trade because they are chasing after a few extra pennies. Stocks have a funny way of going in the wrong direction right after you've made a fantastic paper profit. With the bull put spread, if your objective is to close a profitable position and keep most of the credit you received, then do it when the target is achieved. Close both legs of the spread before the expiration date. Although you won't receive maximum profit from the spread, you will avoid any complications that occur from assignment.
4. Don't be tempted to take small money off the table quickly. The goal is to make enough profit to justify taking the risk.
5. Before you do your first spread, practice. When you are ready to invest real money, start off with a 1 by 1 spread (one long and one short put). Choose the expiration date, strike prices, and premium that suit your directional bias for the underlying stock.

Credit Spread: Bear Call

Because you learned about the bull put spread, the *bear call spread* should be fairly easy to understand. Why? They are both credit spreads. One is bullish, and one is bearish, but the mechanics of entering into the trade are identical.

The bear call spread (also referred to as a *call credit spread*) is the strategy you can use if you are moderately bearish about the underlying stock. To be specific, you buy one *call* option while simultaneously selling another *call* option. In exchange for limited risk, rewards are also limited. The expiration date of both calls is the same (it is a vertical spread), but the strike prices are different. Again, with this strategy you are selling the short leg and buying the long leg for protection. It's really that simple.

With this strategy, you profit when the underlying stock *falls* in price. Like other spread strategies, you are hedging risk (by buying one call option to hedge the risk involved with selling the other call option). And just like the bull put spread, you hope that the cash you receive turns out to be the profit from the trade. Your goal is to manage risk, monitor the position, and chalk up the premium as your profit.

This spread always involves receiving a higher premium for the call sold than is paid for the call bought. You sell the more expensive call and hope that it decreases in value, perhaps even expiring worthless. You do not care about the call owned. It serves only one purpose—to limit risk.

Characteristics of a Bear Call Spread

Before you initiate your first bear call spread, let's look at the following criteria:

- *Underlying stock*: You are moderately *bearish* about the stock and want weak, underperforming stocks. The success or failure of the strategy depends on the stock not moving much higher.
- *Strike price*: For this strategy to be successful, you must bring in enough premium to justify the risk being taken.

. . . .

Short call: Typically, the strike price for the short call (the call you sold) is out of the money.

Long call: Typically, the strike price for the long call (the call you bought for protection) is farther out of the money.

. . . .

Just as with the previous credit spread (bull put), you want to start with out-of-the-money calls because this makes it more likely that the options will be out of the money when expiration arrives.

Note: Some investors choose an at-the-money strike price for the short call, which provides more premium, but it also increases the probability of losing money on the trade. Once again, find a position that you are comfortable holding based on how you expect the underlying stock to behave.

Note: If you're a beginner, start with the criteria listed above.

Rule: The larger the distance between strike prices, the more premium you collect and the greater the size of any potential loss. For example, if you sell the 55 call and buy the 60 call, that 5-point difference is bearish. If you sell the 55 call and buy the 65 call, that 10-point spread essentially increases the potential reward, but doubles the money at risk. The underlying stock would have to remain below the lower strike price in order for you to achieve the maximum profit.

Expiration date: Just as with the previous strategy, you may decide to use a short time frame (30 to 45 days), thereby increasing the odds that the options will remain out of the money at expiration. With any of these vertical spreads, time decay works in your favor.

When you initiate a bear call spread, your goal is for the underlying stock to remain *below* the strike prices of the calls that make up the spread so that both calls are out of the money at expiration and expire worthless. If this happens, the credit you received from selling the call spread is your profit.

Note: You do *not* want the underlying stock to rise above the strike price. Once again, the value of the call spread is what matters. Don't pay attention to the prices of the individual options in the spread.

Implied volatility: When selling options, you want implied volatility to be high so you can receive more cash. Once you own the position, you gain when implied volatility declines. There are no guarantees that this will happen, but it would be ideal.

How Much Can You Lose (or Make)?

Maximum risk: The maximum risk for the bear call spread is the difference between the strike prices and the premium received from selling the spread. Therefore, the greater the distance between strike prices (in the spread), the more money you could lose (or make). A 10-point spread will be costlier than the 5-point spread if you are wrong in your market opinion.

Now let's look at specific examples.

Your First Bear Call Spread

In November, you believe that YYY Manufacturing Company, which is currently $53 per share, will drop below $45 per share over the next month or two. Because you are bearish about the prospects for this stock, you want to profit on a decline, but you also want to limit risk. The bear call spread is an appropriate strategy.

You enter a limit spread order to sell 1 YYY December 55 call (short call) and buy 1 YYY December 60 call (long call) for a net credit of $150 or better.

Instructions to your broker: If you place a bear call spread with your brokerage firm, you might say, "I would like to do a credit call spread on YYY. I'm selling one December 55 call and buying one December 60 call for a net credit of $1.50 or better."

Alternative: You could also say, "I want to sell one YYY December 55/60 call spread for a credit of $1.50 or better."

Reminder: In this example, both calls are out of the money with the call you bought being farther out of the money. The strategy is to start with out-of-the-money options so that there is an increased chance that both options finish out of the money. If both calls expire worthless at expiration, the initial premium that you received is your profit.

Maximum profit: In this example, the premium, or credit, that you received is $150 less commission. This is your credit and the most you can earn on this trade.

Note: No matter what happens, you keep that initial cash of $150. How much you initially received is important as it represents your best possible result.

Remember: As a realistic trader, don't count on making the maximum profit on any trade.

Maximum loss: In this example, your maximum loss for the trade is $350 ($500 difference between two strike prices − $150 net credit received = $350) plus commission.

Therefore, in the worst case, you could lose no more than $350 on this trade. In real life, the worst that could happen is the stock being above $60 at expiration.

Note: Before initiating a spread, always calculate the maximum profit and maximum risk and write a trading plan.

Right or Wrong?

Now let's look at what could go right, or wrong, with the bear call spread.

....

To review, YYY is currently at $53 per share. You sell 1 YYY December 55 call and buy 1 YYY December 60 call for a net credit of $150. Your maximum loss is $350.

....

Example 1: The underlying stock, YYY, remains below the December 55 strike price on the expiration date.

This is exactly what you wanted. As YYY moves down in price (or at least doesn't move higher), both calls lose value. As long as the underlying stock stays below the strike price, you can keep the entire premium you received as the profit.

If YYY stays below $55 at the close of trading on the expiration date, both calls expire worthless. In this example, three weeks after you initiate the position, the long call might fall to $0.90 and the short call to $2.05. At this point, the spread is worth $1.15 and you are ahead (in paper profits). In an ideal world, if you continue to hold the position, both calls will continue to lose value and eventually expire worthless.

Closing a Winning Trade

Before the expiration date, you have several choices in managing a winning trade. First, you could wait until the expiration date and possibly earn the maximum profit. In this case, both calls must expire worthless.

Second, you can close both legs before expiration and take the profits, if any. Using the above example, you might be able to pay $115. This is also a decent outcome. Although the $35 profit ($150 − $115 = $35) is not as satisfying as achieving maximum profit, there is always risk involved when you are holding any position.

To avoid complications, beginners should close both legs of the spread before expiration once their target price has been reached.

Example 2: YYY rises above the December 60 strike price before the expiration date.

This is not what you wanted. In the trading world, trades don't always work out as you hoped. If the underlying stock goes up, not down, you could lose money with the bear call spread.

Your goal was to keep as much of the $150 premium you originally received as possible. In this example, you are currently losing money on the spread. When the call you own is in the money at expiration, you could lose the maximum amount—$350.

Closing a Losing Trade

You manage a bear call spread the same way you manage a bull put spread (because they are credit spreads). Closing both call options is usually the best risk-management plan. If YYY rises to $55 per share, it is not what you want. The higher the stock rises, the more it will cost (subject to the $500 maximum for a 5-point spread) to close the position.

Before the expiration date, it's suggested that you close both legs of the spread. In this example, if you can, buy back (buy to close) the spread by paying a debit of $3.40. You initially received a credit of $150, so your total loss is $190. In real life, the loss could be greater (or less).

Note: The riskiest choice you can make is to do nothing as expiration approaches.

Example 3: The underlying stock, YYY, rises to $57 on the expiration date (between the 55 and 60 strike prices).

Sometimes the underlying stock lands between strike prices. There is also the chance that the long call expires worthless while you get assigned early on the short call. This is not a huge problem. Just buy the shares to cover the short stock position (you get short when assigned on a call option), and sell your long call, if it has any value.

Assignment Risk

As mentioned previously, the long call and short call work together as a team. If you are holding a winning (out-of-the-money) position on the expiration date, both call options expire worthless.

In addition, if you are still holding an in-the-money long call position on the expiration date, the short call will be assigned automatically, and your long call will be exercised automatically. The two stock trades cancel each other out, and you no longer own any position. You will incur the maximum possible loss when this happens.

The problem occurs if the long call is sold or expires worthless and you are left holding the short in-the-money call. (Once again, brokers will not allow this if you are a novice.) Nevertheless, it is not a huge deal as long as you remember this: never sell the long call while still short the other call.

To prevent being assigned an exercise notice on the in-the-money short call when your long call is not in the money, simply cover the short call before the market closes on expiration Friday. Do not forget to do this. You do not want to own a short stock position after expiration.

Reminder: Once again, it's possible that you are assigned on a short call when you do not own the underlying stock. If assigned, you are obligated to sell shares short. You can avoid all these problems by not waiting until the last day to make a decision. If you have a losing position, think about closing both legs of the spread and salvaging what you can.

Early Assignment

It is also possible to be assigned on the short call *before* the expiration date, that is, early assignment. It is not likely but possible. If you are assigned early, you can buy the shares and sell your long call. Suggestion: Call your brokerage if you're not sure what to do next.

Debit Spread: Bull Call

Now that you understand how to initiate credit spreads, let's learn about the *bull call spread*, also known as a *debit call spread*. This strategy is popular because it allows you to profit from a rising stock price without too much out-of-pocket cost.

Unlike buying a call, with the bull call spread you are buying one *call* option and then financing part of the cost by selling another *call* option. You are paying out-of-pocket cash for the spread up front.

You will typically use a bull call spread if you are moderately bullish about the underlying stock (if you are wildly bullish, you can simply buy a call). To reduce the cost and risk of the trade, initiate a bull call spread.

Once again, you buy one call option while simultaneously selling another call option. The expiration date of both calls is the same, but the strike prices are different.

The bull call spread is ideal if you have a strong conviction about the underlying stock. You buy the call at one strike price and finance part of the cost by selling another call with a higher strike price. By buying the more expensive option, you pay cash out of pocket for the spread. This is referred to as a *debit spread* because you pay a debit.

If the underlying stock surpasses both strike prices, then your strategy returns the maximum possible profit at expiration. With the call debit spread, the outcome you are looking for is for the stock to move, or remain, above the strike price of both options at expiration. You may decide to close the position before the expiration date.

Your ultimate goal: To sell the call spread for a price that exceeds the purchase price.

Note: Some investors like debit spreads because they cost less to initiate when compared to buying a call option. Also, you don't need collateral to open the position (unlike credit spreads). You need just enough cash to pay for the position.

In addition, because debit spreads cost less than calls, your potential gain and loss are less compared with buying the call option. In other words, instead of paying $3 for one call, you may pay $2 to buy the spread.

Think about this: Unlike credit spreads, the debit spread has no option to provide protection. Why? Because no protection is needed. When you are long an option, there is no potential for a gigantic loss, so protection is not needed. In the credit spread, however, because you are short an option, you buy another to prevent that large loss. With the debit spread, the option is sold to reduce the cost.

Risks and Rewards of the Bull Call Spread

Like other spread strategies, you can calculate both your potential profits and losses in advance. In addition, with this strategy you have limited loss, but also limited gains. More aggressive traders may prefer buying a call outright. Still, this strategy involves less capital than simply buying a call, and provides more winning trades.

The most you can lose with the bull call spread is the premium paid for the spread. Of course, there are also risks. Note that time is working against you when you buy out-of-the-money options but this is not true for an in-the-money debit spread. Do you know why that is true? With an out-of-the-money spread, the stock must move in your direction (up), or the options will become worthless. However, when both options are already in the money, the passage of time is good because you do not want the underlying stock price to move lower. Therefore, the less time remaining, the better your chances of seeing both options expire in the money (where the spread reaches maximum value).

Remember, in order to be profitable, you have to overcome the cost of the spread. If the debit is too expensive, it becomes harder for the trade to be profitable, and you could lose most or all of your investment.

Suggestion: Before you initiate a bull call spread, think of a realistic price target for the stock and create a strategy based on that forecast. If you are bullish and want to reduce risk by hedging your bet, then the bull call spread may be the right strategy for you.

Characteristics of the Bull Call Spread

Before you create your first bull call spread, let's look at the following criteria:

- *Underlying stock:* Since you are moderately bullish about the stock, you'll want to find strong, leading stocks that will rise high and fast (not easy to find). Your outlook for the underlying stock determines what strikes you are going to choose.
- *Strike price:* There are many strike price combinations that reflect your outlook for the underlying stock. Most important, you want both the long call and short call to be in the money at expiration. This is how you achieve maximum profit. What is the best way to make this happen?

    Hint: Even though the low cost of out-of-the-money options makes them attractive, it is speculative because the stock must move higher for you to make money. No stock movement is required when using in-the-money options. Nevertheless, in-the-money options cost more, so much thought must go into choosing the strike prices for your options. Choose options that suit your realistic outlook for the stock. For many investors who are using this strategy, buying in- or at-the-money options will make more sense than buying out-of-the-money options.

The spread: The difference between the strike prices of the call options in the spread determines your maximum gain or loss. For example, if you buy the 45 call and sell the 50 call, that 5-point difference is the most your spread can be worth (and don't forget to subtract the premium paid when calculating profit potential.)

If you buy the 45 call and sell the 55 call, although your potential reward has increased, so has your potential loss (because the debt paid is higher). The larger the distance between call strike prices, the more you can gain from a large bullish move.

> *Question from a reader*: When trading bull call spreads, is time my friend or enemy?
>
> *Answer*: It's both. When you buy an out-of-the-money bull call spread, you pay a debit. The problem, of course, is that time is working against you. In this case, time is your enemy. However, when you buy the bull call spread and both options are in the money, then time is your ally because the stock price does not have to move any higher for the spread to move to its maximum value.

Premium: Think in advance about the amount of premium you want to spend. The lower the premium, the greater your potential profits, but the smaller your chances of earning any profit. You do not want to pay too much premium in seeking a profit.

Expiration date: Typically, this is a short-term strategy for investors who are bullish about the prospects of the underlying stock. As mentioned earlier, if you buy an out-of-the-money call spread, time decay hurts the position. (If you buy an in-the-money call spread, time decay helps your position.)

Implied volatility: Generally, you want to enter debit spreads when implied volatility is low because option prices are low. Then it will cost less to buy the spread. Buying low implied volatility requires your being aware whether implied volatility is high or low at the time you plan to trade.

How Much Can You Make (or Lose)?

Maximum profit: The most profit you can attain on this trade is the difference in strike prices minus the amount you paid (debit).

For example, if you bought one 30 call and sold one 33 call, that's a 3-point difference. Your maximum gain is $300 (3-point difference in strike prices × 100) minus the premium, or debit, you initially paid.

Maximum loss: The most you can lose on this trade is the cash you initially paid.

Your First Bull Call Spread

Now that you have a general idea of how a bull call spread works, let's look at specific examples.

In August, you believe that YYY, which is currently at $44 per share, will rise to $47 per share or higher over the next two months. You decide to initiate a bull call spread to take advantage of this move. (*Note:* In this example, the option we buy is only slightly out of the money, giving us a decent chance to earn a profit—if the stock behaves as expected.)

Using a spread order, *buy* 1 YYY October 45 call and *sell* 1 YYY October 50 call. The limit price is $2.00.

Cost: Your total cost, or debit, for this trade is $200 plus commissions.

If you wanted to initiate a bull call spread with your brokerage, you might say, "I'd like to buy 1 YYY October 45 call and sell 1 YYY October 50 call for a net debit of $2.00 or less."

Right or Wrong?

Let's take a look at what could go right, or wrong, when you initiate a bull call spread.

Example 1: The underlying stock, YYY, rises above the 45 strike price before the expiration date.

This is what you hoped and expected. If the underlying stock, YYY, rises above $45 before the expiration date, the spread will increase in value.

Note: As the long call option goes farther in the money, the spread between the two call options widens, but it will never go beyond that maximum $5. When expiration arrives, the stock has to be at least $47 for you to earn a profit. Why? At $47, the long call is worth $2.00 (intrinsic value), and the short call is worthless. Net value for the spread is $2.00, and that is your breakeven point (you paid $2.00).

Closing a Winning Trade

Since the underlying stock performed as expected, you may want to close both legs of the spread before the expiration date. In the above example, if you enter a limit order, you may sell (sell to close) the October 45/50 call spread for a net credit of $3.20. Your profit is $120: ($320 − $200 = $120).

Although you can attempt to achieve a higher profit on this trade by holding longer, you must still have a bullish opinion on the stock. However, holding for the maximum is not recommended. The stock would have to move above the upper strike price ($50) at expiration. Since the stock does not appear to be moving that high, close both legs of the spread before expiration once your profit target price is reached.

Closing a Losing Trade

When the market does not go according to your plans, it may be desirable to cut losses, as you will see in the following example.

Example 2: The underlying stock, YYY, remains below the 45 strike price before the expiration date.

If YYY is below $45 and expiration is still in the future, both legs of the spread will drop in price because of time decay. This is not what you expected. For example, the debit spread may decrease in value from the original $2.00 to $1.40, resulting in a paper loss of $60. Your choice is to take that $1.40 or continue to hold as time decay accelerates.

Before the expiration date, you may elect to get out of the trade by selling to close the October 45/50 call spread at a limit price of $0.55 (making you wish you had closed earlier when the premium was still as high as $1.40). The net loss is $145 ($200 − $55 = $145).

Note: If you wait until expiration Friday to close your position, you could lose your entire $200 investment. Sometimes we have to take the loss and move to the next trade.

Assignment Risk

A problem can occur if the underlying stock lands between the two strike prices at expiration. However, in that case, you own the in-the-money option and thus, there is no assignment risk. Sell your in-the-money option before trading stops for the day on expiration Friday.

For the sake of managing risk, you will have to buy back your short call (by paying $0.05 or less) because your broker will not allow you to own a naked call option, even when there are only a few minutes remaining before expiration.

The worst that could happen if you do not sell the call: On Monday, you would be holding a long position on a stock that is going down. Why put yourself in this situation? This is not the risk/reward you wanted when you bought the call spread. Sell the call spread no later than expiration Friday.

Think About This

If you liked selling covered calls on stocks you own, what about using the same strategy on a stock you don't own? If this sounds good, then the bull call spread might be for you. It's essentially a similar concept, but you aren't tying up a lot of capital.

For example, if YYY is at $58, and you believe it will go to $65, you can initiate a 55/65 bull call spread: You buy the in-the-money 55 call and sell the 65 call. One advantage is that your cash isn't tied up in a stock position. The biggest advantage is that downside losses are limited. One disadvantage, however, is that you are paying time premium to own the 55 call, and that cuts possible profits.

Note: I used a lot of examples with out-of-the-money options. This is not a recommendation, but a convenience because it is easier for beginners to understand. It is up to each of you to decide which is an appropriate option to buy or sell. My opinion: If you're a beginner, you can start by choosing a slightly in-the-money option. Why? The probability that the long call will end in the money is higher.

Debit Spread: Bear Put

The last of our four vertical spreads is the *bear put spread*, also known as a *put debit spread*. This is one of the strategies you can use if you want to profit from a declining stock without too much out-of-pocket cost. Because you are paying cash, it is a debit spread.

With this strategy, you are buying one *put* option and then financing part of the cost by selling another *put* option. In other words, the put you sell helps to pay for the put you buy. By selling the put, cost is reduced, but it significantly reduces potential profits.

This is the strategy to use if you are moderately bearish about the underlying stock (if you're wildly bearish, you can simply buy a put).

For this strategy to return the maximum possible profit, both options must be in the money on the expiration date. As you know from previous examples, it's often better to close the position early. If the stock price moves lower (as you expect), you can make a profit, although the gains and losses are limited.

Your goal is for the underlying stock to drop low enough so that the spread earns a profit. In fact, when both put options are in the money on the expiration date, you earn the maximum. The stock must drop far enough so that you can earn more than the cost of the spread.

And just like other spread strategies, you can calculate your potential profits and losses in advance. This strategy comes with limited losses, but also limited gains. To repeat, if you believe that the underlying stock is going to plunge, you may prefer to buy a put outright, but this spread strategy involves less capital than buying a put.

The most you can lose with the bear put spread is the premium you paid for the spread. Just as with the bull call spread, the biggest risk is that time works against you and that the options may expire worthless. If the underlying stock doesn't fall below the strike price of the put that you own before the expiration date, you could lose your entire investment.

Also, if you pay too much for the spread, it limits potential profit even more. A lot of the potential risk depends on the strike prices you choose. In the real world, it's unlikely that you'll achieve the maximum reward because this involves holding the position until the options expire. You not only have to be right about the direction of the stock, but it must happen before the expiration date.

Your ultimate goal: To sell the spread for more than you paid to own it.

Characteristics of the Bear Put Spread

- *Underlying stock:* You'll want to find weak stocks that you believe will continue to decline (and soon). This is not easy to do, unfortunately.
- *Strike prices:* You want the long put and short put to be in the money on the expiration date. This is how you achieve maximum profit.
- *The spread:* As you know from reading about other spreads, the greater the difference between strike prices, the more the positions cost (increasing risk), but also the more potential profits.

For example, if you buy the 50 put and sell the 45 put, the 5-point difference represents a typical bearish spread. If you buy the 50 put and sell the 40 put, this is more bearish and allows for larger gains (and losses).

Both options do not have to be in the money at expiration for you to earn a profit. This is only required to earn the maximum profit.

Your First Bear Put Spread

Let's look at some specific examples of the bear put spread.

In June, you believe that YYY, which is currently $41 a share, will fall below $37 per share over the next one or two months. You decide to initiate a bear put spread.

Enter a spread order to *buy* 1 YYY November 40 put and *sell* 1 YYY November 35 put. In this example, the strike prices of the long put and short put are out of the money, and the premium paid is $1.50 plus commissions.

Maximum profit: To calculate your maximum profit, take the difference between the strike prices ($5 × 100) and subtract your initial net debit ($150). The most you can gain on this trade is $350 ($500 difference in strike prices − $150 net cost of option = $350).

Although it's possible for you to make the maximum profit, don't count on it, especially when you do not expect the stock to move below $35.

Maximum loss: The most you can lose on this trade is the initial debit paid, or $150. As with all vertical spreads, your maximum loss is defined in advance. Although this strategy is less risky than some other strategies (such as selling short), it provides limited reward.

Right or Wrong?

Let's take a look at what could go right, or wrong, with the bear put spread.

Example 1: The underlying stock, YYY, falls below the $40 strike price before the expiration date.

This is exactly what you expected and planned for. Remember that you paid $150 for this spread and that the stock must be at least $1.50 below $40 (the strike price of your put option) at expiration for the spread to be profitable.

Note: As expiration nears, and the long option goes farther in the money, the spread between the two put options widens (that's good), but never surpasses $5.

Closing a Winning Trade

Since the underlying stock performed as expected, you could decide to close both legs of the spread before expiration. In the above example, you could enter a limit order to sell (sell to close) the November 35/40 put spread at a limit price of $360 or better. The profit is $210 ($360 − $150).

Once again, it's not recommended that you try to achieve the maximum profit by holding until the end. Close both legs of the profitable trade before expiration. Remember that there is no assignment risk when you own the more expensive option because you control the exercise decision.

Example 2: The underlying stock, YYY, stays above the 40 strike price before or near the expiration date.

If YYY stays above $40 before expiration, the spread will drop in price. This is not what you expected or wanted. For example, the value of the spread could decline to $0.80.

To avoid losing the maximum with a losing position, close both legs of a losing spread before the expiration date. If you lose confidence that the underlying stock will perform as predicted, it's best to cut your losses and move on. If you wait until expiration, you could lose your entire $150 investment.

Closing a Losing Trade

Before the expiration date, close both legs by selling (to close) the spread. Enter an order to sell the November 35/40 put spread at your specified limit price.

Assignment Risk

As mentioned with the bull call spread, there is no risk of assignment when you're in control of the exercise decision. However, you must be careful when the underlying stock lands between the two strike prices at expiration.

Do not forget to sell your spread, and this means selling the long option and buying the short option. If you forget, the long leg would automatically be exercised, and the short leg would expire worthless. As a result, you would be short stock.

In other words, on Monday morning after expiration, you'd be holding the underlying stock short. You can always turn around and buy the stock (sometimes for a gain and sometimes for a loss), but why suffer through the weekend worrying? As I've said repeatedly, it's much more efficient to close the spread before expiration. You won't get maximum profit, but you also avoid all exercise complications.

Early Assignment

Occasionally, the short put is assigned early. This is not a huge problem because you'd call your brokerage firm and exercise the long put (which is even farther in the money than your short put). Then both put positions would no longer exist, the stock trades would cancel each other out, and you'd earn the maximum possible profit with no remaining position.

The good news: It's unlikely you'll be assigned early. Remember that if assigned, you can exercise and lock in the maximum, but it will probably never happen.

•••••••••••••••••••••••••••••••••

Now that you have learned about spreads, let's take a look at two intermediate option strategies—straddles and strangles. When *buying* straddles and strangles, they work best when the underlying stock makes big moves in either direction.

20

Buying Straddles and Strangles

If you have a good reason to believe that the underlying stock will make a big move in either direction (up or down) and are willing to bet on that happening, then the straddle might be what you're looking for.

For example, let's say that you know that an earnings report, a drug test result from the FDA, or a Fed announcement is pending. Any of these events could move the market or your stock. The problem is that you don't know if the results will be good or bad. With the straddle, you can potentially make money no matter which way the stock moves. You are speculating on how big the price change will be, but you don't care which direction. Sounds great, doesn't it?

To take advantage of the anticipated move, you can buy a two-legged straddle, which allows you to simultaneously take a bearish and bullish position. The higher the implied volatility of the underlying stock's options, the greater the expectation that the move will be big. It will also cost you more to participate. After all, you are not the only one who wants to wager on the news, and the straddle will not be cheap.

The allure of the straddle is that you can make a profit if the underlying stock moves far enough in either direction. On paper, the long straddle offers potentially high returns with limited (but not small) losses. In the real world, however, it's difficult to make a profit with this strategy, primarily because the options are often overpriced.

Profiting from straddles is more difficult than many traders realize. Because of a variety of factors (mainly implied volatility), the underlying stock often doesn't move far enough for the options to return a profit.

If the stock doesn't move much in either direction, you could lose a very large portion of your investment overnight. The straddle is a hedged position, so the goal is to profit from one side of the straddle by more than you lose on the other. In addition, buying both a call and a put on a volatile stock is costly, and this makes it more difficult to come out as a winner.

And as you know, if you pay too much for implied volatility, even if the stock makes a strong move, you could lose money. For all these reasons, buying the straddle is a strategy you may use occasionally, but probably not more often than that.

Note: You can buy (*long straddle*) or sell (*short straddle*) straddles. In this chapter we discuss only the *long straddle* (buying). The short straddle provides profits more frequently but is an incredibly risky Level 5 strategy (with the potential for unlimited loss) and is not recommended for most investors.

Characteristics of the Straddle

Underlying stock: The ideal stock is one that is likely to make a big move in either direction, the sooner the better, but definitely before the expiration date. Identifying the right stock is the key to success with this strategy.

Options: The call and put have the same strike price and expiration date.

Strike price: Typically, investors attempt to buy options with at-the-money strike prices. For a stock trading at or near $40 per share, you might choose the December 40 call and the December 40 put. As always, it is your decision which strike prices to choose, but straddles should be at the money unless you want to begin the trade with a market bias (more bullish or bearish).

Expiration date: With long straddles, time is your enemy. As the options get closer to the expiration date, time decay accelerates (and that's painful). You don't want to hold the straddle to the expiration date when both options could expire worthless.

Implied volatility: Volatility is an important factor that affects option prices but is crucial for straddle buyers. For straddles, some investors attempt to buy when volatility is low and is expected to increase. However, in our example (pending news), implied volatility is seldom, if ever, low. When implied volatility is low, option traders are not anticipating a big move.

Therefore, by the time you hear market-moving news about a stock, more than likely, implied volatility (and option prices) has already risen. Even if the stock moves, you might have paid so much for implied volatility that you'll lose money.

Once the exciting news is no longer expected, implied volatility and option prices can get demolished overnight. This will create losses for the straddle owner if the stock does not undergo a good-sized price change.

Your First Straddle

In September, you believe that YYY, which is currently $50.74 per share, will rise or fall dramatically on breaking news about an earnings report that will be released in a week. Therefore, you buy 1 YYY October 50 straddle and pay $4.25. In this example, the call and put option are at or near the money.

The total cost, or debit, for this trade is $425 ($250 for call + $175 for put = $425) plus commissions.

Maximum profit: Theoretically, the profit potential is unlimited for the life of the options, but in real life stocks do not rise hundreds of points on news. In addition, you will probably take your profits early. Once the news is released and the stock moves (or fails to move), there is no reason to own the straddle. Sell it.

Maximum loss: The most you can lose on this trade is the initial amount you paid, $425. You will lose the maximum if YYY closes at or near $50 at expiration, and if you made the mistake of not selling the straddle.

Breakeven at expiration: In this example, the total cost of the straddle is $425. Therefore, the lower breakeven is $45.75 ($50 − $4.25). The upper breakeven is $54.25 ($50 + $4.25).

Figure 20.1 is an example of a straddle entry screen.

Right or Wrong?

Let's see what can go right, or wrong, with the straddle.

Example 1: Based on a positive earnings report, the underlying stock, YYY, rises to $55.30 per share on the day that the news is announced.

This is what you expected. YYY rose above the $54.25 breakeven price, and you have a paper profit. You were rewarded, so it is time to exit the trade. The October 50 call option is worth $6.50 ($5.30 in intrinsic value plus $1.20 in time value), and the October 50 put option is trading at $0.15. As the underlying stock rises in price, the call option increases while the put option decreases. The farther the underlying stock moves away from the strike price, the higher your potential profit.

Underlying	Strategy		Last	Change	Bid	Ask
YYY	Straddle		$50.74	0.875	50.68	50.79

Leg	Action	Qty	Expiration	Strike	Call/Put
1	Buy to Open	1	May 18	50	Call
2	Buy to Open	1	May 18	50	Put

Figure 20.1 The straddle entry screen

Closing a Winning Trade

Before expiration, you decide to exit. In the above example, you may sell the straddle, possibly collecting $6.60 ($6.45 plus $0.15). Your total profit would be $235 ($660 − $425 initial investment) = $235 less commissions.

Important note: Because of time decay, most traders do not hold straddles to expiration but take their profits, or cut their losses, quickly. It's easy to turn a profit into a loser by waiting too long. With straddles, take the money and run.

Note: Some experienced traders will close the profitable leg but keep the losing leg open, hoping for a sudden reversal. There is nothing wrong with this idea when the price of the other leg is *small*.

For example, holding the October 50 put is likely to result in losing the remaining $15, but it is only $15. (If you want to speculate with $15, feel free to do so.) However, the biggest mistake you can make with this strategy is holding both options to expiration.

Note: Be sure to exit the trade prior to expiration to prevent automatic exercise of an in-the-money option.

Example 2: The underlying stock, YYY, falls to $34 based on a negative earnings report.

This is what you hoped would happen. Because YYY fell below the $45.75 breakeven price, the October 50 put option is now worth $16 (intrinsic value). Conversely, there are no bids for the October 50 call, and it is essentially worthless. This trade has been a huge success. Sell the October 50 put and collect your profit of $1,175 ($1,600 − $425 = $1,175 less commissions).

Example 3: The underlying stock, YYY, rises to $51 two weeks before the expiration date.

This is not what you wanted. In this example, although the underlying stock went up, it did not rise above the $54.25 breakeven price.

Both options will have deteriorated in value, which is the worst-case scenario when trading straddles (and not selling the position immediately after the news release made it worse).

With two weeks left, and not as much time value, it is way past time to give up on the trade. The YYY October 50 call is worth $1.45, and the YYY October 50 put is $0.45. You have a decision to make: Wait until expiration, hoping for a sudden increase, or close both legs immediately to salvage your remaining value.

Note: If the underlying stock remains near the strike prices, you will lose almost all your money on the position. To be profitable, the stock has to surpass either the upper or lower breakeven point.

How to Manage a Losing Trade

Since YYY didn't perform as expected, you decide to cut your losses and close both legs of the straddle. This is a smart move. Your total loss for the trade is $235 [$425 initial cost of straddle minus $190 ($145 call option + $45 put option)] = $235 plus commissions.

If you had waited until expiration, it's possible that you would have lost nearly all of the entire initial investment of $425. Although unlikely, YYY could have made a sudden move below $45.75 (very unlikely) or above $54.25 (small, but reasonable possibility), salvaging your trade.

As an options trader, you can only rely on probabilities. Unless you expect the stock to jump for some unknown reason, close the position and salvage some spread value rather than wait until the expiration date. This is a choice only you can make.

Let's now take a look at *strangles*, another intermediate options strategy that is similar to straddles.

Buying Strangles

There are two possible trades in strangles: the *long strangle* (buy) and the *short strangle* (sell).

Long Strangle

To create a long strangle, you typically buy one out-of-the-money call and one out-of-the-money put with the same expiration date but with *different strike prices.* (Remember that the *straddle* had options with the same strike price.)

For example, let's say that YYY is $62 per share in January. You *buy* 1 YYY March 65 call and *buy* 1 YYY March 55 put for a net debit of $4.55.

> *Upper breakeven:* $69.55 (65 strike price + $4.55 debit)
>
> *Lower breakeven:* $50.45 (55 strike price − $4.55 debit)
>
> *Maximum loss:* The most you can lose on this trade is the total cost of the strangle, or $455.

If the stock is trading between the 55 and 65 strike prices when expiration arrives, you will have the maximum loss. Before expiration arrives, the strangle value declines every day, and the residual (left over) premium depends on how much time remains before the options expire.

In this case, both options will expire worthless if they are held to expiration. It's suggested that you close the position at some point and salvage some cash. Holding until the expiration date is a high-risk play.

If the stock is lower than 55 or above 65, you may or may not have a profit, depending on the stock price (remember those breakeven prices) and time remaining.

Bottom line: Just as with straddles, the underlying stock has to make a huge move in either direction, or you will experience losses.

Maximum gain: The reason that some investors like to buy strangles is that their gains are theoretically unlimited during the life of the option.

Note: Strangles are similar to straddles except for the difference in strike prices. Also, it's even more difficult to earn a profit when the position is held to expiration. Investors like them for all the wrong reasons—for example, they are cheaper than straddles. They ignore that the underlying stock has to make an even bigger move.

The time to initiate a strangle (like a straddle) is when there is upcoming news such as an earnings release or a Fed announcement, *and* the implied volatility is not too high. (Unfortunately, this is also when the strangle costs the most.) Unless you know something about the underlying stock that no one else knows, strangles may return an occasional large profit, but losses are far more common.

Many things can go wrong such as a drop in implied volatility (which will happen once the news is out), time decay, or that the stock makes a too-small move on the news. Nevertheless, profits are potentially big if the underlying stock behaves as you hoped.

The odds of making a profitable trade are not very favorable with a strangle. This is a strategy best left to experienced traders because the chances of winning are small.

Short Strangle: Not Recommended

To be blunt, the *short strangle* (selling a strangle) is an extremely risky trade that is not recommended for beginners. (Brokers won't let you make this trade unless you are approved for Level 5 trading.) This strategy consists of *selling* an out-of-the-money call and *selling* an out-of-the-money put.

For example, let's say that YYY has been trading in a range between $32 and $34 per share. You forecast that YYY will not be trading out of this range in the near future. You then could initiate a short strangle by selling one January 35 call and one January 30 put. The premium might be $1.50.

Because you are selling a call and put, you receive premium from each leg. The strangle works best on stocks that are not going anywhere. By the way, if you do a short strangle on a volatile stock, you are the one who could get strangled (which is how they created the clever name, strangle).

In the above example, there are two possible outcomes. If YYY stays between $30 and $35, you keep the strangle premium as the options expire. However, what if YYY makes a significant move in either direction? For example, what if YYY falls to $23 per share? In this case, the premium on the put would rise to more than $6 (the intrinsic value) while the premium on the call would be near zero. *Result:* A loss of $450 ($600 − $150 = $450).

To unwind a strangle, you buy the options that you had sold to initiate the position. Nevertheless, in a worst-case scenario, you could lose money on both legs, which is why you *always* cover both sides when exiting the trade. How can you lose twice? For example, let's say you become frightened when the stock rallies, so you buy the call at an elevated price. Then when the stock suddenly reverses direction, you become frightened again and pay too much for the put.

Ask yourself this question: Why would anyone take on a complex trade with limited revenue and unlimited loss? As one of my acquaintances said, "If you think that selling naked is bad—with the short strangle you are double-naked!" And it's true—you are naked on both sides. This is the kind of strategy that gives options a bad name because it causes too many traders to blow up their accounts.

. . . .

In the next chapter, you will be introduced to two fascinating strategies: how to sell cash-secured puts, and selling naked puts.

21

Selling Cash-Secured and Naked Puts

The next two strategies, selling *cash-secured puts* and selling *naked puts*, are often misunderstood but are extremely useful. If you want a strategy that allows you to buy a stock at a discount while receiving income, then you should look at these strategies.

The trades are identical, but with cash-secured puts, you must have enough collateral set aside to pay for the stock if assigned. When you sell naked puts, however, you only need enough collateral to meet margin requirements. Selling cash-secured puts is a Level 2 strategy, while selling naked puts is Level 4, primarily because it requires using margin.

What It Means to Sell Cash-Secured Puts

Let's say that you are interested in buying stock but below the current market price. By selling cash-secured puts, you may be able to buy shares of the underlying stock at a discount, but you could also wind up earning income.

In other words, selling a cash-secured (or cash-covered) put is a strategic way of purchasing stock you would like to own at a discount. The catch is that you must have enough money in your account to buy the stock if you are assigned an exercise notice on the put option. (We get into assignment a little later.)

When you sell cash-secured puts, you want the underlying stock to go *up* so that the option expires worthless and you get to keep the premium as your profit. If in the short term the stock drops in price, you may have a temporary loss but you get to buy the stock at your target price (strike price). That price is the strike price, reduced by the premium you received.

Risks and Rewards of Cash-Secured Puts

The main benefit of the cash-secured puts is that you keep the cash (premium) for selling the put. No matter which direction the stock goes, up or down, you get to pocket the cash while getting the chance to buy the stock at a lower price.

If you want the stock, this is your opportunity to collect a premium while waiting to see if you will buy the stock. As long as you have the money in your account as collateral, you can sell cash-secured puts.

While selling cash-secured puts seems to be a brilliant strategy, there are risks. The main risk to using this strategy is when the underlying stock falls dramatically below the strike price, and your trade will be losing money. Then you will no longer feel that you bought shares at a discount. However, this risk is actually a bit less than the risk of someone who owns the stock. You both lose when the stock price plunges, but your loss is reduced by the premium collected.

In the absolute worst-case scenario, if the stock goes to zero, you would lose all the cash put up as collateral. However, this is the same fate that befalls any stockholder. During market crashes or corrections, you will wish you had used another strategy.

Hint: If you use this strategy, do not sell too many puts.

Use this strategy only for stocks that you want to buy, and for the number of shares that you want to buy. If the underlying stock suddenly plunges and the stock is "put" to you, then you're not disappointed. After all, you must believe that this stock is worth owning or you wouldn't have made the effort to buy it.

Finally, selling puts also means that your gains are limited to the premium collected. In return for those limited profits, you receive cash. If the stock suddenly zooms higher, then you might wish you had bought the stock rather than sold a cash-covered put, but you have a nice profit for your trouble.

Let's take a closer look at the characteristics of this strategy.

Characteristics of the Cash-Secured Put

Underlying stock: When selling puts, if the underlying stock goes up, you pocket the premium, and you don't buy the stock. On the other hand, if the underlying stock goes down, it's possible that you'll be obligated to buy the stock at the strike price. Either way, the strategy works. The key to using this strategy is that the stock you choose must be one you're willing to own.

Remember, if the stock goes up too much, you may be disappointed by your relatively small profit. Do not let that bother you: You chose to sell the put rather than buy stock, and there is nothing you can change now. And if the stock plunges, although you get to buy the stock at a discount, you own a position that is losing money. Just know that it is a smaller loss than if you had bought the stock instead.

> *Strike price:* It's suggested that you start by selling out-of-the-money puts (unless you want to own that stock very badly). Why out-of-the-money puts? There is a higher probability that the option will expire worthless. Then you keep the premium as your prize. After all, most option traders believe that it's better to make a profit than to own the stock. So if you want to trade options, it is important to think like a trader. But only you know how badly you want to own the stock.
>
> *Hint:* It does not pay to use in-the-money options for this strategy because the time premium tends to be small.

Which is best? Before initiating the trade, think about the premium. You must weigh the premium you can receive against how urgently you want to buy the stock. If you are eager to buy stock, sell an option that is at the money. (If you're very eager, forget about selling options and just buy the stock.)

On the other hand, if you sell an option that is too far out of the money, you will not receive much premium, and there will be little chance of buying the stock. If you are eager to own stock, sell a put option that is not too far out of the money.

Bottom line: If this is the first time you are selling cash-secured puts, choose an out-of-the-money put. Ask yourself this: "Am I willing to buy the underlying stock at the strike price of this put option?" If the answer is yes, you probably picked an option with the correct strike price. It is more than likely that it will be slightly out of the money.

Expiration date: Your goal is for the option to expire worthless, so be certain to choose an expiration date that fits your expectation for the stock price. If you are slightly bullish and have no specific time period in mind, then sell a relatively short-term put option, perhaps three to five weeks.

Assignment: With this strategy, if you planned to buy the underlying stock at a discount, then assignment will be welcome, not something to avoid. It means that the stock is "put" to you at the strike price, and you are obligated to buy it. The main risk is if the stock continues to fall after you buy it. If this happens, then you must manage risk and decide whether to continue to hold the stock. (You could also write covered calls on the underlying stock to slightly reduce the risk of stock ownership.)

Note: Because this is a strategy where you welcome assignment, you'll probably not want to close the trade early.

Your First Cash-Secured Put

Now that you have a general idea of how this strategy of selling cash-secured puts works, let's look at specific examples.

In March, YYY is selling for $48 per share. If you could buy YYY for $45, you would buy it. You decide to initiate a cash-secured put with a 45 strike, allowing you to either buy YYY at $45 or collect the premium as your profit.

Trade: You *sell* 1 YYY May 45 put for $3.00, receiving $300 in premium ($3.00 × 100) less commission. In this example, the option is out of the money. This is decent premium with reduced risk of assignment.

Because it is a cash-secured put, your broker will hold $4,200 ($45 strike price × 100 minus the $300 premium) in your account as a cash reserve (collateral) to be used in case you are assigned. In fact, you would welcome assignment because it forces you to buy YYY at $45 per share. The $300 premium reduces your cost basis to $42 per share ($45 minus the $3 premium).

Right or Wrong?

Let's see what can go right, or wrong, when you initiate the cash-secured put.

Example 1: The underlying stock, YYY, stays at or above $48 per share on or near the expiration date.

This is a desirable outcome. If YYY remains at or above $48 at expiration, the put option will expire worthless, and the $300 premium is your profit. You are not assigned, and, therefore, you do not buy the stock. For the majority of cash-secured put sellers, this is an ideal scenario because they have earned a nice profit with no future risk. You are free to sell another cash-secured put for the following month.

Maximum gain: The $300 profit is the most you could have earned on this trade.

Closing a Winning Trade

To close this trade, you would cover the short put prior to expiration. For example, if you pay $0.20, then your profit would be $280. The $4,200 held by your brokerage firm is released.

Note: If YYY unexpectedly rallies much higher than the $45 strike price, don't kick yourself for missing out on a profitable opportunity by not buying the stock outright. You still made a profit (but do not get greedy).

Example 2: The underlying stock, YYY, is below $45 per share on the expiration date.

This is a desirable outcome. If YYY is below the strike price at expiration, you will be assigned an exercise notice and be obligated to purchase shares of YYY at $45. The total cost of the trade will be $4,200 plus commission. For tax purposes, your cost basis is the price paid (strike price) minus the option premium ($3). The $4,200 that was set aside will be used to purchase the stock.

If you sold a cash-secured put because you wanted to purchase YYY, then you will welcome assignment and are comfortable buying 100 shares.

Maximum loss: If YYY unexpectedly plunges to $35 per share, you are still obligated to buy the stock at $45 per share. In this example, a 10-point drop in YYY would be an unpleasant surprise to stockholders (and you are now a stockholder).

The maximum loss occurs when the stock drops to near $0, which is possible but unlikely. In this case, you'd be obligated to buy a worthless stock at the strike price. Nevertheless, stock corrections and crashes can result in dramatic losses, and the once attractive $300 premium will not look so good now. This is the reason why it's important to sell puts only on a stock you want to own.

Assignment Risk at Expiration

When you sell a cash-secured put, you will either own the stock (assigned), or you won't. It's that simple. Either way, you keep the premium.

If the put option is out of the money and you do nothing, the put option expires worthless. If the put option is in the money at expiration, you will receive an assignment notice and be obligated to buy the stock, which is what you wanted to happen.

Early Assignment

Although it is unlikely, when selling cash-secured puts, there's always a chance that you'll be assigned early (before the expiration date) on the put you sold. Always plan for the possibility the stock will be "put" to you (you receive an assignment notice and will be forced to buy the stock). This is not a bad outcome.

Note: After being assigned, you may decide to immediately sell (write) a covered call on the newly purchased stock.

Selling Naked Puts

Let's discuss what happens when you sell options naked (now you know the truth: option traders have a sense of humor!). One of the allures of selling naked puts is there is an opportunity to make a good return on your investment. When there is no up-front money required (other than margin), the investment is relatively small, allowing for a high percentage return (but the risk is as high as ever).

The reason you are naked (or uncovered) is that you are not backing the position with collateral. In fact, from your perspective, selling naked puts is the same as selling cash-secured puts. For your broker, the difference is that you may not have enough cash in your account to buy the stock, and you are using margin. (By the way, people also refer to this strategy as *writing puts*.)

Keep this in mind: If the stock drops too far and the put price surges, you will be called upon to meet a higher margin call. Please be certain you do not sell too many puts so that you can meet that margin call. If you fail to meet that call, the puts will be bought at the market price.

Because some people do not fully understand the risks of selling naked puts, brokerage firms do not encourage customers to use this strategy. If you are a beginner, I strongly urge you to avoid margin and sell cash-secured puts instead.

As you gain experience, you may consider selling naked puts, as long as you fully understand the risks. It's easy to misuse margin when selling puts (and trade a larger position size than is prudent), which is why this strategy has so many restrictions. If you don't understand what you're doing, you can severely damage your account.

Note: Technically, selling cash-secured puts is no more risky than owning stock and is popular with many experienced option traders. *Selling naked calls*, on the other hand, is not recommended for inexperienced investors or traders. (It's similar to buying stocks on margin.)

Suggestion: If you are a novice, it's recommended that you do not sell any naked options (but it won't hurt to learn the strategy).

What It Means to Sell Naked (or Uncovered) Puts

If you want to know how to sell naked puts, first read about selling cash-secured puts. The strategy is identical except that when you sell naked, you use margin. Unfortunately, many people misuse margin and end up selling many more puts than they can afford. At first, it almost seems as if you are getting easy money—that is, until the market plunges.

You manage naked put positions just as you do when buying stock on margin. This is not the kind of strategy you initiate right before you go on vacation. (If you do, you might not have much money left in your account when you return.) It's also not the kind of strategy you can put on autopilot—closely monitor the underlying stock.

If used properly, naked put selling makes sense for experienced traders who are willing to thoroughly research the underlying stock and market conditions. Nevertheless, some people have been talked into using this strategy without being fully aware of the risks.

When selling naked puts, you receive premium, or revenue. In return, you accept all downside risk below the strike price.

When the Stock Gets "Put" to You

One of the unique features of selling cash-secured puts and naked puts is that the stock can get "put" to you and placed in your brokerage account. That happens when your account is assigned an exercise notice.

You won't mind if this was part of your trading plan. However, if you are using this strategy for speculation, the last thing you want is to own the stock. You just want to earn a profit by selling the put. But if the stock goes down, then you could find yourself in trouble. What you really want is for the option to expire worthless and to never hit the strike price.

Let's summarize what all of this means. You received money for selling a put option on a stock. That is your monetary reward for taking risk. But by the rules of the contract you are also required to buy the stock at the strike price (if the option is exercised).

What if you made a bad decision or something unexpected happens? What if the stock falls by 80 percent? Your obligation to buy stock at the (higher) strike price is still in force. If you're a speculator, you lost. All you can do now is cover the short put and end the agony. Do not get trapped into holding the option and eventually buying the stock. Just get out.

Note: Before the stock is put to you (assigned), you have another choice. You could buy back the put contract you sold because you want to avoid assignment.

How to Lose a Million Dollars

I don't want to talk you out of selling naked puts, but I know a guy who lost millions of dollars selling naked puts on stocks he didn't want to own. His strategy worked brilliantly for a few years. He told me it felt like he was receiving free money.

When the unthinkable happened and the market crashed, he was obligated to cover the options on sinking stocks, but at sky-high prices (because demand for those puts pushed implied volatility much higher). Since he traded on margin and didn't have the cash to back up his obligations, he was forced into bankruptcy.

If you sell naked puts, remember these five rules:

- *Lesson 1:* Plan for the unthinkable (i.e., worst-case scenarios).
- *Lesson 2:* Sell naked puts only on stocks you plan to buy. Better yet, sell cash-secured puts instead.
- *Lesson 3:* Manage margin wisely and understand your obligations.
- *Lesson 4.* Don't sell more puts than you can afford. In other words, be very aware of potential losses.
- *Lesson 5:* Don't forget Lesson 1.

· ·

Congratulations for finishing another important chapter. In the next chapter, you'll learn about the Greeks.

22

Delta and the Other Greeks

You should know that the Greeks are derived from complicated formulas using option pricing models such as Black-Scholes and Cox-Rubenstein. Fortunately, the information that is displayed on your computer is straightforward. As retail options investors, we will probably look at no more than two or three of the Greeks.

Note: You can find the Greeks on the option chain on your brokerage firm screen or find them on the OIC or CBOE website.

What Are the Greeks?

You already know that option prices are affected by many factors such as volatility, time to expiration, and their relationship to the underlying stock. Wouldn't it be helpful if you could measure how the price of your option is expected to change as market conditions change, such as a $1 move in the stock?

What if you could determine how much risk you are taking on before you initiate an option position? The Greeks provide the numbers you need. They also help you decide how to manage that risk and help you make decisions such as whether to hold, close, or adjust your option position.

The most common Greeks used to describe the relationship between the option price and outside factors are *delta, gamma, theta, rho*, and *vega*.

Experienced option investors use the Greeks to find important information. Each Greek tells a different story, and understanding the Greeks will help you compete with other option investors, but more importantly, it helps traders manage risk.

Here is how the Greeks are displayed on the screen. As you can see, they are simply numbers. The trick is learning what the numbers mean.

Hint: Use no more than the first two decimal places.

Delta	Gamma	Theta	Vega	Rho	Action	Strike ▲
0.6896	0.0567	-0.0298	0.0998	0.0563	Select ▼	85
0.5353	0.0676	-0.0317	0.1117	0.0449	Select ▼	87.5
0.3654	0.0662	-0.029	0.1061	0.0312	Select ▼	90
0.2158	0.0528	-0.022	0.0838	0.0187	Select ▼	92.5
0.1164	0.0348	-0.0149	0.0574	0.0102	Select ▼	95

Figure 22.1   The Greeks

Source: Fidelity Investments. © 2002 FMR LLC. All rights reserved. Used by permission.

For retail investors, the most important Greek is delta.

Delta

Delta measures how much an option price is expected to change when the price of the underlying stock changes by one point. Every change in the stock price affects the delta.

For example, if you buy an option that moves a penny when the underlying stock moves $3, this means that the delta is very small and owning that option is not likely to produce any profits. You would earn $0.02 when the stock moves by $6. Once you realize how helpful delta is when estimating profit or loss potential for your option trades, you won't trade without it.

Misconception: Although delta is incredibly useful, it is not a silver bullet. Delta is what it is: a number that helps you understand the relationship between the stock price and option premium, providing clues as to how the premium might behave as the stock moves up or down. In other words, delta provides a good estimate of how much money you will make, or lose, when the stock price changes.

Using Delta to Determine Price Changes

The next part is a little technical, but once you understand the numbers, it will be relatively easy. Calls have a positive delta between 0 and 1, while puts have a negative delta between 0 and –1. Let's use delta to determine how much a call option will increase for every $1 increase in the underlying stock.

For example, if a certain IBM call option has a delta of 40, it should increase by $0.40 while IBM moves up a dollar. Note that it will not be exactly 40 cents because other factors (such as other Greeks) also affect the option price. Or if an option has a delta of 50, as the stock goes up $1, the price of the call option should go up by $0.50. If it's a put option that has the 50 delta, the price of the put will go down by $0.50.

Note: Many people drop the decimal point and instead of saying it has a delta of .4, or .5, they will say, "40 delta," or, "50 delta," and so on. On computer screens, however, the decimal will usually be included.

Misconceptions: Many people wrongly believe that if a stock goes up or down a dollar, the option will *always* move the same amount. This will happen only under certain circumstances (when the option is deep in the money and the delta is 1.0). Delta is not constant. It changes as the stock price changes. (More on this below.)

Advanced note: The option price almost never changes by more than the change in the underlying stock price. (The rare exception occurs when other Greeks are more powerful than delta in affecting the option price.)

Using Delta to Determine Probabilities

Another way to use delta is as a rough estimate of the probability an option will be in the money at expiration. For example, 40 delta suggests that the option has a 40 percent probability of being in the money at expiration. If the stock continues to rise, then the delta of the call option would also rise because the probability of finishing in the money is increasing. The delta of a put option declines as the stock moves higher.

Using this method, a 25 delta option has a 25 percent probability of being in the money at expiration assuming that market conditions don't change. A 50 delta suggests that an option has a 50–50 chance of being in the money at expiration. And finally, 80 delta options have an 80 percent probability of being in the money at expiration.

Although many investors use delta to estimate the odds an option will be in the money, not everyone agrees that delta should be used in this way.

Suggestion: Use delta as a general guide to determine the chances that an option will be in the money at expiration.

Remember, just because an option is in the money doesn't mean that it will be profitable for the buyer or unprofitable for the seller. Whether you make a profit or not depends only on the price you initially paid for the option and the price at which it is eventually sold.

Delta Reveals More Clues

Many beginning traders ask why the underlying stock makes a huge move and the option price didn't move very much. Delta provides the best answer. When buying low delta options, beginners must realize that a one-dollar rise in the stock price will not boost the option price by very much. If you look at delta before trading any option, you'll discover that cheap out-of-the-money options are truly a long shot for buyers. When time is short and the option is far out of the money, the stock could move $3 and the option might not gain anything. Such options have a delta near zero.

Note: As you will see, other Greeks affect option prices, and they could add to, or subtract from, the effect of delta.

Delta Examples

Let's take a look at different ways to use delta so that you can understand this concept better.

Example 1: You own YYY and the stock price is $60 per share. You buy an at-the-money call option with a strike price of 60, and there are 60 days left until the expiration date. What is the delta of this option?

If you answered approximately 50, you'd be right. At-the-money options have a delta near 50.

Example 2: Using the same example, you are holding the YYY option with a 50 delta. If YYY stock rises from $60 to $61 per share, the delta of this option increases as the stock moves up. If the call option were priced at $1.75, it might increase to $2.25, which is a $0.50 increase.

When you look at the delta again, it may have increased from 50 to 60 delta (.50 to .60) as the stock moved in the money. In theory, if the stock rises by another dollar, the option should increase by $0.60 (because its new delta is 60).

Example 3: Let's say that YYY drops from $60 per share to $59, and the call option price was initially $1.75 and drops to $1.25, a decline of $0.50. This is to be expected when the delta is 50. Expect the option price to change (approximately) by its delta regardless of which way the stock moves. With the stock at $59, the new delta might be 40. For the next $1 drop in the stock, the call option price will fall by $0.40.

In this example, if the stock drops another 2 points, the option will theoretically drop by roughly $0.80, but this is only an estimate because we just learned that delta changes as the stock price changes (and other factors may influence the premium).

Example 4: YYY is $50, and you think it will go to $55
before January. You buy a 55 call option, which has a delta
of 20. For the first $1 gain in YYY, the call option gains
$0.20 (ignoring the effects of time decay).

If YYY went above $60, for example, and the option went deep in the money, the option would have a delta near 1 (100 delta). At that point, for every $1 increase in YYY, the call option will gain approximately an equal amount as the stock.

Example 5: YYY is $30 per share. The 30 call has a delta
of 50, while the 25 call has a delta of 90. Therefore, if YYY
goes up by a dollar, the 25 call, which is in the money, will
appreciate by $0.90, while the 30 call will go up by $0.50.
You already know that an in-the-money option has a higher
delta, and now you can quantify it.

Delta Facts

Now that you have seen a few examples, let's look at some facts about delta.

Fact: Each option has its own delta, which is constantly changing.

Fact: If you own an option when its delta is positive or sell an option whose delta is negative, you can say you are *long delta*.

Fact: Before expiration, deltas vary. A deep in-the-money option has a high delta, perhaps 80 or 100. A far out-of-the-money option may have a delta of 0 to 20. Puts are the opposite. A deep in-the-money put option may have a delta of −80 to −100. A far out-of-the money put option may have a delta of 0 to −20.

Fact: At expiration, an in-the-money call option has a delta of 1 (100). An out-of-the-money call option has a delta of 0 at expiration. When exactly at the money, the delta is 50.

Fact: As the expiration date approaches, delta changes. If the underlying stock is above the strike price, call options are in the money, and delta will approach 1 (delta 100) rapidly as time passes, and the option will move point to point with the stock. [The reverse occurs with puts, i.e., if the underlying stock is below the strike price and the option is in the money, delta approaches –1 (minus delta 100). When this happens, the option moves point to point with the stock.]

Fact: When you buy an out-of-the-money option, there is a high probability that it will expire worthless. Why? The delta is small, and it is harder for it to move far enough to become in the money before the expiration date.

Fact: When an out-of-the-money call option approaches the expiration date, its delta will approach 0. Why? At expiration, all out-of-the-money options have no delta. The delta of an option that is far out of the money will be low. With every $1 move in the stock, the option will change little.

Fact: If you are long a 50 delta call and short 50 shares of stock, you are *delta neutral.* In this example, you are long calls and short stock, and total position delta is zero. Traders like delta-neutral positions because there is no market risk as they wait to produce a profit.

Fact: Delta is often referred to as a *hedge ratio* because it tells you how many shares of stock you need to sell when buying one call option (or how many shares to buy when buying one put option) in order to have a *delta-neutral* (i.e., market-neutral) position.

Fact: Call owners may lose money even when delta is increasing. The passage of time or decreasing implied volatility often affects option prices by more than the change in the stock price.

Fact: Traders must also understand gamma because it defines how delta changes as the stock price changes.

Gamma

You already know that delta changes as the stock price changes. Gamma describes that change. Therefore, if the underlying stock went from $45 to $46, its delta would change. How fast does it change?

The answer is found by looking at gamma, which measures the rate at which delta changes when the underlying stock moves $1.

Here's an analogy that might help: If you are driving a car, then delta is your speed. For example, if your speed is 45, that is your delta. Gamma, on the other hand, is how fast you are accelerating. For example, let's say you accelerate from 45 to 60. Gamma measures how fast you go from 45 to 60.

Here's a real life example: Let's say that the delta of an option is 55 (.55). When we look at our underlying stock, YYY, we see that it just moved higher by one dollar to $47 per share. We notice that delta is now 60. That change in the delta from 55 to 60 (or from .55 to .60) is because of gamma. In other words, gamma was 5. (Another example: If the stock moved from 57 to 60, this is gamma 3.)

How does this help? It allows you to estimate the price change (and new delta), and this gives you a good estimate of expected profit and loss. Gamma alerts you to the fact that gains and losses will accelerate as the stock continues to move.

Advanced note: If you have high gamma, delta will change dramatically even if the move in the stock is only one or two points. High gamma is a two-edged sword. It can bring tremendous profits when you are long gamma (i.e., the total position gamma is >0), but also cause huge, unexpected losses when you are short a lot of gamma (total position gamma is <0).

Here are some facts about gamma:

Fact: Gamma for each option is always a positive number.
In other words, the delta of both calls and puts changes as the stock price changes. Remember to subtract an option's gamma when you are short (i.e., you sold) that option.

Fact: If you notice that gamma is suddenly getting bigger, it means that the risk or reward is increasing. Gamma increases as the expiration date approaches. Gamma also increases as the option moves nearer to being at the money. The pros call it "exploding gamma," which means that position delta (and profits and losses) is growing quickly.

Fact: When an option has high gamma, options prices are more sensitive to price changes in the underlying stock.

Fact: Options have the highest gamma when the option is at the money a few seconds before expiration. At expiration, delta is either at 0 or 100, so within seconds, delta can swing by 2.0 (going from –1 to +1) or vice versa as the stock moves by only two cents (one cent in the money to one cent out of the money).

Theta: Think "T" for Time

Do you remember that clicking time clock I talk about in the first chapter? Theta measures how much the time value (or premium) declines in one day. Specifically, theta tells you how much the option decreases in value as the option gets closer to expiration by one day. Theta is the cost of doing business for option owners and the reward (for taking on risk) for option sellers.

Here are some facts about theta:

Fact: Theta is highest with at-the-money options and then gradually declines as the options move out of the money and in the money.

Fact: When you buy an option that is quickly losing time value, your market expectations must occur quickly or the option will lose all of its time value.

Fact: Options with high time premium (high volatility stocks) have higher theta than options with small amounts of time premium (low volatility stocks).

Vega: Think "V" for Volatility

You already know that options on volatile stocks are more expensive than options on other stocks, and as volatility rises, the option price rises. Conversely, if volatility falls, option prices fall. Here's where *vega* enters: Vega, which is always a positive number, measures the amount that an option price changes when volatility changes by one point.

Here's exactly what it measures: For every 1 percent change (i.e., changing from .20 to .21) in implied volatility, vega measures how much the option price changes. Therefore, vega measures risk of a sudden and large change in implied volatility. Market makers who hold huge option positions adjust those positions to trade with a portfolio that is near vega-neutral.

Here's a fact about vega. Vega is not a real Greek letter.

Rho

Rho is the least important Greek and one that you probably won't use. It measures how much option premium will rise or fall as interest rates rise or fall by one point. Rho is more important when interest rates are high for LEAPS (because interest rates affect long-term options more than short-term options).

It answers this question: If interest rates rise or fall by one percentage point, how much will the option price change?

Here is one fact about rho. Call options have positive rho. Put options have negative rho.

Don't Ignore the Greeks

Delta, as well as the other Greeks, cannot be ignored. For example, delta helps you to manage risk and gives you an idea of how much your position might earn (or lose). Most important, before you initiate an option position, look at the Greeks to help you choose which options to trade. Market makers are aware of the Greeks, and if you're serious about trading options, so should you.

Fortunately, once you learn the Greeks, you don't have to spend hours studying them before taking on a position. You can glance at the Greeks and decide what action to take next.

Note: The more complex the option position, the more important it is to consult the Greeks.

Caution: Some traders get so obsessed with the Greeks that they lose sight of their ultimate goal—to make money. The Greeks are a useful tool, but should not be treated as gospel.

• •

Now that you have been introduced to the Greeks, it's a good time to learn how to trade options with ETFs, indexes, weekly options, and mini-options.

23

Trading Options with ETFs, Indexes, Weeklys, and Mini-Options

For many of you, this will be an exciting chapter, especially if you don't know about these unique products. In this short chapter, you will be introduced to trading options on ETFs, Weeklys, mini-options, and indexes. Remember this: Anything you do with standard options can be done with any of these.

Options on ETFs

Exchange-traded funds are similar to mutual funds but are traded like stocks, that is they can be bought and sold during the trading day rather than only once per day at the net asset value.

Using Options on ETFs to Speculate

You can buy options on exchange-traded funds (ETFs) to speculate on the direction of the underlying index. Buying call or put options on indexes such as SPY (S&P 500), the Dow Jones Industrial Average (DJI), QQQ (Nasdaq 100), and IWM (Russell 2000) is the same as buying options on individual stocks. It's an efficient way to participate in the broad market without having to guess which individual stocks will rally or decline.

The risks are the same as with standard options: You have to be right about the timing as well as the direction of the underlying index. Also, when the expiration date arrives, you may lose your entire investment if the underlying index hasn't performed as expected.

You can also buy options on specialized ETFs such as the Chicago Board Options Exchange volatility index (VIX), which measures the implied volatility of SPX (S&P 500 index) options. The SPX, representing shares of the top 500 capitalized stocks, is essentially the U.S. stock market. The underlying assets for these options are VIX futures contracts. That's right, you are literally buying options on volatility. These are tricky to trade so avoid them unless you are certain you know what you are doing.

Strategy: You can also buy a LEAPS call on ETF indexes such as the S&P 500, Nasdaq, or Dow Jones Industrial Average for a long-term bullish strategy. On the other hand, a LEAPS put would allow you to hedge a long-term stock position. The downside to LEAPS, as you remember, is the higher cost.

Using Options on ETFs to Protect Stock Portfolios

Instead of buying and selling options on individual stocks, you can hedge long positions with exchange-traded funds (ETFs) such as SPY, DIA, IWM, or QQQ.

For example, to help protect a $50,000 portfolio that invests primarily in large capitalization stocks, you would need to buy three puts. Why? See below.

For example, let's say that you bought 3 SPY put contracts with a $150 strike price (or 1,500 on the S&P 500) that expire in June and cost $449 each. That totals $1,347 plus commissions ($449 × 3 contracts), and is the cost for three months of protection. If the market plunges any time before June 22, the puts limit your losses.

Your risk: In this example, the most you could lose is $1,347, which is the cost of the three puts. Why three put contracts? Each put represents 100 shares. Since you have the right to sell 300 shares at $150 per share, this is $45,000 worth of stock, or enough to hedge 90 percent of your $50,000 portfolio.

Long-Term Protection

If you want ten months of protection for a $50,000 portfolio, then buy three LEAPS puts on the SPY with a $150 strike price that expires nine months later. We looked up the price of the contracts and discovered that they cost $939 each for a total of $2,817 ($939 × 3 contracts). That's the cost when you truly fear a market correction or crash.

As you know, LEAPS are long-term option contracts that are identical to standard options except for the longer time before they expire (from nine months to three years).

Your risk: Again, it is the cost of buying the options (and they're not cheap).

Exercise: Remember, if SPY drops in price, you may have a winning put position (but you will definitely have a losing stock position) on the expiration date. If your option is in the money, do not exercise. Just sell it. You bought the puts as insurance, so sell the puts and cash in the insurance policy.

Bottom line: The next time you fear an impending crash, consider buying puts on ETFs to hedge against the risk, assuming you do not want to sell your stock position. Often, simply selling the stock is the easiest and most cost-effective solution. Just because you know how to use puts doesn't mean that buying them is the best (or even a good) choice.

Trading Options on Indexes

Instead of buying options on ETFs, you could also buy options on market indexes. Indexes are basically a theoretical (they are not real and cannot be traded) basket or portfolio of stocks that is composed of each of the stocks in the given index.

When you buy index options, you are participating in the market that consists of the components of that index. Major indexes include the S&P 500 (SPX or INX), Dow Jones Industrial Average (DJI), Russell 2000 (RUT), or Nasdaq Composite (IXIC). There are numerous indexes available for trading.

Note: Even though buying index options is a Level 2 strategy at many brokerage firms, the options tend to be costly because the price of the underlying index is high. These are the most actively traded options, and both individuals and large institutions trade index options.

There are two main differences between buying options on ETFs and on market indexes. First, most index options are *cash-settled.* (That is, exercise or assignment is settled in cash, not in shares.)

The other difference is that index options are European style, which means that there is no early exercise. Because of that, you don't have to worry about getting assigned early when you are selling options.

Let's compare buying options on ETFs and indexes. If you were going to hedge a $300,000 stock portfolio using put options on SPY, you would have to buy 20 puts (assuming SPY is $150 per share).

On the other hand, if you hedged that same portfolio with index options, two (2) puts are adequate because SPX trades at roughly ten times SPY. Here's the math: $300,000 divided by $150,000 (or $1,500 for SPX) = 2 index put options.

For example, instead of paying $450 per contract for a SPY ETF, an SPX index option would cost approximately $4,500 per contract for a strike price that is 10 times the value of the SPY strike price. The options expire at the same time.

> *Hint:* A strike price of $150 on SPY is equivalent to a $1,500 strike price on the SPX (S&P 500). In other words, SPY is roughly 1/10 of the SPX, and it takes 10 SPY contracts to provide the same hedge as 1 SPX contract.

There is a third difference: SPY options pay a significant dividend while index options do not pay a dividend.

If you do trade index options and even options on ETFs, it's highly recommended that you exit all positions before the expiration date. If you want to experiment, though, feel free to open a practice trading account on the CBOE or your brokerage firm's website.

Trading Weekly Options

One popular product for active traders is weekly options. Just like the name suggests, Weeklys expire one week (actually eight calendar days) after they are listed for trading. You can use Weeklys on every strategy included in this book, but with a shorter time frame. They are also the same as any other option you learned about (except for their fleeting existence).

The only caveat: Not all underlying stocks, ETFs, or indexes have weekly options (only the most actively traded ones do).

Note: Weeklys are also available on all the major indexes, such as the S&P 500, Nasdaq 100, Dow Jones Industrial Average, and Russell 2000.

Why would you want to trade weekly options? First, Weeklys are ideal to purchase if you believe a stock will make a dramatic move within a few days. It will cost you a lot less premium. On the other hand, if you sell covered calls, you can earn that premium very quickly, but these options provide little in the way of downside protection.

Second, the shorter time frame equals less cost for option buyers. Lower premium is one of the main reasons weekly options are so popular with traders (volume continues to surge). Day traders are especially excited by Weeklys, and they are good plays for people willing to pay the much higher rate of time decay.

What is the downside of weekly options? First, be careful of the wide spreads, which can eat into your potential profits. Second, time is not on your side when you are the option buyer. If you are not immediately correct on your expectation for the underlying stock, expect to lose your entire investment. The smaller premium of Weeklys may be attractive for buyers, but sellers collect that small premium and come up short.

Bottom line: Weeklys are not for everyone, but they are worth studying.

Trading Mini-Options

As you already know from reading this book, one option contract controls 100 shares of stock. That can be a problem for high-priced stocks: For example, one 30-day, at-the-money option for an $800 stock could be costly (perhaps $30 per share for one contract). The mini-option was created to help investors who lack the resources to trade such costly options.

Here's how the minis work: With the mini-option, one option contract represents 10 shares of stock (rather than 100 shares with a standard option). Therefore, if you wanted to sell a covered call on an $800 stock, you could buy 10 shares of stock and then sell one mini-option on the 10 shares. For call buyers, instead of paying thousands of dollars per call or put, it would cost 10 percent as much to buy the mini-option.

For example, if YYY is trading at $500 per share, it would cost $50,000 to buy 100 shares. Now you can buy 10 shares of that same stock for $5,000 and sell one mini-call. Other option strategies can also be used with the minis.

Remember: Minis are not bargain contracts, and option prices are not less per share. They are only 1/10 the size of regular options. Because mini-options will be listed on the option chain, you must be careful not to inadvertently buy or sell a mini-option when you really wanted a standard option. Mistakes like that could be costly, so verify you have the correct option symbol.

Bottom line: The mini-option is exactly the same as a standard option except it represents fewer shares. It gives option investors a chance to buy or sell options using less money, and also to test various strategies. The flexibility to buy or sell options on 10, 20, or 30 shares (rather than 100) has made mini-options popular.

• •

And now, I'll introduce advanced option strategies, the most difficult chapter in the book. If you want, feel free to skip this chapter and go to Part 6. You can always come back to the advanced strategies later.

24

Advanced Strategies

Taking the time to understand the intermediate strategies learned in this section should keep you busy for months, if not longer. But if you want to experiment with advanced strategies, then this chapter should meet your needs. As I mention at the beginning of the book, trading options is like playing chess. But when you use advanced strategies, it's similar to playing 3D chess. With these strategies, there are multiple ways to make—or lose—money.

The advanced strategies included in this chapter are the playground of the experienced trader. Instead of buying and selling positions with one or two legs, some of these strategies involve three or more legs. This is what makes these strategies intriguing and powerful.

Although this is technically an introductory book, it's useful to learn about advanced strategies. There is nothing wrong with experimenting as long as you trade small (one or two contracts).

Note: This chapter is meant to be an introduction to advanced strategies. To learn more about the risks and rewards of these strategies, read the recommended list of advanced trading books in Chapter 26.

And now, hold onto your seat as I give you an overview of advanced trading strategies.

The Iron Condor

Iron condors are extremely popular with experienced traders. You can either buy iron condors (long) or sell them (short), but most traders sell iron condors, which is what I discuss in this chapter.

When you sell an iron condor, the trade consists of two vertical credit spreads: a put credit spread and a call credit spread. They have the same expiration date, but each option has a different strike price.

When you chart a profit-loss graph of this strategy, it looks like a large bird, thus the name, "iron condor." The name is cool, but using the strategy can be challenging.

This is considered a market-neutral strategy because it works well when the underlying stock makes neither a bullish nor bearish move. Therefore, this strategy is for anyone with a *neutral* (i.e., nondirectional) outlook for the underlying stock.

Before attempting the iron condor, it's essential that you already know how to trade basic spreads. After all, iron condors combine call and put spreads into one strategy. For that reason, iron condors may require some mental exercise for you to understand how they work, which is why you should practice this strategy before risking real money. In addition, because the iron condor consists of two credit spreads, you will need to use a margin account to initiate this strategy.

Selling an Iron Condor

When you sell an iron condor, you typically sell out-of-the-money put spreads and an equal quantity of out-of-the-money call spreads. Just as with other credit spreads, the long options are a hedge against losses from the options sold.

Goal: Your goal is for the call and put spreads to expire worthless so that you can keep the credit received from selling the options as your profit. You are speculating that the price of the underlying stock will land between the two short strike prices (as you'll see in the example below).

Maximum gain: Your maximum profit is the credit initially received from selling the call and put spreads.

Maximum loss: Your maximum loss is the same as the maximum loss for credit spreads. Do you remember what that is? It is the difference between the strike prices of the two calls (or two puts) multiplied by 100, minus the premium collected.

Risk: When the position is held to expiration, you can lose money on only *one* of the spreads, but never on both. Nevertheless, it is possible to lose more than the theoretical maximum if you mismanage the position, that is, pay too much to close the call spread and then, after a market reversal, pay up to close the put spread. Therefore, if you do take a loss by covering either the call or put spread at a high price, give serious consideration to paying the low cost required to get out of the (now inexpensive) other half of the iron condor.

A lot of things can go wrong with this strategy (i.e., the stock could make a strong move in either direction), but unwinding two spreads is just as easy as unwinding a single spread. Just enter your orders carefully. Nevertheless, it takes skill and experience to make money using this strategy, and managing iron condor risk can be challenging.

Example of an Iron Condor

You notice that YYY stock has been trading between $55 and $65 for the last few months. Right now the stock is $62 per share. In February, you decide to sell an iron condor.

Trade: Enter an order to sell the April 65/70 call spread and the April 50/55 put spread for a total net credit of $2.05.

If the trade works as expected, YYY will stay between $55 and $65 until the April expiration date. In this example, all the options expire worthless, and the $205 credit is your profit.

In a worst-case scenario, YYY will drop below $50 or rise above $70 (the long strike prices). Therefore, you could lose the difference between the call strike prices (when it is above $70) minus the premium received or the difference between the put strike prices (when the stock is below $50).

In this example, the maximum loss would be $295 ($500 difference between strike prices minus $205 net credit = $295).

Calendar Spreads (Long)

With calendar spreads (also known as *time spreads* or *horizontal spreads*), you attempt to capture time value on options with different expiration dates. The goal is to exploit the difference in the rate of time decay between the front month and distant month options. Calendar spreads are considered less risky than simply buying a call or a put, but they serve a completely different purpose. Like other option strategies, you know in advance your maximum risk. However, the maximum gain can only be estimated because you cannot know what the value of the option you own will be when the trade ends.

The long calendar spread consists of two options with different expiration dates. You can use either puts or calls, and calendar spreads are often a nondirectional strategy, although they can be played directionally.

For example, you might sell YYY August 40 calls and buy November 40 calls. For the calendar spread to work, the August calls must decay faster than the November calls. When you close the position, your potential gain depends on how much premium you can collect for the spread. This is the same for every trade using any strategy.

The strategy is flexible depending on your outlook for the underlying stock. You might initiate an at-the-money calendar spread if you were neutral about an underlying stock and believe it will trade sideways for the next month or two. If the underlying stock were unchanged during the life of the option, you would expect to make a profit.

It's a debit trade because you are paying more for the November options than you receive for the August options. The calendar trader predicts where the stock will be at or near August expiration because the spread is most profitable when the front-month option expires when it's right at the money.

Example of a Calendar Spread

Trade: In May, YYY is trading at $50 per share, and you believe it will trade sideways for the next two months. You sell 1 July 50 call and buy 1 August 50 call, paying a debit of $2.00.

As you know from studying time premium, the shorter-term (July) call (the option you sold) will be less expensive than the back month (August) call. With this strategy, you want to take advantage of time, so you want the short option to expire worthless and the long option to retain as much of its value as possible.

Maximum risk: You know in advance your potential loss, which is the initial premium that you paid. In the above example, your maximum loss is $2.00.

Maximum profit: Maximum profits can be substantial but are unknown because they depend on implied volatility at the time the position is closed. As with other spreads, it's recommended that you close the spread early.

As time passes, the time value decreases for both options. When the calendar is working as planned, the short option decays more quickly. With a month until expiration, the spread might be worth $2.45.

In this example, you could make a $45 profit by selling the August call and buying the July call for a net credit of $245. Because you paid $200, the profit is $45.

With experienced traders, this strategy offers a number of flexible plays, but don't attempt this strategy until you have mastered the four basic spread strategies.

Advanced note: A variation of the calendar spread is the *diagonal spread*, in which a calendar spread is combined with a credit spread. With this strategy, you buy a call or put with a longer expiration date, and sell a call or put with a different strike price and a shorter expiration date. Although potential gains and losses are limited, this is a complicated trade geared for more experienced traders.

Example of a diagonal spread: Buy 1 YYY October 75 call. Sell 1 YYY September 70 call. Note that the option you bought (October) expires later than the option you sold (September). Also note that the option you bought (October 75) is farther out of the money than the option you sold (September 70).

Note: This may not necessarily be a credit spread. Depending on volatility levels, this spread could provide a cash credit or require payment of a cash debit.

Butterfly (Long)

The butterfly is a combination of a bull and bear spread and offers limited risk and limited profit. Investors often initiate a butterfly to take advantage of low volatility. The name, "butterfly," was created because the profit-loss graph appears to have the body and wings of a butterfly.

You establish a long butterfly by buying one call at a lower strike price, selling two calls at a middle strike price, and buying one call at a higher strike price. All three options have the same expiration date. The two options bought are an equal distant from the middle strike.

The goal of the long butterfly is to have the underlying stock at or near the middle strike price as expiration approaches. If volatility is low and the stock doesn't move too much, the trade may be very successful. If the underlying stock makes a sharp move in either direction, you could lose money. Because the butterfly involves three legs, it can be commission costly.

Example of a Butterfly

Here's an example of a long butterfly spread: YYY is trading at $60 per share. Buy 1 February 55 call, sell 2 February 60 calls, and buy 1 February 65 call. This is an at-the-money call butterfly.

Note: The goal is for YYY to remain close to the 60 strike price where your 55 call would be worth $5 (as the other options expire worthless). The profit would be the $5.00 minus the net debit paid when initiating the trade.

Note: The optimal result is rare in this example (because this occurs only when the underlying stock is exactly at $60.00 when expiration arrives).

Enter the order as one butterfly spread, and do not trade the individual options with separate orders. The butterfly can be suitable for option traders with some experience (it's considered one of the simplest of the advanced strategies). The trap you want to avoid is paying too much for a butterfly. Also, although potential losses are limited, so is the maximum gain.

Even more important, it's not easy to choose an underlying stock that changes little before the expiration date. For that reason, you can buy an out-of-the-money call butterfly when you believe the stock will move higher or an out-of-the-money put butterfly when bearish.

> *Hint:* Choose your target stock price for the middle option's strike price.

Congratulations! You have now been introduced to intermediate and advanced trading strategies. (It will take considerable time for you to fully understand how they work.) Be sure to study and practice before using real money.

. . . .

You are now entering the opinion section of the book. Although it's beneficial to listen to other people's opinions, in the end you have to do what you think is best. With that in mind, in the next chapter you will read a fascinating interview I had with Sheldon Natenberg on the importance of volatility in options trading. This should give you additional insights into the mind of a professional trader.

SINCERE ADVICE

25

Sheldon Natenberg:
Professional Options
Trader

If you ask professional traders for the title of one of the most influential books about options, more than likely Sheldon Natenberg's book *Option Volatility & Pricing* (McGraw-Hill) will be mentioned. Although geared primarily to the professional trader, his insights into the importance of volatility in determining option prices were a breakthrough in the options world.

Natenberg started his career as an independent market maker in equity options at the Chicago Board Options Exchange (CBOE) before moving to the floor of the Chicago Board of Trade (CBOT). He has been the director of education in charge of training professional options traders for the Chicago Trading Company, a proprietary derivatives trading firm. I caught up with Natenberg when he was between classes.

What is the most common misconception about options?

The big problem for all options traders, including professionals, is this idea of volatility, the speed of the market. If someone thinks the market is going up, he or she will tend to buy calls. And if it turns out these people are right and the market did go up, they might end up losing money. Why did they lose money? Buying calls is supposed to be a bullish position, and the market went up. But of course what was happening was that the market was going up slowly, not sufficiently fast to offset the decay in the option. This idea of volatility is unique to options markets, but it is the overriding consideration in many strategies.

So should retail traders be aware of volatility?

There are two things you can trade on in the options markets. You can trade on the direction of the market—you have an opinion that the market is going up or down. Or you can trade on the speed of the market, which is volatility. How fast is the market going to move? Two typical volatility strategies are a straddle or strangle.

Most professional options traders have decided they're not very good at picking the direction of the market so they focus on the other characteristic: the speed of the market. Generally, people focus on one or the other. For retail customers, I think direction is the most important consideration. Most professional traders trade on volatility.

In my opinion, a nonprofessional needs to combine a price outlook with an understanding of volatility, and it's not easy. It's hard enough just to deal with the price, but to deal with the price and volatility together is more than most people are willing to do. If someone is really good at picking the direction of the market, my feeling is forget about options and buy or sell the stock.

Can you explain volatility so a novice can understand it?

You could say there are two basic interpretations. One is the volatility of the underlying market. Is the stock moving $5 a day or $1 a day, $0.05 a day, $0.10 a day or sitting still? The other idea is implied volatility, which is what the marketplace thinks is going to happen, and this is what determines options prices.

Here's an example that we use a lot in our business. You're trying to figure out what to wear when you are getting up in the morning. In other words, you're trying to determine what the weather is going to be today. Obviously, it's the future weather.

Let's say you think it's going to be sunny because that's what the weather report said. You look out the window and everyone is carrying an umbrella. What are they saying? They are implying through their actions what they think the weather is going to be. And basically, when you trade, you are betting your judgment against the marketplace's judgment. You're betting it's not going to rain even though everyone is carrying an umbrella.

Let's relate it to options trading. The marketplace thinks that certain things are going to happen, and they price options accordingly. The price of the option is based on what people think will happen. And what they think is going to happen can be translated into volatility—an implied volatility.

So, you use volatility to determine the value of an option?

Exactly. The value of an option in theory is dependent on the volatility of the underlying market—how fast it moves. What traders try to do is try to make their best estimate of what the volatility is going to be over the life of the option—that is, how much the underlying stock is going to move around.

The actual volatility, which no one can know, will determine the value of the option. Perhaps I can put it this way. Everything that is traded—it doesn't matter whether it is options or anything else—is a question of price versus value. If you see something with a high value and a low price, you want to be a buyer. Something with a high price and a low value, you want to be a seller.

Options traders are making the same judgments, but we calculate the value using a theoretical pricing model like Black-Scholes. The theoretical pricing model requires us to make a judgment about the volatility of the underlying market over the life of the option.

However, we can work backwards and say, "Suppose I know the price. What volatility does the marketplace imply by looking at this price?" Traders usually think of the theoretical value as being the volatility over the life of the option. They think of the price as being the implied volatility.

Can a novice use this to his or her advantage?

Anyone in options trading should be familiar with the basics of theoretical pricing. The question is how do you use it? If most retail traders think the market is going up, there are several things they can do.

They can certainly buy the stock. They can also buy calls. The question is should they buy calls or not? They should be buying calls if they think the calls give them an advantage.

For example, if retail traders use a model that says the call is worth $6 and it's trading for $4, in theory they have a $2 advantage in buying the calls. Once they have made the trade, they would treat it differently than would a professional, who would do certain types of hedging. In the long run, the retail trader would still come out better by buying the calls. If the calls were $6 and the price is $6, they might as well just buy the stock.

Most retail customers start with an idea that a stock is going up or down. And they have a directional opinion. The next question is if they should take advantage of their directional opinion in the options market. They can use a theoretical pricing model like Black-Scholes to do that.

How does a pricing model like Black-Scholes work?

Assuming the input is correct, the model gives you a value for the option. The trader will compare it to the price in the marketplace and decide whether he or she should be buying or selling. The difficult part is you have to enter a volatility number. Most traders look at graphs of volatility from the past (historical volatility) to come up with a prediction of the future.

What conclusions did you make about volatility and pricing?

The simple answer is people don't pay enough attention to it. They don't realize how dramatically options can be affected by changes in volatility. It's confusing because volatility is unique to options trading and is something most people have never come across before. You watch the evening newscast, and they say the market is really volatile today. The options trader asks: how do you quantify that? What number says that the market is more or less volatile?

I will give you an example. The idea of volatility is based on the assumption that the world looks like a bell-shaped curve. In other words, if you graphed the distribution of price changes, in theory they should look like a bell-shaped curve. The question you have to ask is: Is that true? And everyone knows it isn't true.

Volatility is another name for standard deviation. If you look in a textbook, sometimes it won't say volatility but will say standard deviation. But of course the standard deviation is based on the assumption you are working with a normal distribution: a bell-shaped curve. Nothing that we trade is exactly a normal distribution. So everyone is trying to make adjustments to make the model better fit the real world. What is the probability of the underlying stock going to this level, which will cause the option to be worth this? The options pricing models are just probability-based models. If you get the probabilities correct, you will get the value correct.

How do the pros manage risk?

If you looked at a professional trading firm, went in, and analyzed what the traders are doing, you'd find they are spending a lot more time worrying about the risk of the position they have taken than trying to figure out exactly whether they got the right values in the marketplace. Perhaps the biggest mistake made by traders is the lack of risk management. People are not sufficiently sensitive to the ways that market conditions can change and how that can affect options.

Think of Long-Term Capital Management (a hedge fund run by a group of academics and traders who specialized in options and other derivatives). These guys were as smart as they come. And they were primarily trading on relationships and volatility, and their losses were significant.

How could that happen?

In our business, the intelligent trading of options from a purely pro's point of view requires people to focus on two things. Number one, how do you figure out what an option is worth? Do you use a Black-Scholes model or some other model? But all those models are based on the laws of probability. The fact is, you can have all the probabilities right and still lose money—because you can be unlucky in the short run.

You hear about all the bad things that happen to individual traders and firms—it's mainly a lack of discipline. Everyone makes mistakes.

Number two, can you accept your mistake, take your loss, and go on? Some people just can't accept their mistake and make it worse and worse.

I'm thinking of Nick Leeson (the futures trader who single-handedly wiped out the 233-year-old Barings Investment Bank). From what I read, he is not a bad person. He just started to lose money for the firm in a way that he wasn't supposed to, and his ego wouldn't let him admit what was happening.

So how do you plan for what could go wrong?

It's not just asking what bad things can happen, but it's also asking what action to take if you run into bad luck. You must be prepared. If you're not prepared, then you freeze. That's happened to almost every trader. Things go against you, and you hadn't thought about it, and you have no idea what you are going to do. And it's not only the bad luck. Professional traders also ask: If things go my way and I get really fortunate, what should I do to maximize my profits? It's not only what I am going to do to minimize my losses when things go bad, but what I am going to do to maximize my profits when things go well.

Does software help?

You couldn't trade options without the software—it is invaluable. But you also can't be a slave to the software. The software isn't any good unless you understand what is behind it. For example, you can get software that tells you what an option is worth under certain conditions. And what makes these models like Black-Scholes really valuable is that you can ask: What if conditions change in this way? How will my position work or how will it look? You have to consider a wide variety of possibilities. You can't plan for every scenario, but you have to broaden your horizon beyond what people normally do.

I will use the software to determine how my position will look if the market price changes, if volatility changes, if time passes, if interest rates change. All of these different things can occur in the market. You have to ask yourself what worries you the most. And what am I going to do if things start to go against me?

Is it better to buy options on indexes or on stocks?

We find it's easier to trade index options than individual equities, although we do trade individual equities. You have to do a lot more research with equities. It really depends on how you are trying to trade. A professional market-making firm wants to make a lot of small profits on a large turnover, whereas the average retail trader is trying to make a large profit on a small turnover.

As one trader said, "Professional trading is like picking up dimes in front of a bulldozer. You can make a lot of money but you better keep your eye on the bulldozer." You'll get run over if you don't.

We trade on high volume. We try to make money from the bid-offer spread, buying at the bid and selling at the offer. We're happy to make small profit many times over, whereas a retail customer wants to buy the next hot stock. For us, it's easier to hit a lot of singles in the index markets or interest-rate markets because the characteristics of these markets are easier to deal with.

What other advice would you give traders?

The most important advice, which I also give to the pros, is that you should learn as many strategies as possible. You should go out and do every possible strategy you ever learned, but you should do it really small. If you go out and do one or two contracts, you will not get killed. By doing them in the real world, you will learn a lot. The problem with a lot of traders, even the pros, is they get a little knowledge and want to trade in bigger sizes, and they don't realize the bad things that can happen.

I'm not trying to discourage anyone from trading options, because I think it's a fascinating field. But you have to be realistic. It's not easy, and there is a lot to learn. At our firm, Chicago Trading Company, you will learn for at least a year before they even let you trade.

Is there a secret the pros know that we don't?

No! Occasionally I see an ad in the paper that announces someone is coming to town and invites readers to learn the secrets of the pros. There are no secrets. The only secret is hard work.

Most retail customers look at options trading as a hobby. There is nothing wrong with that, but you can't expect to be as good as a professional trader if you're not willing to put in the time and effort. A pro will put in more time and effort because his or her livelihood depends on it.

Let's say someone reads your book and wants to trade professionally?

Regardless of how good a book is, it can't give you all the aspects of trading unless you go into the real world and do it yourself. It's like taking a class. No matter how good the instructor, no matter how good the class—it just gives you a foundation to go into the real world, but it doesn't give you every unique situation you are going to encounter.

But you have to follow the first rule of beginning trading. Do it small. Whatever you do, do it small, that is, until you understand the different things that can occur and the relationships between options and different strategies.

What does it take to be a successful trader?

From the professional point of view, you have to be good with numbers. You don't have to be a mathematician, but you have to manipulate numbers quickly. We found in options trading that people who like probability-based games, like chess, bridge, or poker, tend to do well in options because they can appreciate the different probabilities and the way things fit together.

To be successful in this business, you have to be disciplined and willing to accept losses. You also have to make new decisions every day. Let's say I buy a stock at $100 and the stock is now at $98. I have to forget about whether I should have bought the stock at $100. I have to put yesterday's decision behind me and look at the new conditions today. Maybe I think the stock is going up. Maybe I think I should buy more stock. Or perhaps I realize I made a mistake, take my $2 loss, and look for another stock. The minute you fall asleep, however, is when the market comes up and bites you.

· ·

Now that you've gotten some insights into how a professional thinks and trades, the next chapter contains my list of recommended books and classes, as well as my opinion about expensive options seminars.

26

Where to Get Help

After researching, trading, and studying options for several years, I have a few observations that might be helpful. You may or may not agree with my conclusions, but keep in mind that they are my opinions. Let's begin by looking at some of the places you can go if you need additional help, or, better yet, if you want to pursue an even more advanced options education.

Phone Number

1-888-OPTIONS (1-888-678-4667)

This is the phone number of the Options Industry Council (OIC), the educational arm of the U.S. options exchanges and the Options Clearing Corporation (OCC). If you have questions about trading options while reading my book, this is *the* number to call. The staff is extremely knowledgeable and helpful (but don't call for investment advice). You can also e-mail questions to options@theocc.com. From the basics to butterflies, staff members will answer your questions promptly.

Online Resources

www.optionseducation.org

This is the website of the OIC, an excellent site filled with educational material and free options quotes. It also has special options calculators that give you important information such as implied volatility and delta. In addition, it offers free online options classes, videos, webcasts, podcasts, research papers, and live seminars. From this website, you can also chat online with very experienced staff members. Finally, there are hundreds of articles about options on everything from taxes to the Greeks.

www.cboe.com

This is the website of the Chicago Board Options Exchange (CBOE), an informative site containing free options quotes, an options chain, and a calculator for determining the theoretical value of any option. It also offers online option classes, live seminars, and webcasts. The site is filled with useful educational information. It also has a convenient option chain app so you can look at quotes from a mobile device. Almost everything you need to know about options will be on this site.

In addition, the following websites contain detailed articles and news about stocks and options:

Finance.yahoo.com (Yahoo! Finance)
Money.cnn.com (Money)
www.barrons.com (Barron's)
www.bloomberg.com (Bloomberg)
www.briefing.com (Briefing)
www.cnbc.com (CNBC)
www.fool.com (Motley Fool)
www.foxbusiness.com (Fox Business News)
www.forbes.com (*Forbes* Magazine)

www.ft.com (*Financial Times*)

www.google.com/finance (Google Finance)

www.investopedia.com (Investopedia)

www.investors.com (*Investor's Business Daily*)

www.kiplinger.com (Kiplinger)

www.marketwatch.com (MarketWatch)

www.money.msn.com (MSN Money)

www.moneyshow.com (The Money Show)

www.morningstar.com (Morningstar)

www.nasdaq.com (Nasdaq)

www.nyse.com (New York Stock Exchange)

www.quote.com (Quote.com)

www.sec.gov (SEC)

www.seekingalpha.com (Seeking Alpha)

www.smartmoney.com (*SmartMoney*)

www.stockcharts.com (Stockcharts)

www.thestreet.com (The Street)

www.tradersexpo.com (Trader's Expo)

www.valueline.com (Value Line)

www.wikiinvest.com (Wikiinvest)

www.wsj.com (*Wall Street Journal*)

Options Calculators and Software

Most of the large brokerage firms have software that compares, analyzes, and evaluates options and option strategies. More than likely, you can get the software at no cost when you open an account. If you can't, both the CBOE and the OIC have online and mobile options calculators that should meet your needs.

In addition, if you need to see the Greeks, implied volatility, or an option chain, almost all brokerage firms have online and mobile applications.

Additional Reading

Beginner to Intermediate Option Trading

After you've read my book, I recommend the following two option books:

The Rookie's Guide to Options, 2nd Edition (2013)
by Mark Wolfinger

Wolfinger's book is well researched and aimed at experienced rookies. The best part: he discusses at length your choices for each trade and the reasons why you should take, or not take, action. There are few people as knowledgeable about options as this author. Full disclosure: I know him personally.

Options for the Beginner and Beyond, 2nd Edition
(FT Press, 2013) by W. Edward Olmstead

Olmstead does an excellent job of summarizing the most popular options strategies in understandable language. The best part: the book includes numerous real-life examples of various strategies.

Characteristics and Risks of Standardized Options
(Options Clearing Corporation)

This is the must-read brochure published by the Options Clearing Corporation (OCC) that can be found for free on the OCC or CBOE website. The brochure is required reading for options traders, although it's extremely technical. After you've read my book, you should be able to understand this brochure.

Advanced Trading

Options as a Strategic Investment, 5th Edition
(Prentice-Hall, 2012) by Lawrence G. McMillan

This 900-page classic is used as a textbook in many college classrooms. It's not as technical as other advanced-level options books, so it's an easier read, and it is still a must-read for anyone pursuing a career as a professional options trader. McMillan introduces every conceivable option strategy.

Options, Futures and Other Derivatives, 8th Edition
(Prentice-Hall, 2011) by John C. Hull

This classic 800-page book is considered the bible of options and derivatives. The author is a recognized expert in the field and gives many examples of how options are constructed and priced.

Option Volatility & Pricing (McGraw-Hill, 1994)
by Sheldon Natenberg

This is a thought-provoking book on the effect of volatility when pricing options. It is recommended reading for experienced options traders who need insights into implied volatility. I was so impressed with Natenberg's book that I interviewed him for this book.

Seminars and Classes

www.optionseducation.org

The OIC website includes loads of educational material and useful information. It also offers free online classes and free seminars throughout the country that teach the basics as well as advanced strategies. The best part is that it teaches you what you need to know for free without any strings attached.

www.cboe.com

You can sign up for classes at various price levels (from $0 to $2,000) that will teach you everything you need to know about options from beginning to advanced strategies.

Continuing Education Classes

Check your local college or high school for reasonably priced options classes. The colleges either teach options as a separate course or include the subject as part of a finance class. In addition, if you are preparing for a broker's license, Series 7, you will need to be thoroughly familiar with constructing and pricing options. Many schools offer Series 7 classes, which include a detailed options discussion.

Investment Clubs

Check on the web for local investment clubs and seminars. Usually, they invite knowledgeable guest speakers to the meetings. You can also meet other option investors, giving you an opportunity to share ideas and ask questions.

What About High-Priced Options Classes for Retail Traders?

In my opinion, you should think twice about attending high-priced classes for retail investors that charge between $4,000 and $30,000 (or $15,000 if you sign up today) for two- to five-day classes that teach strategies that you can learn in this book.

The instructors at these classes mainly teach speculative strategies that are designed to make money when you have little or no money. They also lead you to believe that the more complicated the strategy and the sexier the name, the more money you'll make. So the only way you can make a profit is by taking additional classes and buying their software.

I was invited to a free workshop designed to convince me (and 30 other attendees) to sign up for an expensive options seminar. The instructor literally said anything to get us to sign the four-page contract. He justified the $4,000 cost for the seminar by reminding us that we'd spend at least that much money on a big screen television set. "And we can guarantee you'll make all your money back within a year of trading," the instructor promised the crowd.

Actually, the funniest thing the instructor said was that we shouldn't read books on options trading because we won't remember what we read. The second funniest thing he said was that they only teach low-risk, high-return strategies in the seminars.

At the workshop, the instructor said the secret to successful trading involves buying cheap out-of-the-money call options on low volatility stocks like Walmart a few weeks before earnings are announced—and selling as soon as the stock goes up 2, 3, or 4 points. "You can make $3,780 in one day!" he shouted.

I asked this question: "What is the probability of a low volatility stock like Walmart going up that many points after an earnings announcement?" His answer: "I'll get back to you later." Then he added, "But you can always do a bull call spread."

Note to instructor: It's been years since Walmart went up more than a point after an earnings announcement. And a bull call spread won't save you.

My View

What do I think? Many brokerage firms and independent websites have sophisticated options software programs that can search for multiple criteria and do advanced option calculations—provided free to customers. Call your brokerage firm and see what it offers or search the Internet. So before you plunk down thousands of dollars for software that purports to tell you the best time to buy and sell, use the free software provided by your brokerage firm.

There is also a difference between attending a school that teaches options trading and a seminar that helps you learn speculative strategies. Learning how to trade options is not as simple as buying a software program. If someone really did create a software package that magically picked the correct options to buy or sell, it wouldn't be shared with you or me.

In addition, how can these software programs (as well as web-based services that are offered for a monthly fee) compete with the million-dollar programs provided by brokerage firms or option exchanges? The truth is there is no secret system that will make you rich.

At the seminars, people are always intrigued by spreads. The selling point is that you are using the premium from one leg to finance the other leg. Everything works brilliantly in the classroom, but in the real world of trading, no strategy turns out so perfectly.

Some instructors at these seminars ask, "How much money do you want to make?" You should immediately reply: "How much money could I lose?"

In the classroom, under laboratory conditions, it's very easy to find options that fit your strategy. In real life, however, finding options that fit the criteria you are looking for is a lot harder than you think. And the more complex the strategy, the more variables you will have to consider.

There is one basic truth that many instructors fail to tell you. Many speculators lose money, although the exact percentage is hard to pinpoint. On the other hand, you can do very well if you use options as part of a planned strategy to increase income or as a method for buying stocks, all with reduced risk.

Another truth is that many people think that the more costly something is, the more valuable it is. Therefore, you may believe that the $30,000 class will be more beneficial than a free course. Not true. You should be very cautious about enrolling in those overpriced classes. You can get the same information for almost free at the OIC or CBOE, your brokerage firm, or an online class.

· ·

Now that you know where to get help, I will tell you some of the lessons that I learned about options.

27

Lessons I Learned About Options

Just as I believe people should learn about, and participate in, the stock market, people should learn about, and participate in, the options market. There are times when you need options for all of the reasons I've mentioned in this book: income, speculation, hedging, and insurance. If used properly, options are an excellent tool for managing your portfolio and increasing your returns.

In my opinion, you should start by selling covered calls. If you ask me whether I'd rather be the options buyer or the options seller, I would choose the options seller. Selling covered calls is a defensive options strategy that won't make me lose sleep (as long as I choose the right underlying stock). I personally believe that anyone who is interested in owning stock should use the covered call strategy, at least when you're first learning to use options, and when the stock market is slightly bullish.

Another suggestion: Check with your brokerage firm to see if you are allowed to sell covered calls in your 401(k) or IRA. Not only do you receive premium from selling covered calls in a tax-deferred plan, but you won't pay taxes until you take the money out (always check with a tax advisor or the plan administrator to confirm this). As long as you are aware of the risks, this strategy makes sense for many long-term investors.

I also believe that more people should look at buying protective puts, especially put options on ETFs. Protecting long stock positions and index funds with ETF put options is an effective insurance policy and can help reduce fears. Although protective puts don't give 100 percent protection, they are portfolio savers during a crash or correction. Unfortunately, protective puts are expensive, so you don't want to use them too often.

On occasion, a speculative opportunity (such as a market-moving event) comes along that you can pursue. It probably doesn't happen often, but when it does, you should be prepared to take advantage of it.

What are these opportunities? Sometimes they are recommendations from a financial professional, but it's more than likely they are the result of your own research. To consistently make money as a speculator, however, you'll have to work hard. Although it's possible to be part of the minority that consistently makes money speculating in options, it's also not easy.

There are also times when you will want to purchase a stock but don't want to commit the capital. The options market allows you to make a relatively small investment with a chance at a large return. As long as you thoroughly research the underlying stock and correctly choose which option to buy and how much to pay, your trading could be profitable, and you might even hit that elusive home run once in a while.

Suggestion: Before you enter a position, plan for what could go wrong. This is why you must have rules for getting into a trade and rules for getting out. If your trade is not working out as you planned, cutting losses is one of the smartest moves you can make.

One guideline is to close your position at a predetermined target price. If you're not careful, a small loss could easily turn into a major one. You must have valid reasons (hope is not a reason) to hold the position. Otherwise, cut your losses and look for another trade.

On the other hand, if your trade is working out as you planned, think about taking money off the table. One of the most important actions you can take is to protect your profits. By protecting profits, you'll have enough money to trade another day. Don't let a winning position turn into a loser.

Even more important, you must protect yourself from large losses. Don't forget that sometimes the most profitable trade you can make is not trading at all. Sitting on the sidelines is often the best strategy.

When I told Daniel, my friend who had made and lost $130,000 trading options in three days, that I was writing this book, he passed along this advice. "Tell your readers that if they are going to trade options, they better monitor their own account. You have to do what you think is right and not rely on anyone to tell you what to do." Good advice.

Before I go, I'd like to make six observations:

1. When trading, if you lose more money than you make, something has to change. Perhaps a new strategy will work.
2. It's not how much money you make that's important, but how much you keep.
3. No one cares more about your money than you do (and believe me, I speak from experience).
4. Never stop learning, and do not believe you know everything about options.
5. Practice trading before investing real money.
6. Congratulations! You are no longer a beginner.

The Closing: What You Should Do Now

Thanks again for taking the time to read my book. I hope that I was able to teach you about options without making them sound confusing or boring. As I said in the beginning, my goal was to be the first person to write a book about options that was easy to read. Now that you've finished my book, other option books should be easier to understand. I have a secret: I used techniques I learned as a teacher to write this book. Hopefully, they worked.

By now, you might be thinking of trying out these strategies with real money. First, there is no rush. Don't feel pressured to enter the options market until you are ready. Although my book gives you a solid start, there is much more to learn.

When you're ready, you'll be amazed at how your attitude changes when you invest real money. You may experience a thrill when you make a profit, but also anguish when you lose. One of the keys to trading success is being levelheaded and disciplined, even under volatile conditions. It's hard to teach discipline in a book, but with more experience, you'll learn what not to do.

Most important, if you can use what you learned in this book to make consistent profits or even a huge gain on occasion, then your time was well spent. (And I'd be really happy for you.) Good luck, and I wish you great success trading options.

··

If you have comments or questions about my book, feel free to send me an e-mail at msincere@gmail.com. In addition, if you notice any errors, please let me know so I can make corrections in the next edition. Finally, if you have time, feel free to stop by my website, www.michaelsincere.com. I hope to hear from you soon.

Index

Note: Italic page locators refer to figures and tables.

Acknowledgments

Thanks to Earn, my wife, for her devotion and patience.

To Zach Gajewski and Peter McCurdy, my editors at McGraw-Hill, for working with me to develop this book and helping me to see it through to completion.

I want to thank options expert Mark Wolfinger for fact checking the entire book, and for making exceptional suggestions and corrections. Without his help, the second edition would not have been completed.

I want to thank Sheldon Natenberg for taking the time to discuss volatility and options pricing with me.

I also want to thank Joe, Dave, Darren, Bill, and Juanita at Investor's Services at the OCC for patiently answering all my questions on the help line.

Hazel Garcia, for being an excellent assistant; Paula Florez, for helping to transcribe tapes; web designer Ryan Saunders, for creating top-notch websites; Jonathan Burton of MarketWatch.com, for the writing opportunities; Steva Kail, for pointing me in the right direction; and Laura Libretti at McGraw-Hill, for her wise advice about the publishing world.

I also want to thank my friends: Lourdes Fernandez-Vidal, Harvey Small, Sanne Mueller, Karolina Roubickova, Karina Royer, Bob Spector, Bruce Berger, Lucie Stejskalova, Jarle Wirgenes, Lene Wirgenes, Jason Zimmer, Rayna Exelbierd, Evrice Cornelius, Ron Weisberg, and Maytee Martinez.

About the Author

Michael Sincere interviewed some of the top traders and financial experts in the country to find out the lessons they had learned in the market so that he could help others avoid the mistakes he had made. He wrote a book about these lessons, followed by more books, including *Understanding Stocks* (McGraw-Hill, 2nd Edition), *All About Market Indicators* (McGraw-Hill), *Start Day Trading Now* (Adams Media), and *Predict the Next Bull or Bear Market and Win* (Adams Media).

Sincere has written numerous columns and magazine articles on investing and trading. He has also been interviewed on dozens of national radio programs and has appeared on financial news TV programs such as CNBC and ABC's *World News Now* to talk about his books. In addition to being a freelance writer and author, Sincere writes a column for MarketWatch, "Michael Sincere's Long-Term Trader."

You can visit the author's website and blog at www.michaelsincere .com.